"What a wonderful book on a difficult subject—an enjoyable read and a refreshing, natural, and straightforward approach to negotiation. Business anywhere is conducted on the basis of relationships, and in my experience the best business is based on superior relationships. We would all do well to be reminded of these principles that transcend markets, business types, culture, and geography."

—Lane Kagey, COO, LG International

"The greatest business lesson of the 21st century is that we have to think sustainably. *Beyond Dealmaking* demonstrates persuasively how this process can and must start at the negotiating table. Melanie Billings-Yun's smart, friendly style makes her the perfect guide to show you how to negotiate long-term success by thinking beyond the deal."

—Russell Read, senior managing partner,
C Change Investments

"*Beyond Dealmaking* gets you thinking about what 'the deal' means to a long-term business relationship—much like the wedding is to a successful marriage, it is only a first step. Melanie Billings-Yun gives the reader the insight and tools needed to plan for and negotiate agreements that will be the basis for longstanding and mutually beneficial business relationships."

—Matthew Gerber, president and CEO, SprayCool

"In Asia we have long known the importance of relationships in creating a successful and sustainable business. Unfortunately, this lesson is lost on many in the West who go after the quick deal, only to see their fortunes fall just as quickly. *Beyond Dealmaking* is a great antidote to this short-term thinking. I highly recommend it to all who negotiate in Asia or anywhere in the world."

—Young-Ho Park, president and CEO, SK Holdings

"*Beyond Dealmaking* is a practical guide on how to think differently (and positively!) for lasting results, whether at home, in your community, or in corporate boardrooms around the world."

—William Tung, vice president of Latin America/
Asia Pacific, Columbia Sportswear

"Melanie Billings-Yun's insight and experience as a leading negotiation consultant have given her the unique opportunity to develop an innovative vision and a simple yet effective approach to negotiating, which will drive you and your business to higher levels of success."

—Ellen Devlin, former general manager, Nike Korea and
Nike Thailand

BEYOND DEALMAKING

FIVE STEPS TO NEGOTIATING
PROFITABLE RELATIONSHIPS

MELANIE BILLINGS-YUN

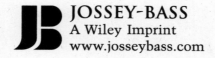

JOSSEY-BASS
A Wiley Imprint
www.josseybass.com

Published by Jossey-Bass
A Wiley Imprint
989 Market Street, San Francisco, CA 94103–1741— www.josseybass.com

Jossey-Bass books and products are available through most bookstores. To contact Jossey-Bass directly call our Customer Care Department within the U.S. at 800–956–7739, outside the U.S. at 317–572–3986, or fax 317–572–4002.

Jossey-Bass also publishes its books in a variety of electronic formats. Some content that appears in print may not be available in electronic books.

Library of Congress Cataloging-in-Publication Data
Billings-Yun, Melanie.
  Beyond dealmaking : five steps to negotiating profitable relationships / Melanie Billings-Yun.
    p. cm.
  Includes bibliographical references and index.
  ISBN 978-0-470-47190-6 (cloth)
1. Negotiation in business. 2. Deals. 3. Success in business. I. Title.
  HD58.6.B53 2010
  658.4'052-dc22
                                        2009038854

Printed in the United States of America
FIRST EDITION
HB Printing   10 9 8 7 6 5 4 3 2 1

Contents

Preface   ix

Introduction   xiii

Part One
WHY RELATIONSHIPS MATTER   **1**

1. The Goal Is Not a Good Deal, but a Good Outcome   3
2. Even Monkeys Demand Fairness   29
3. The Power of Us   49

Part Two
THE MIND OF THE NEGOTIATOR   **73**

4. The Four Pillars of Relationship Negotiation   75
5. Don't Feed the Bears!   99
6. Be Prepared   117

Part Three
FIVE STEPS TO SUCCESS   **131**

7. Goals—What You *Really* Want   133
8. Routes—How to Get There   157
9. Arguments—Making Your Case   181
10. Substitutes—The Backup Plan   203
11. Persuasion—Winning Them Over   225

Part Four
CONCLUSION   **249**

12. You Can Negotiate!   251

Appendix A: GRASP Negotiation Planner   257

Appendix B: Post-Negotiation Evaluation   263

Notes   265

Acknowledgments   269

About the Author   271

Index   273

*To Joe, my husband, adviser, and lifetime negotiation
counterpart*

Preface

Why do so many people dislike negotiation? For most it calls up the grueling and nerve-racking image of buying a used car. In fact, many seem to equate negotiation with behavior that is at best morally questionable. "I'm not any good at confrontation," I have been told by countless nervous clients at our first meeting. "You've got to be clever at outwitting the other side, bluffing, reading minds, spinning information, fast-talking." Or they may say, "I'm too nice/honest/soft-spoken to be a negotiator." Or simply, "I don't like fighting."

It's time to clear up these paralyzing misconceptions. Negotiation is not the art of war. That's fighting. It's not about outfoxing people. That's trickery. It's certainly not fast-talking, which is, well, simply annoying. Rather, as you will see over the following pages, negotiation is the process of connecting with another person or persons, resolving your differences, and coming up with solutions that will allow you to collaborate profitably and satisfyingly beyond the signing of the deal. In short, it's about creating a relationship.

As hundreds of nice, honest, soft-spoken people have found through my training programs, approaching negotiation as the first step in building a mutually beneficial working relationship changes everything. Relationship negotiation draws on a constructive skill-set. Destructive behaviors—aggression and deception—may be effective methods for getting others to agree to what you want (people will promise just about anything under torture), but they almost never inspire others to faithfully carry out those agreements, to be fair and honest with you, to work with you willingly, to give you the benefit of the doubt when problems arise, to do business with you again, or to speak well of you to others. Those cooperative actions are built not on coercive terms, or even on contractual terms, but on trust, affinity, and a belief that you are concerned about the other's interests as well as your own.

How does relationship negotiation differ from the standard approach to negotiation? Many negotiation books, starting with the groundbreaking *Getting to Yes* (which was being conceived just down the road at the Harvard Law School while I was directing a research program on the lessons of history at the Kennedy School of Government), have recognized that building friendly and open relationships is an important step in gaining agreement. These authors are on the right track but are still aiming short of the goal. (Perhaps my different perspective originates from the longer-term view of the historian as opposed to the contractual focus of lawyers, for whom the signing of the deal brings closure, a black-and-white snapshot of terms to be carried out. Historians look at human actions, especially at what happens after an agreement is signed—often finding results to be quite different from the promises that preceded them.)

Closing a deal and creating an understanding that will be implemented fully and freely present two very different objectives for the negotiator, with vastly different payoffs. If your eye is on the higher-value target of ensuring that the agreement is implemented, relationship-building cannot be seen as a mere step toward the immediate aim of getting a "yes." To achieve the greatest long-term value from a negotiation, *relationship-building must be the goal*, with the negotiation of agreements being positive steps toward achieving that goal.

This is an important distinction, because few of the negotiations you will take part in over your lifetime will involve onetime transactions such as buying or selling a car. Mostly you will negotiate with people with whom you have ongoing relationships: regular suppliers, repeat customers, bosses, employees, team members, co-workers, neighbors, family members. If you negotiate with these relations transactionally, focusing only on getting your terms, you will find yourself at an increasing distance from the people with whom you regularly deal, and less and less able to get them to give you what you want. If, on the other hand, you approach them from the perspective of the relationship, each encounter will become easier, more positive, and ultimately more productive.

This book will provide you with the why and how of relationship-negotiating. It is based on my observations from nearly two decades as a negotiation consultant and trainer in the United States, Asia, Europe, and Australia with clients from a broad range of nationalities and professions, as well as my experience teaching in business schools in Asia and the United States. Most of these observations have been direct, from negotiations in which I was personally engaged. Some come from the experiences reported to me by people I have trained, with whom I have stayed in touch over the years. Every story or example in this book, except where clearly indicated otherwise, is a true account drawn from those negotiations.

That said, I have made three modifications, which I will disclose at the outset. First, to preserve my clients' confidentiality, the identifying elements in most cases have been altered. The story is real, but the person and company have been renamed. Second, I have made the stylistic decision to use quotation marks to give certain examples more immediacy. While the spirit and overall content of those quotes match what the speaker said at the time, the wording is based solely on my memory. I lay no claim to word-for-word historical accuracy. Third, I have simplified some of the examples to make a specific point. This is a sin of omission rather than commission. What is described is true, but I have left out what I felt to be irrelevant or needlessly confusing. Negotiations tend to be lengthy, convoluted, rambling, and quite often tedious. When a point could be made without introducing unnecessary complexity, I have done so.

Finally, in hopes of making these lessons as straightforward and as easy as possible to absorb and apply, I have focused on two-party negotiations. While managing group dynamics is an important advanced negotiation skill, it's more useful to start by learning how to uncover a single counterpart's goals, for example, than by imagining the possible needs, desires, and aspirations of an entire committee. In this book my aim is to help you build confidence using the tools of the five-step GRASP negotiation method in one-on-one situations so that you can quickly begin reaping the many benefits of relationship-based negotiation.

Whether you're reading this because you're tired of being taken advantage of, are fed up with having hard-fought negotiations collapse before they can bear fruit, or are looking for a more positive way to resolve differences, I assure you that if you follow the methods and lessons in this book you will reap tangible, even amazing, results as negotiation goes from painful and punishing to positive and rewarding. Even those who cringe at the sound of raised voices can learn to be master negotiators, while discovering that the greatest victories come not through fighting battles but through establishing profitable and satisfying relationships.

Introduction

If the recent economic collapse has taught us anything, it is that the pursuit of immediate gain with no attention to the long-term consequences is a recipe for financial disaster. The gains accumulated were primarily on paper, but the losses have been painfully real. The problem was that far too few people were looking beyond the deal to see whether it would result in a positive outcome. Mortgage brokers got paid bonuses for signing off on loans, regardless of whether those loans could ever be repaid. What did it matter if the borrower, who had been passed off onto some other institution, defaulted down the road? The answer became agonizingly clear when banks and mortgage companies began to sink under unpaid debts, when borrowers who didn't lose their homes saw their house values plummet, and when the brokers who had generated those billions of dollars of paper profits found themselves on the street.

The folly was in thinking that the deal itself is the goal, that a promise is the same as an outcome, and that once you get a signature on a piece of paper, your relationship with the other party is over and the money will begin flowing in of its own accord. Sounds silly in retrospect, doesn't it? Yet that is the way most books still portray the objective and process of negotiation. Your target, they say, is a deal.

Unfortunately, that narrow focus misses the real point. As anyone knows who has done business in Asia or the Middle East, sold a mortgage to someone who had no realistic way to pay it, or, frankly, has been married, getting to "yes" is not the same as getting results. The other parties may say yes to be polite or to make you go away when they feel cornered by forceful tactics. They may agree to promises they have no intention of keeping, because they feel no connection and therefore no moral obligation to you. The challenge for business, government, and society is not in getting people to make promises but in getting them to carry out those promises fully, willingly, and consistently. That can only be accomplished through changing your negotiation target from making a deal to building an honest and mutually committed relationship with the people who will be carrying out that agreement.

Negotiating Relationships

In the same way that the vows made in a wedding ceremony don't guarantee a happy marriage, contractual terms won't ensure smooth and successful business. The marriage license only "closes the deal" to the extent that it opens the door to a potentially fruitful union. The success of the marriage—or the business partnership—depends on the parties' willingness to make it work because they feel committed to the relationship and satisfied that they are benefiting from it.

Have you ever agreed to something, but the negotiation process left you so annoyed or demeaned that you were just waiting for a way to back out of the deal or even the score? Imagine that your boss calls you into his or her office to tell you that the company needs you elsewhere, so you either accept a transfer or you lose your job. You may agree to the transfer as a stopgap measure, but are you secretly looking for another employer? Even if you find nothing else and so are forced to accept the transfer, are you as committed an employee as you once were?

Let's take a less clearly personal case. A customer's procurement manager drives your professional service firm's contract down to a rock-bottom price by continually reminding you of their company's negotiation power and threatening to drop you for a cheaper competitor. You may reluctantly sign on to the deal, but wouldn't you secretly want to get even by socking them with variation orders for every little extra they request, things you would willingly throw in for other, more likeable clients?

And those are just the deals that got to yes. I would lay odds that you can remember walking away from a potentially profitable transaction simply because you didn't like the attitude of the negotiator on the other side. The terms were acceptable, but the way you were being treated was not. You felt so accosted or demeaned or ignored that you didn't want to have anything more to do with that person or that company. At bottom, you felt the deal just wasn't worth the emotional cost.

You can't expect people to carry out agreements faithfully when one moment you call them valued partners and the next you treat them as mere tools, or obstructions, in your quest for short-term profitability or convenience.

A new negotiation paradigm—away from negotiating a deal and toward negotiating a relationship—is needed for the twenty-first century, because the business landscape has fundamentally changed. Businesses can no longer stay on top by negotiating short-term victories. Nor can any organization hope to navigate the increasingly complex economy by pursuing an endless cycle of zero-sum transactions. The key to winning unbeatable, long-term results is to negotiate solid, long-term relationships.

Thousands of companies and individuals have profited hand-somely from the concept of "relationship selling." Yet I was struck painfully by the words of Jim Cathcart, one of the founding fathers of that movement, who distilled his sales philosophy as the rejection of a negotiation mentality. "Business should be practiced as an act of friendship, rather than merely as a process of negotiation. It is about connecting with people profitably, not merely persuading them to buy," Cathcart writes.[1] Where does that leave negotiation? As the opposite of friendship and good business practice? Sadly, the notion of negotiation as hostile, self-interested, and manipulative has been reinforced by negotiation "experts" who advise you to "start from 'no'" or who promise to teach you "how to beat the opposition every time." It is precisely this thinking that has led to so many unprofitable or unworkable deals and that makes negotiation stressful and distasteful to the great majority of people.

It doesn't have to be that way. All we need to do in order to move from transactional, deal-centered negotiation to relationship-centered negotiation is turn the relationship sales philosophy slightly around: *Negotiation should be practiced as a process of profitably connecting with people, rather than merely as an act of persuasion.* Only then will we be on our way to achieving truly winning results.

Taking the Fear out of Negotiation

"That's great in theory," I imagine many of you thinking as you read this, "but what if I'm not a gifted speaker? What if I don't think quickly under pressure or I become emotional when confronted?"

Here's the good news. Relationship negotiation doesn't require you to be eloquent, cunning, tough, quick-witted, or fast-talking. There are no prizes for speed or sleight of hand when laying a strong and rewarding foundation for the future. Instead, the basis of your negotiating power is advance preparation, openness, empathy, patience, and a sincere effort to reach a mutually successful agreement. These are competencies to which even the humblest among us has equal access—but only a select few use to their greatest advantage. This book will provide you with the tools to develop and get the most out of those competencies.

Preparation also helps keep undesired emotions (whether your own or the other party's) in check. Emotional reactions are very like nerve reactions: they're set off by shock. Just as we can't tickle ourselves, because our brains know what's coming, we're far less likely to become upset if we anticipate that others may react negatively at some point in the negotiation—whether it's because they generally have volcanic personalities or they're likely to feel upset by some specific aspect of the discussion. And we're far less likely to set off that negative reaction if we have considered in advance, for example, that Ben generally gets flustered when he's under time pressure or that Sarah, who has put a good deal of effort into formulating her proposal, will probably feel hurt and angry when we reject it. By anticipating problems, we can change our approach in an effort to avoid or at least mitigate them: when we negotiate with Ben, we first ensure that we have set aside sufficient, uninterrupted time; when we reject Sarah's proposal, we give her a full explanation why as well as positive suggestions she can take away. This book will show you how to understand the other side and, through understanding, to anticipate reactions. The payoff of preparation and empathy is not just that they enable you to allay negative reactions and deflect confrontations before they occur; you will also find a marked reduction in your fear of negotiation.

Over the years, I have trained thousands of negotiators from all walks of life—men, women, old, young, businesspeople, social activists, public servants, Asians, Americans, Europeans, Middle Easterners; the list goes on. Almost all started out admitting that they disliked, even feared, negotiation. Yet those same people reported a stunning change after becoming skilled at the GRASP relationship negotiating method (see Part Three). Negotiation, they told me, had gone from being a painful, even humiliating, experience to a rewarding one, not just improving their effectiveness on the job but enhancing the relationships in their private lives as well. I assure you, those people were no more naturally gifted than yourself. What enabled them to be so successful was that they had learned to approach negotiation in a new way, just as you can by following the steps in this book.

Organization of the Book

Beyond Dealmaking has two objectives divided among three parts. Part One, "Why Relationships Matter," sets out to demonstrate the importance of negotiating open, mutually beneficial, and trusting relationships—and the terrible risks we run by ignoring them. Why do so many deals jump from handshake to heartburn? Why is it that "yes" so often fails to lead to positive action? Real-life examples drawn from every possible type of negotiation will show the impact of fairness, honesty, empathy, flexibility, and problem-solving on the success or failure of negotiation outcomes. From those stories and lessons you will see that

- Negotiation isn't a battle or a game—it's simply finding a way to work profitably together.

- People do business with people they connect with.

- Cooperation is based more on a sense of fairness than on contracts.

- Building a positive relationship starts with the first date, not after the wedding.

- Healthy relationships have to work both ways.

The second aim of the book is to provide a practical guide for achieving outstanding and sustainable negotiation results, whether across continents, within your own organization, or among family members. This objective is covered in Parts Two and Three.

Part Two, "The Mind of the Negotiator," focuses on the basic approach to negotiating value-enhancing relationships. It stresses the importance of planning, connecting, understanding, problem-solving, reciprocity, and holding firm against one-sided demands.

Part Three, "Five Steps to Success," presents the step-by-step GRASP negotiation model, a method for negotiating profit-maximizing and durable partnerships that has been used successfully by thousands of businesspeople, public officials, NGOs, and private men and women around the world. (If you want to get straight to the GRASP method, you can skip over Parts One and Two; however, I strongly recommend that you read Chapters Two, "Even Monkeys Demand Fairness," and Five, "Don't Feed the Bears!" before you start negotiating.)

The GRASP model breaks down negotiation into five steps:

- **G**: Understanding the **Goals** of *all* parties, beyond the immediate deal

- **R**: Developing **Routes** to those goals that will maximize the benefit of *all* parties

- **A**: Promoting fairness, trust, and common understanding through valid **Arguments**

- **S**: Benchmarking your current relationships against possible **Substitutes**

- **P**: Increasing your **Persuasion** through open and empathetic communication

The name "GRASP" is more than a memory device; it symbolizes the primary focus of this book. To grasp means both to hold on to something firmly and to understand. The GRASP method creates firm commitments because they are built on understanding, not on gamesmanship. By learning this simple but powerful method and using the GRASP Negotiation Planner at the end of this book (see Appendix A) as an aid in planning your next negotiation, you will discover that negotiation can be a positive, creative, and, most important, genuinely rewarding experience. I welcome you onto this journey.

BEYOND DEALMAKING

Part 1

WHY RELATIONSHIPS MATTER

Chapter 1

THE GOAL IS NOT A GOOD DEAL, BUT A GOOD OUTCOME

When I began working as a professional negotiator, I envisaged myself making deals: helping companies reach strong and profitable commercial agreements. Instead, I was inundated with contractual disputes, business alliances in trouble, partnerships on the rocks. The disputes ranged from relatively small local purchase and sales transactions to multimillion-dollar international ventures bound by detailed contracts; from recent fallings-out to old battles that had nearly exhausted the parties in courts. Yet, despite this diversity, they had one important thing in common: they had all started out with "yes."

The phenomenon transformed my view of negotiation. Until then I had focused on negotiation as a transaction, with a concrete set of objectives and a definable end. The negotiator's goal, according to every book I read, was to secure a set of terms that would maximize "our side's" gains while giving enough value to the other side to win their agreement. The end of the negotiator's line of sight was an agreement. While he or she might anticipate and try to reduce implementation problems by peppering the contract with performance guarantees, liquidated damages clauses, and so on, the focus remained firmly on the deal.

Yet experience showed me plainly that getting a deal, even a "good" deal, was not enough. Every one of these expensive and emotionally draining disputes had started out as a deal that both parties had felt was good—at least good enough to sign on to at the time. So why were so many going bad? The answer was clear: they were failing to create successful working relationships. A deal is nothing but a promise. A relationship—marked by open, two-way communication, respect, empathy, trust, reliability, and sincere efforts to promote long-term mutual benefit—is what will see that promise through implementation and beyond.

Short-Term Fixation, Long-Term Loss

My first consulting client opened my eyes to the importance of looking beyond the deal. Choi had a thriving business importing American meat, which he sold to the many Western restaurants and chains that were popping up across Korea. For several years he had bought beef from a single supplier in Texas, his orders more than doubling each year. However, things changed suddenly in November 1997 when Korea was hit by the Asian financial crisis.

Virtually overnight, Korean currency dropped to less than half its value against the dollar. Banks desperately called in loans in hopes of avoiding collapse. To stave off national bankruptcy, Korea had to accept an IMF bailout and trusteeship, a painful humiliation. Worst of all for Choi, the Korean public reacted to the crisis with an intense wave of nationalism: boycotting all foreign products and businesses. By December, usually the busiest time of year in the food industry, the only people to be seen in foreign-linked restaurants were the staff.

Reeling from the one-two punch of currency devaluation and customer desertion, Choi called his supplier to say that he would have to cancel the orders he had contracted for the next several months, until the economic situation in Korea improved and the boycott was called off. He expected some sympathy, even words of support for his plight. It was, after all, a national crisis, not a business failure—and the supplier, as it had stated many times, was his "valued partner." Instead, he was stunned a few weeks later to receive a letter of demand from the beef exporter's lawyer, telling him that by failing to pay on time for his last order and canceling his precommitted next order, he was in violation of their contract. If he didn't immediately rescind his cancellation, the letter said, they would sue.

When Choi came to see me to help him negotiate a settlement, he was gripping the letter tightly in his hand and shaking it as he spoke. "I've been giving these people my business for four years," he fumed. "I went to visit their ranch. I even invited them to stay in my home. MY HOME! Now, the first time I have a problem they send me this?" He flung the letter onto the table in disgust.

I tried to explain to Choi that the supplier was just switching into automatic contract-compliance mode, not specifically picking on him, and that the language in the letter was standard legalese, not a personal insult. But it was clear that neither explanation took away the sting. More helpfully, I told him that I thought we could resolve the matter by coming up with a plan to extend the payments and orders over a longer period. He agreed, but kept repeating numbly, "I have given them my business for four years. I had them into my home."

In fact, we easily resolved the business dispute. Within months, Korea was on its way to economic recovery, and Choi was able to recommence business and complete the contract. However, once he had fulfilled his order, he refused to do business with the Texas supplier ever again. Over the next years the Korean economy thrived and Choi's business boomed. However, it was another meat supplier who reaped the benefits.

The Texas company had thought transactionally. While they were fully within their rights to enforce the terms of their contract, they missed the bigger point. By treating a business partner as nothing more than a set of agreements and showing concern only for their own interests, they failed to connect with him as a human being trying to do his best under difficult but temporary conditions. By focusing exclusively on the deal at the expense of the relationship, they sacrificed much greater long-term business profits.

Looking beyond the deal doesn't mean ignoring commitments. Commitment is what differentiates relationships from one-night stands, or healthy business partnerships from single transactions. For the beef supplier to have said, "Okay, never mind. Times are tough. Let's just drop the whole thing," would be no more relationship-oriented than shouting, "Pay up or else!" However, there are a number of things the cattle company could have done to strengthen the relationship and maximize long-term business gain during this difficult time.

Most important, the president, who had negotiated the original deal with Choi, could have spoken to him personally and collaboratively, as a partner facing a crisis that was hurting both their businesses. This would have opened the door to joint and productive problem-solving, possibly even to finding new areas for mutual gain, such as taking advantage of the Korean currency's weakness to import to America ranch machinery or vehicles at reduced prices. Instead, by sending a letter of demand through the company's lawyers, the president conveyed the messages that "I'm not interested in your problems," and "I only posed as your partner to get the contract." The result was that the Texas company not only lost Choi's loyalty and the profits their relationship would have generated over the long term, but also suffered a reputational loss as Choi recounted his tale of fair-weather friends throughout his wide business network.

Deals Versus Relationships

Negotiating relationships is a process, not an act or a transaction, because it doesn't have a clear beginning or end. Nor, like a contest on the playing field or in the courtroom, does it have one winner and one loser. Your goal is to reach an agreement to work with another party *in the future*, under conditions that enable both sides to prosper.

Traditional deal-based negotiation is transactional. It's about this deal, these terms. Get a signature, and you're done. With its emphasis on winning and losing, transactional negotiation is frequently compared to a game (of wits) or a battle (of nerves). But there is a crucial difference between reaching an agreement and competing in a game or fighting a battle: games and battles don't require cooperation once they are concluded.

There are other critical differences:

- In a deal, the goal is confined to getting an agreement. In a relationship, the goal is working together profitably, starting from the first agreement, then building far beyond it.

- In a deal, the party you are negotiating with is, to a large extent, your opponent. In a relationship, the other party is your preferred partner.

- Deals are about getting as much of what you want as you can carry away. Relationships are based on fair division and joint burden-sharing.

- In a deal, you hold yourself aloof from the other party: hiding information, guarding your responses, pressing your position. In a relationship, you are more relaxed, open, and natural: sharing information and truly seeking to understand and resolve differences.

- In a deal, you may exaggerate the strength of your position or try to trick the other side into giving in. Successful relationships are based on honesty, reliability, and follow-through.

- Deals are static, inflexible, with exhaustive contracts intended to guarantee that every term and condition will remain "carved in stone" until the transaction is completed. Relationships are also based on fundamental agreements, but they are more accommodating, less rigidly detailed. Because relationships take place over time, change needs to be anticipated and managed constructively rather than ignored because it falls outside of the scope of the initial agreement. Relationships are dynamic, not carved in stone.

Not all deals require relationships in order to succeed, of course. When you sell your old car through an online ad or bargain over a ceramic pot in a foreign market while on vacation, it truly is a transactional activity. The goods are delivered the moment the deal is sealed, and you are unlikely ever to see that person again. But such cases are the rare exception. Most negotiations—from mergers and acquisitions, to supplier contracts, to interdepartmental meetings for allocating funding or agreeing on where to hold the company picnic—are for arrangements that will be implemented over time (sometimes years) or that will lead to future arrangements. Even when you are unlikely to meet that individual customer or supplier or even colleague ever again, the relationships you build throughout the negotiation and implementation process will have an impact on your future business by shaping your reputation and the number and type of references you receive.

Here is an example. Last year I bought a houseful of furniture for our new home in Oregon. The salesman was wonderful to work with. Even though he knew that this was a onetime deal (I had made it clear that there were no more rooms in the house to furnish!), he treated it as a relationship. He asked me how I wanted to work with him. When I said I preferred to be left alone until I had made up my mind, he honored that request. He gave me information and pointed out other possible options

I could consider, but he never forcibly steered me toward a more expensive line or pressed me to buy unwanted extras. Because it was a large order, I was able to negotiate free delivery and assembly. The negotiation was pleasant and professional. At no point did the salesman make me feel like he was doing me a favor. Most impressive, a week or so after the delivery he called to make sure that everything had been installed to my satisfaction.

Had the salesman treated this as a transaction, wringing the most he could out of the sale, he might have come out with a higher immediate gain. (On the other hand, I might have walked out of the store having bought nothing, as I had at two previous furniture showrooms with overbearing salespeople and take-it-or-leave-it attitudes.) However, by treating this as a valued relationship, he came away with a number of longer-term benefits. First, I wrote a note to his boss, saying what a great salesman he was and crediting him for the size of the purchase. When the furniture arrived a bit late, I took it in stride, having enough stored goodwill toward the company to accommodate a few small difficulties. Since then I have regularly recommended the store—and that salesman by name—to family and friends who are looking for furniture. I even made it a point to try out his parents' restaurant, which he had mentioned when we were chatting after the sale.

Let's compare this to the very different experience my friend Jeremy had with the agent managing the commercial property where he had his office. The property market had boomed in his area, and landlords were feeling their power. Hoping to lock him in at the current peak price, three months before Jeremy's initial lease was to expire the landlord sent him an e-mail informing him that they were planning to raise his rent by 80 percent and warning that if he didn't commit to another two-year lease within the next week they couldn't guarantee the "goodwill" rate. The tone could best be described as officious. When Jeremy called the landlord's agent to discuss ways to reduce the increase, the agent was unashamedly rude. "We have people lining up for this property," she said. "There's nothing to discuss. Do you want the deal or not?"

Feeling trapped because he had just paid for some expensive office renovations, Jeremy reluctantly signed the lease. But after that, he made it a point to document every failure of the management or minor problem that occurred, from elevators breaking down to undue noise during office hours. When people asked him if there was space available in his building, he warned them away from "those bloodsuckers." Six months later, when the property market started to decline, Jeremy couldn't stand it anymore. Although he knew that by breaking the contract he risked legal action and would suffer expensive relocation costs, he moved out. When the landlord threatened to sue to collect the amount remaining on the lease, Jeremy shot back with his evidence of the building management's negligence and said he was ready to go to court and make it public. The landlord settled, with Jeremy forfeiting only his initial rent deposit.

Who benefited more? The furniture salesman, who approached a onetime deal as a relationship, or the landlord, who approached a multiyear relationship as if it were a transaction?

Rules of Relationship

Relationships exist at many levels of intimacy. They are not all deep or lasting. No doubt in your own life you have experienced a wide variety of personal relationships: from classmates or colleagues you work with on a daily basis for a fleeting time, to the hairdresser or barber you see once a month for years, to family and friends with whom you share intimate bonds throughout your lifetime. Obviously, these very different relationships require different levels of trust, openness, and commitment.

Commercial relationships run the same gamut: from small customers who purchase limited quantities of your product, to giant retailers who buy up nearly all of your output; from suppliers who sell you readily available commodities, to high-tech manufacturers who provide you with customized components. You have relationships with business partners, service providers, clients, consultants, employees, bosses, and colleagues. Despite the vast differences among these relationships, they all involve people with whom you work and share a mutual dependence.

Every relationship, regardless of depth, requires words, attitudes, and behavior that express a positive connection. Here is my top-ten list for negotiators:

- Respect, friendliness, a sense that you like the other person as a human being, not merely as a means, or obstacle, to your end

- Fairness in distributing and carrying out both responsibilities and benefits

- Honest, open, and positive communication

- Care and concern for the other's well-being, both within and beyond the immediate transaction

- Empathy and understanding

- Collaborative efforts toward mutual success

- Reciprocity, returning favors, responding to trust with trust

- Open-mindedness, flexibility, and willingness to adapt to different ideas and to changes

- Appropriate commitment at each stage of the relationship

- Dependability, maintaining your understandings, and following through with your promises

This may seem to be an overwhelming list, but it's actually the way we approach normal human relations. Think of even a casual friendship—say with a colleague or neighbor—and you will see that you instinctively follow all of these rules to some extent. You want nothing from these informal associations besides the general benevolence of the other party, and yet you take the positive steps needed to gain and maintain their goodwill. You smile and say good morning; you show concern and care when he appears with his arm in a sling; if she offers you a gift of some vegetables from her garden, you share something with her some other time. This is the natural way human beings interact to create smooth and cooperative relationships.

Why then should it be less natural or intelligent to show the same positive manner toward the person on the other side of the negotiation table, whose active collaboration you are pursuing and whose cooperation you will rely on for your own success in carrying out the agreement? Simply stated, it's not. The grave danger is becoming so focused on the deal that you forget the human being with whom you have to fashion the deal, the person who will say "yes" or "no" to the terms you propose, and the people who will implement any final agreement.

Let's look at each of these attitudes and behaviors within a negotiation context.

Respect, Friendliness, and Liking

Whether you are negotiating a deal or trying to resolve a dispute, it almost never pays to be nasty or to demean the other side. It's such common sense that it's hard to understand why so many people choose a hostile approach. Ask yourself: Do you feel more cooperative toward people who put you down or who, while you are talking to them, scowl at you or roll their eyes? Does having someone reply to your friendly overtures with a silent poker face make you feel more relaxed and creative or more defensive? You wouldn't be in the negotiation if you didn't share a common interest in working together, so why pretend otherwise? Unfortunately, many people seem to believe that acting surly gives them an edge. Mostly, it just creates resistance.

I have seen negotiations fall apart because one side comes on aggressively or dismissively, such as perpetually reminding the other how much bigger their company is than their counterpart's or using body language that signals contempt. All this does is set off a defensive reaction, along with alarm bells over how unpleasant any working relationship with that party might be. In extreme cases it leads to direct retaliation. A very successful Indian businessman told me how he had walked out of an acquisition negotiation because the attorney on the other side, a white South African, had opened the meeting by shaking everyone's hand but his, the only dark-skinned person in the room. When I asked him if he had damaged his interests by passing up what he admitted was a lucrative deal, he replied nonchalantly, "There are so many fish in the ocean. Who needs a rotten one? I just made the deal with someone else."

Disrespect also leads to indirect retaliation. A supplier to Ford Motor Company found a unique and very effective way of getting back at the automaker for what he felt was its procurement department's bullying negotiation tactics. He shared his experience in an article published in the *Harvard Business Review*, whose U.S. circulation runs to a quarter of a million. The automaker, he complained to all who would hear, "seems to send its people to 'hate school' so that they learn to hate suppliers. The company is extremely confrontational. After dealing with Ford I decided not to buy its cars."[1] He may have continued to work with Ford for economic reasons, but he had exacted his revenge.

On the other hand, people are far more compliant with someone who is likeable and behaves as if he or she likes and respects *them*. You create liking through affiliation (establishing likeness) and affirmation (giving praise).[2] Affiliation is as simple as finding something you have in common with the other person.

Informal conversations before the negotiation uncover those points of connection, reducing emotional distance and creating the beginnings of a relationship. I may be American and you Russian, but if we both love Tolstoy or have studied in Paris, we become less wary of each other. As the connections grow, so does our willingness to help each other out.

Offering praise is the other building block of liking. Some people are afraid to praise, feeling that it weakens them in a negotiation. In fact, it's quite the opposite. Of course, you mustn't get carried away: fawning and flattery are simply annoying. But offering a genuine compliment to another's attributes ("What a beautiful office you have!"), accomplishments ("We are very impressed with the quality of your prototype"), attitude ("I really appreciate your efforts to resolve this"), or actions ("That's a great help. Thanks!") makes the other feel appreciated. Appreciation opens the door to cooperation.

At a minimum, whether you are negotiating a deal or a dispute, you will come out ahead by being pleasant and respectful to everyone at the table, using their names, starting off with a smile, listening politely and sincerely, and continually sending off positive signals that you want to work with them. Friendliness does not mean that you can't be firm or that you'll only say things the other party wants to hear. It doesn't require acceptance of their viewpoint or acquiescence in their wishes. It simply means never being personally insulting or pointlessly disagreeable.

Fairness

Fairness will be dealt with at length in the next chapter. However, it deserves a quick mention here in the context of friendliness. A common negotiation misstep is to use cooperative language while pursuing utterly one-sided gains. A negotiator might start off with a big smile and say, "I'm looking for a win-win deal," then do everything in his or her power to win the whole lot.

To be effective, friendly words have to be matched with discernibly fair treatment. The two add up to sincerity. Friendliness without fairness appears as mere wolfish manipulation and can create a powerful sense of revulsion that may not only destroy long-term relationships but even overturn a signed deal. In fact, experiments performed by neuroeconomists on negotiators connected to MRIs found that perceptions of unfairness cause the brain to light up in the same area as when one is physically affronted by a repulsive taste or smell.[3] When the unfair demand follows a friendly lead-in, the reaction is particularly bitter—like taking a spoonful of what you thought was honey, only to get a mouthful of motor oil!

Honest, Open, and Positive Communication

When I teach negotiation, I am regularly astonished by the number of otherwise decent people who approach their first role plays by shutting down all honest communication. They may seek to mislead the other side by hiding their true objectives, pretending they want things they don't actually want and claiming that they don't want things they do. Or they will clam up, revealing nothing at all. When asked what their priorities are or what price they're looking for, they will answer with vacuities such as "That depends." Then silence. The result in the first instance (misleading) is that they end up with things they don't want. In the second (stonewalling), if they reach any deal at all, it will be of low value, since they never asked for what they wanted.

Negotiating is an attempt to reach a mutually rewarding arrangement that maximizes your goals. You can rarely attain a goal by aiming in the opposite direction or by refusing to aim at all. Whether you need delivery by a certain date, want to keep a house purchase within a set budget, or would prefer to settle a dispute out of court, you will get the results you are after most reliably and efficiently by first asserting what it is that you want. Saying otherwise will just send the negotiation on an unproductive path.

At minimum, bluffing, misdirection, and stonewalling are wastes of time. Worse, these behaviors are generally understood by society to be hostile and morally repugnant. Unlike at the poker table, where bluffing is part of the game, social expectations don't disappear at the negotiation table, especially when the negotiation is intended to create a cooperative bond. As with any relationship, business demands honesty and openness.

Moreover, even from the most Machiavellian perspective, the chances that you will get caught giving false information are higher now than at any point in human history. In the linked world of the twenty-first century, information has become remarkably easy to obtain and verify. You might be able to get away with deception on occasion, but over time being known for not playing straight will ruin your reputation and destroy your business.

While honesty and openness are prerequisites to effective negotiation, they alone are insufficient to create a mutually satisfying relationship. The negotiator across the table could, for example, honestly and openly tell you that he thinks you are stupid or that she is not the least bit interested in your needs, but those negative approaches would not likely lead to a successful outcome. Communication that builds relationships also must be positive.

A former student wrote me for advice after failing to negotiate a higher job title to go with the new position and transfer she had been offered. She sent me the e-mail traffic that had led to the communication breakdown. In her last message, after being told by the COO that securing the title she had asked for would be difficult, she had fired back, "I know you *think* that, but you've never given me an acceptable reason to believe it." The COO didn't reply. My guess is that he was questioning whether he wanted to work with her after all.

Although her words were open and honest, they were also attacking and demanding. They led in no positive direction. After we discussed the likely impact of her first message, she wrote a follow-up e-mail the next day apologizing for hitting "Send" too hastily. She wrote, "I know and appreciate you are working hard to give me the best package you can within company guidelines.

However, it is difficult to justify leaving my community and taking on more responsibilities unless I can clearly see it as a step forward. Can you help me understand why the proposed title is a problem? If it's just a matter of wording, I am certain that we can work together to find language that would suit all parties." He responded with an apology of his own for not explaining himself earlier. Within two days, they were able to settle on a mutually acceptable title and job scope.

Care and Concern

To build a rewarding relationship, you need to demonstrate that you care about your counterpart's well-being. Care is more than honest and positive communication or even the fair division of benefits. It is a visible sign that you value others as more than a source of revenue, that you are personally concerned about them.

Care can be shown in a thousand little ways within a negotiation. You might start by asking your counterpart where it would be most convenient to meet. I assure you that this will earn you far more negotiating pull than if you insist that he comes to your office, then stick him in an uncomfortable chair a few inches lower than your own in an attempt to establish dominance. Moreover, the need for care doesn't exist only during the negotiation. To gain the most out of the deal you need to make sure that someone in your company is responsible for the relationship expectations that have been raised during the negotiation.

Several years ago I met a man who produced foreign language versions of leading international magazines. He told me about his very different experiences with two of his suppliers: the publishers of a well-known American men's magazine and an equally popular French women's monthly.

"The Americans," he said, "were very friendly during the negotiation. They showed a great interest in my knowledge of the publishing business. They asked me lots of questions about my experience and said I was just the partner they were looking for. I really got a warm feeling. But after we signed the deal, I never saw them again. Every month they would send me the copy to translate and ask for my accounts. That was it. When I asked them if they wanted to see the local edition before we went to print, they said, 'No, we trust you know your market.' It was a nice way of saying, 'Don't bother me. Just send the royalties.'

"The French, on the other hand, are on the phone with me practically every week, checking on what I'm doing and offering their suggestions. They want to see each month's edition before it goes out, though they probably can't read it, just to make sure we're in alignment on the look. Last year they asked me to add a men's magazine from their line. That would mean dropping the American magazine, because the market was too small for both. It was a tough choice, because the American magazine was well established, but eventually I went with the French publisher."

"Why was that?" I asked.

He answered in three words: "Because they care."

Empathy and Understanding

Negotiation is about resolving differences, so there will invariably be times when you see things differently from the person on the other side of the table. However, that does not mean that you need to vilify other parties, denigrate their beliefs or ideas, or insist that they are wrong to feel the way they do. Empathy is a great bridge-builder. As with liking, it doesn't require agreement, just an understanding that there are more shades in the world than black and white.

For example, the owner of the professional firm you are seeking to acquire may have put a higher value on her client list than you consider valid. You are certainly correct to question the legitimacy of her estimate, to point out the different considerations that have gone into your calculation, to explain why you believe your valuation is more reasonable, even to make it clear that you are unwilling to pay the price she has asked. At the same time, you can empathize with the pain she must feel in giving up a business she has spent so many years building, understand the value she has attached to every one of those hard-won clients, and imagine the fears she might feel about her economic future. Showing fellow feeling will get you a good deal farther than saying, "You're crazy if you think your business is worth that much!"

Even in disputes, it is important not to let your anger over the issues translate into personal resentment against the other negotiator. Casting the other side as the embodiment of the problem increases resistance to any settlement while it decreases your perspective and creativity. It may be a truism, but a fight really does take at least two. If before negotiating a dispute you spend some time thinking about how the other side will see things, how he will feel, and why he will feel that way, then you will be prepared to empathize with rather than react to any hostility. By validating his right to be unhappy and appreciating the difficulties he (as well as you) has faced, you can help him open up to a different perspective, even to begin to empathize with you. It is amazing how quickly this will move the conversation from accusation into problem-solving.

Although people may *behave* unreasonably from time to time (and some may do so on a regular basis), it is rarely true that they *are* utterly unreasonable. You just have to find the doorway into their reasoning.

Collaborative Efforts Toward Mutual Success

A relationship is founded on the understanding that we're in this together. I need steady customers, and you need reliable suppliers. I need skilled labor, and you want work that rewards those skills. You and I are each looking for a quiet roommate to share the cost of rent. The more effectively we fulfill each other's needs, the more we both prosper. Indeed, the relationship is only viable as long as we *both* feel it is satisfying our interests. If you think I am pushing only my own benefit at your expense, you will respond in kind until there is no mutuality left.

Unfortunately, while the reality of implementation is "us," it is common for negotiators to approach dealmaking as "me against you." Especially when negotiators aren't involved in implementation—and their performance is assessed on immediate transactional gains—it's easy to fall into the zero-sum trap of measuring success by how much one side can squeeze out of the other. But it is close to impossible to build a trusting relationship while simultaneously seeking to profit at the expense of the other party.

This mismatch between the transaction and the relationship is one of the most vital reasons that companies need to begin looking beyond the deal and to develop negotiation performance indicators that take profitability, not just price, into consideration. Otherwise, they may end up as Enron did, paying its negotiator a $54 million bonus for hammering through a power-generation deal in India that not only never made a penny but actually lost the company billions of dollars—helping to drive Enron into bankruptcy. (I'll talk about that more in the next chapter.)

Cutthroat transactional negotiation can also destroy relationships with outside parties. Accusations of one top discount retailer's callous treatment of employee claims, for example, have spawned a number of searing documentaries, dozens of protest websites, and literally thousands of lawsuits, not to mention an employee turnover rate that is five times that of the more employee-friendly warehouse store, Costco. Beyond the workplace, the negative publicity about strong-armed negotiation tactics has led to widespread community resistance to store expansion.

Costco, on the other hand, benefits from tremendous goodwill as a result of its more collaborative policy toward its employees. Costco's founder and CEO, Jim Sinegal, has explained that supporting his employees is a long-term strategy. "Wall Street is in the business of making money between now and next Tuesday," he said. "We're in the business of building an organization, an institution that we hope will be here fifty years from now. And paying good wages and keeping your people working with you is very good business. . . . Imagine that you have 120,000 loyal ambassadors out there who are constantly saying good things about Costco. It has to be a significant advantage for you."[4]

Negotiating collaborative relationships with your business partners begins the process of synergy. By working together to ensure mutual long-term success, you can collaborate on ways to reduce costs and increase efficiencies, to develop new or improved products, and to explore market-leading opportunities.

Reciprocity

Balance is at the heart of relationships. If someone buys you lunch or gives you a lift home when your car breaks down, you will typically feel an obligation to repay the social debt, either in kind or through some roughly equivalent benefit. It's human nature. Within negotiation, reciprocity is also the process of exchange that allows us to test the other's reliability and, from that, begin to build trust.

If, on the other hand, a freeloader sticks you with the bill or asks repeatedly for unreciprocated favors, you will begin to distrust, even dislike, that person. Think of the neighbor you never see unless she wants to borrow something or the co-worker who constantly asks you for help but never gives you credit for your contribution. Within negotiation, this would be the person who pumps you for information but refuses to give out any information of her own; who pleads with you to "help me out" but never gives an inch in return. Failing to reciprocate is the quickest way to kill a relationship.

Reciprocity doesn't mean automatically matching concessions, although one assumes some give-and-take on terms. Rather, it takes place on a more personal, behavioral level. If you are friendly, I respond with friendliness. If you open up a bit, such as by sharing your priorities, I open up an equivalent amount—or perhaps a step more. We may take turns hosting the meeting. Each time you respond in kind, you demonstrate that you are reliable, that you will not take advantage of me, and that I can trust you—and vice versa.

In multiround prisoner's dilemma games in which the players can choose either to give or withhold trust, the strategy that wins every time is called "tit-for-tat." The game works as follows. In each round, two players can choose either to cooperate by bidding high (in which case both win a bit) or to try to undercut the other side by bidding low (in which case the low bidder stands to win the whole pot, as long as the other player bids high). If both parties bid low, however, neither wins anything.

Tit-for-tat is a strategy that works to promote positive behavior through the power of reciprocity. Player A opens with a cooperative move, a high bid. If Player B responds with cooperation, then Player A reciprocates by bidding high on the next move. However, if Player B behaves selfishly by putting in a low bid, Player A reciprocates the next round with a low bid. In every new round, Player A consistently pays back Player B's last move. Eventually, Player B will get the lesson that (1) Player A's actions are a direct result of his own and (2) cooperation is more rewarding over the long run than selfishness.

Tit-for-tat is amazingly effective in molding behavior at the negotiation table. For the most part, it's also simple to do. Most negotiators will respond to cooperation with cooperation. Nearly all are happy to retaliate when they feel they have been harmed. The hard part is to respond positively when the other party moves from negative to positive behavior. It's in our nature to hold a grudge for a while when we feel we've been mistreated, and we tend to want to get in the last blow. However, in this case the natural reaction is not in our best interest. If we fail to respond positively to a concession, the other party may get the message that nothing is to be gained from being more cooperative. A spouse or parent may continue making conciliatory gestures in the face of repeated rejection, but it's unlikely the negotiator across the table will be so long-suffering.

Open-Mindedness and Adaptability

As we will explore more fully in Chapter Six, preparation is essential to effective negotiation. However, planning ahead isn't the same as a rigid insistence on how the eventual deal or relationship will be structured. We always need to be open to the possibility that the other negotiator may have a good idea we never thought of. If we listen with an open mind, we may even find that the other's plan actually gives us more of what we wanted than our original plan did.

Rigidity is the antithesis of negotiation, killing creativity and cooperation, transforming the process into hard-selling at best, outright coercion at worst. Although it is vital to be firm in one's goals, firmness must be balanced with flexibility and open-mindedness in how to achieve those goals. Only our basic principles should be unbending.

While it's more or less self-evident that one needs to be adaptable within the negotiation process, it's a thornier issue when it comes to implementation. That said, it is no less essential. While businesses may yearn for predictability, in long-term contracts the only thing that's predictable is that something will change. When a critical change does occur, a contract-centered, transactional relationship will be unable to cope with the new circumstances, as we saw earlier with Choi and the beef supplier.

A relationship, on the other hand, is able to roll with the punches. That doesn't mean accepting change on demand. Reliability is the cornerstone of relationships, whether business or personal. But by incorporating a degree of flexibility, we can actually strengthen reliability. If we sweep potential problems under the rug and rely purely on the enforcement power of the contract, we'll be thrown into dispute every time a change occurs. However, by anticipating change and foreseeing potential problems, we can create methods for working them out before they become crises.

Veolia Water, which negotiates twenty- to thirty-year water supply arrangements with foreign municipalities, always includes provisions in its contracts setting out how the partners will handle problems that are likely to occur somewhere down the road, from drought to currency devaluations. As often as possible, the company ensures that the same people who negotiate the contract are directly involved in its implementation, maintaining close, regular communication with the business partner for the duration of the project. As a result, despite droughts, cyclones, earthquakes, and tsunamis, Veolia's international partnerships have grown without faltering, making it the world's leading supplier of piped water.

Commitment

One reason people are leery of negotiating relationships is that they fear the requirements of trust and openness subject them to greater risk. It is undoubtedly true that relationships entail risk. But so does business. So does life. And certainly so does a transactional mind-set.

The fear of negotiating relationships comes in part from a misunderstanding of what it means. Looking beyond the deal does not mean opening your books or baring your soul to the other party in the first meeting. That would make no more sense than proposing to someone you'd just met. You don't know enough about the other party—or they about you—to make an intelligent commitment. Relationships need time to develop and to test for fit. By rushing intimacy, you not only risk making a dreadful mistake but you actually discourage the cultivation of trust by failing to give the budding relationship the care and devotion it needs.

As in the game of tit-for-tat, the best way to build a trusting relationship is to commit one step at a time, checking to see that everyone is still together after each new step. Most relationships will never warrant complete trust or openness, although they will function very well at a reliable level of cooperation. A few will grow into true partnerships. However, even close alliances need clear, confirmable commitments that can be monitored to make sure that the parties remain on track together and to counter the normal tendency to take comfortable relationships for granted.

Another point of caution on making commitments: most people in the world develop trust bonds with an outsider at a much slower pace than Americans, who are accustomed to forming instant relationships. If you force people from more reserved cultures to make commitments at your pace—especially if they come from one of the harmony-based countries of Asia—they will say "yes" in hopes of satisfying you enough that you will stop pushing. But that doesn't mean "Yes, we agree" or "Yes, we will do it." It's more like "Yes, something like that might be nice someday, once we get to know you." When negotiating internationally, you have to give the other side the time to grow confident in the relationship.

When my firm was negotiating a project with Siam Cement in Thailand, we met a number of times over the span of nearly a year before they felt comfortable authorizing even the first stage of work. Yet, because we had taken the time to reach a solid, mutual agreement—and because we had earned their trust by keeping faith with them through many changes along the way—they resolutely kept their commitment to us, even when less expensive options came along.

Dependability

The final rule of relationships takes us out of the realm of negotiation per se, but it is necessary to make one vital point about implementation. Agreements are successful only when the parties make them in good faith. If you promise more than you can deliver, expect that the deal will break down and that you will wind up in court. If you fail to honor your commitments, expect to lose the trust and loyalty of the other side.

If you are negotiating an arrangement in which you will play no implementation role, it is crucial you make sure that the implementers on your side are committed to carrying out every agreed term precisely as understood by the parties at the time of agreement and to upholding the spirit of the relationship you have created. Your reputation—and the relationships you have created—rest on your credibility.

Why Go to All This Trouble?

Not everyone wants a relationship. Building and maintaining relationships involves a lot more work than simple dealmaking, in which you can be detached, no-nonsense, and unaffected by what comes after. But over time, living off single transactions is downright exhausting and offers ever-diminishing returns. In the long run, you will find that the extra work you put into negotiating relationships will more than pay for itself in tangible gains—and will reward you with a happier life.

In the next two chapters, we will look more closely at how negotiators can avoid serious problems and realize substantial benefits from looking beyond the deal.

Key Lessons from This Chapter

- A deal is merely a promise; a relationship ensures the desired outcome.
- Contracts cannot replace communication.
- Negotiating relationships is a process, not a transaction.
- Every relationship requires positive words, attitudes, and behaviors, including

    - Respect, friendliness, and liking
    - Fairness

- Honest, open, and positive communication
- Care and concern
- Empathy and understanding
- Collaborative efforts toward mutual success
- Reciprocity
- Open-mindedness and adaptability
- Commitment
- Dependability

Chapter 2

EVEN MONKEYS DEMAND

FAIRNESS

Let's start with avoiding problems. The biggest concern of any negotiator should be to ensure that the agreed terms are carried out and produce the desired outcome. But if, after the fact, one side determines that the deal was not fair, all bets are off. As a species, we reject cooperation with those we feel have taken advantage of us.

Several years ago a fascinating story appeared in the science journal *Nature*.[1] A study had been made of monkeys—not the higher-order apes who have been taught to speak in sign language or to use computers, but little organ-grinder monkeys. The experiment showed that they, like humans, get really mad when they are offered what they feel is an unfair deal.

The monkeys in the study were trained to play a barter game with the human researchers. Whenever a monkey would hand over a small rock, a researcher would give it a slice of cucumber in exchange. Trading rocks for food seemed like a great deal to the monkeys, so they happily swapped their rocks and munched on their winnings. However, once the monkeys had mastered the game, the researchers changed the rules. While they continued to "pay" half of the monkeys in cucumber slices for their rocks, they began awarding the other half with grapes in exchange.

The monkeys who got grapes were naturally very happy with their "raise"—grapes, in monkeys' eyes, being a higher-valued currency than cucumbers. The interesting response, though, came from the monkeys who were still getting cucumbers.

For the latter group, what had once seemed like a more than fair deal (cucumbers for rocks) now seemed grossly unfair ("They're getting grapes, and we're supposed to be content with cucumbers!?"). The monkeys who continued to be paid cucumbers went on strike, rebuffing all further dealings with the humans, refusing to eat the cucumbers they had been given, and in some cases hurling their cucumber slices back at the researchers.

What we learn from this experiment, beyond the fact that monkeys reasonably prefer grapes to cucumbers, is that fairness is not merely a nice word or perfect-world ideal. Quite the opposite. It's a constant emotional need, hardwired into our brains. Even monkeys demand it! And when we humans, like monkeys, feel that we have been treated unfairly, we cease cooperating and will often seek revenge.

The monkey study also shows what an avalanche of lawsuits and broken deals should have taught us long ago but still seems to get lost on hardball, win-lose negotiators: *negotiation is not just about sealing the deal.* The need for fairness does not evaporate with the drying of the ink on a contract. Fairness remains fluid, adjusting as circumstances change or as we gain more information. We can trick people or hide information to get a signed agreement, but once the other side finds out the truth, all bets are off on any but the briefest transactions being carried out as promised. New information causes us to recalculate the terms of what is fair. What had once seemed to the monkeys to be a winning trade of a useless rock for a juicy slice of cucumber was instantly recalculated into a losing bargain based on an insipid cucumber and a delectable grape. And with that recalculation, the concept of fairness shifted.

The monkey study teaches us five lessons about relationships, which we all know about ourselves but often forget to apply to others. Every good negotiation should take these to heart:

1. Everyone (not just ourselves) demands a sense of fairness.
2. We feel less obligated to honor contracts we feel are unfair.
3. Fairness is relative (it is affected by what others are getting).
4. The perception of fairness is unfixed (it changes with new information).
5. Technical fairness ("You freely accepted these terms") is not good enough.

Why are these crucial lessons for negotiators? Quite simply because fairness has a tremendous impact on the willingness of the parties to *implement* agreements. Most agreements that fall apart do so because one side—consisting of moral, conscientious, reasonable people in most cases—decides that in the original agreement it was treated unfairly.

Let's look at the case of a professor I will call Beth, who told me how she had felt "cheated" when she got her first job out of graduate school. During her doctoral studies, Beth had worked part-time as a research assistant for one of her professors. After graduation she was offered a job at a respected think tank. She described how thrilled she was to have landed her "dream job." She was so happy to get the offer that she put almost no thought into what she would be paid. So in her final interview, when one of the partners asked what salary she expected, she had to make a quick mental calculation to come up with a number that sounded fair and reasonable. Not knowing the market rate, she based her salary request on what she had been earning as a graduate student. Beth explained that she had been paid an hourly rate by her professor that came to an annual equivalent of $60,000, but she felt that with her PhD in hand she deserved a bit more. As the boss continued to look at her expectantly, she ventured somewhat nervously, "$75,000?" There was a long silence while the partner seemed to ponder whether the new hire was worth it. Then finally, to Beth's immense relief, he nodded and said, "Okay, I think we can do that," and she was hired.

Elated at her new, exciting job, and higher salary, Beth threw herself into her work, putting in long hours on nights and weekends and quickly earning a reputation as an incisive researcher and analyst, sought after by project leaders. Simultaneously, she became close friends with the HR director, a woman a few years older than Beth with whom she would attend concerts and plays from time to time. When Beth's year-end review and salary discussion rolled around, the HR director called her into her office. Without a word the HR director placed two documents on her desk, within Beth's direct line of sight, then excused herself, saying she had to step out for a moment. Naturally, Beth leaned forward and glanced at the documents. Then she looked closer. They were the employment contracts of her fellow analysts, both hired around the same time as she, and both making $90,000–$100,000.

Beth was aghast. She was also embarrassed, hurt, and confused. But more than anything, she was mad. At first she was mad at herself for having asked for so little. "I knew on the one hand that the fault was mine for not having done my homework," she said. She admitted that the salary of $75,000 had been technically fair. That was the amount she had asked for; her boss had not lied to her or actively misled her in any way. Others had asked for more, so they had gotten more. All of that she accepted on an intellectual level. Yet, on a deeper, emotional level, she grew increasingly mad at her employer: for paying her less for the same work as others, for withholding information, and for "taking advantage" of her in order to save a few dollars, when she had been giving her all to the company. He may have honored the technical rules, but he had broken one of the fundamental rules of relationships—fairness—and in so doing had lost her trust.

As much as she tried to justify the difference in strict market or legal terms, she just wasn't able to get over the fact that she was being paid less than her colleagues for the same work—and that her boss had knowingly taken part in this unfairness. It became harder, she recalled, to put in the same long hours. She felt indignant whenever her boss praised her work. She resented the extra work thrown her way, which had once filled her with pride. Even when she demanded and won a substantial raise in her year-end review, her heart was no longer in the job. A couple of months later, when she got an offer to help start up a competing think tank at a nearby university, she left her job without looking back.

Beth's experience is hardly unique, but it is fascinating for the mixed responses it elicits. Many people to whom I've told the story respond by arguing that the deal was fair: Beth, they say, got what she asked for, and it would be unreasonable for an employer to give someone more than that. However—when they are asked to stop thinking of the story being about an anonymous "Beth" and instead imagine themselves, in their current jobs, discovering that every other employee at their level was earning 25–30 percent more than they were—virtually everyone admits that they would not *feel* it was fair and that they would probably look for another job.

While we all feel angry when we are treated unfairly, it's remarkable how many of us have trouble imagining that others would feel the same resentment if it happened to them. Note the number of people who felt Beth's situation to be fair when they considered it in the abstract, but utterly unfair were it to happen to them. Because they focused more on technical or legal definitions of fairness when the issue didn't apply to them personally, they were less able to predict a problem arising from Beth's deep emotional sense of unfairness.

In the same way, many negotiators take pride in outmaneuvering or openly beating the other side as if they were in a sports competition. They may even go out of their way to upset or bully their "opponent" to "put him off his game." All is fair, they argue, as long as you *nominally* play by the rules. A game is over when the closing bell rings (or a referee reaches a decision), so it doesn't matter if the other side likes you, trusts you, or agrees with the outcome. What they forget, however, is that most negotiations are just the beginning of a relationship, in which you need the cooperation of the other party to get the agreed result and to build or safeguard your reputation. Therefore, doubts about the fairness of the agreement or resentment over perceived ill-treatment during the negotiation can lead to a much less positive outcome than the one you thought you had won.

Why do we have to worry about feelings? The simple answer is that even the most hard-nosed among us act more on feelings than on logic or mathematical equations.[2] How many individuals or businesses spend small fortunes in court over disputes worth a fraction of the costs? Once we come to feel that someone has taken advantage of us, we will rarely make the cool, analytical calculations taught in game theory: "Am I still profiting from this deal?" Instead, like the businessman who walked out of the potentially lucrative deal because the lawyer on the other side didn't shake his hand, we will seek to balance the scales and at the same time to punish the person (or organization) who has made a fool of us, by ensuring that he or she no longer wins. Some may dismiss this as irrational, but it is only so if we confine our definition of interests to immediate financial gain. Punishing someone who has caused us intentional pain not only sends out a very sensible message—"Don't think you can do things like that to me and get away with it!"—but also activates the pleasure centers of our brains in much the same way as eating chocolate or having sex.

Whether you agree with their logic or not, the fact is that people who feel that they have been treated unfairly are much less willing to play by the rules in the future. Ethics are a two-way street. We all have an internal honor code that guides our conduct, but when we are treated dishonorably, that code tends to go out the window. A quick example: a study of organizational morale following employee pay cuts showed that internal company theft increased by an average of 500 percent if the employees felt the process had been handled unfairly or without sufficient consultation.[3]

Put yourself in Beth's shoes. Would you work as hard once you found out how much less you were getting than others at your level—or would you start clocking out at 5:00? Would you be as loyal to the company—or would you be looking for another job? Even if you got the pay raise, would you trust or seek to please your boss as much?

Your answers to these questions show why playing fair is important. You can make very profitable deals without it, but you are taking a big risk, especially over the long term. A used-car dealer can sell a lemon on the theory that it's a onetime transaction with a customer he'll never see again, because a new sucker is born every minute. However, Beth's employer's goals involved both sides working together over time. Had her employer thought more about his goals, he would have understood that his priorities were (1) to hire the best employee (2) at an affordable price, who would (3) get the company's work done well and swiftly, (4) please the clients, and (5) help build a more profitable business. His goals were not (or *should not* have been) to save $1,500 a month by hiring a short-term, disgruntled employee who would benefit from a year's worth of on-the-job training that she would then take to another firm—which is precisely what happened.

What Is Fairness?

For something so basic to our emotional needs, "fairness" is an unusually fuzzy concept. Other fundamental needs—food, shelter, even love or recognition—have clear and universally understood meanings. Fairness, on the other hand, exists uniquely within the eye of the beholder. Dictionary definitions just send you in circles: "fair" means "equitable," which in turn means "just," which in turn means "properly due or merited," which leads us to "deserved," and from there to "right," and finally to complete frustration with the alternatives of "consistent with prevailing or accepted standards or circumstances" or "suitable for a particular person, condition, occasion, or place." In other words, "fair." Like pornography, fairness is one of those things that is harder to define in the abstract than the particular.

That said, we do know some things about how fairness is felt in the context of a negotiation. Broadly speaking, our need for fairness kicks in at three different stages in the negotiation and implementation process. It's a long, even daunting, list, but sidestepping any single item on it can break a deal:

1. *Process fairness*—the way the negotiation is conducted. For example, do all parties

   - Have a chance to voice their views and be listened to respectfully and empathetically?

   - Feel their concerns are being taken seriously?

   - Receive accurate and reasonably complete information?

   - Receive sufficient explanations to help them understand and accept arguments made to them?

   - Feel they have a role in the decision-making process?

   - Have sufficient time to make thoughtful decisions?

2. *Equity*—the sense of a win-win deal. For example, do all parties

   - Feel they have received a reasonable return for their contributions to the transaction?

   - Feel that everyone benefits to a degree comparable to what each has brought to the table (balanced against the realities of supply and demand)?

- Feel that their benefits measure up to those received by others in equivalent positions?

- In the cases where there are disparities understand and accept why the disparities are justified?

3. *Conduct in accordance with expectations*—how the agreement is implemented. For example,

- Are promises kept?

- Does the outcome of the deal more or less correspond to claims made during the negotiation?

- Were mistakes corrected?

- Have the partners sought to maintain the spirit as well as the letter of the agreement?

- Do the parties continue to communicate openly and treat one another respectfully?

- Is there reasonable flexibility in dealing with problems, new information, and unforeseen changes?

The third stage takes us beyond negotiation per se, but it underscores the vital point that negotiation and implementation—what we say and what we do—are inextricably linked. The first two stages fall directly within the realm of negotiation, so let's spend a little more time considering them.

Process Fairness

A former client of mine, the "Tan family," owned and operated a company that provided cleaning and food services for a major airline. The airline was a $20 billion public company making over $1 billion a year in profits. The Tans were one of several vendors who serviced its planes between flights. Although they made a tidy income for a small family business—around a quarter of a million dollars a year—clearly there was a significant disparity in power and resources between the buyer and seller. This power disparity regularly spilled over into the negotiation process.

Negotiations between the parties were more of a monologue in which the airline's procurement team laid out the terms: "This is what we want, and so this is what you will do." At first the Tans were so excited to have this blue-ribbon customer that they brushed off the airline's aggressive style as just the way big companies talk. After all, they reasoned, their business was profitable, so what did it matter if their partners were bullies?

Over time, however, the Tans grew increasingly resentful that their interests and genuine concerns were never considered, especially as their partner's actions began to cut into their profits. Several times the airline fined them large sums for damages allegedly caused by their workers but refused to let them investigate the cause or question the damage assessment. And they changed contract terms by fiat. When the Tans warned the airline's contract management team that its new cost-cutting policy of reducing the number of workers cleaning each plane without increasing the turnaround time for cleaning between flights would inevitably reduce the quality of the job, the airline negotiators blew them off, saying, "You should be grateful we're offering you our business. We're not here to help you improve your internal operations. If you don't like the terms, we'll find someone else to do the work."

Pretty tough stuff. Some might even say with admiration that the airline knew how to drive a hard bargain. The problem is that the Tans got so fed up with being ignored, pushed around, demeaned, and bullied that they couldn't take it anymore. The money, in their minds, just wasn't worth the humiliation. Having reached their emotional limit, they announced to the airline that they were closing up shop immediately (easy enough to do when your main overhead is day laborers). Not coincidentally, the walkout took place at the very height of the travel season.

As the airline scrambled to deal with a crisis of dirty planes, the contract manager threatened the Tans' firm with a lawsuit. The Tans replied that because of the fines and the contract changes the airline had imposed, they were on the verge of bankruptcy in any case, so the airline could sue away. A couple of hours later, now desperate, the contract manager called back with an offer to forgive the fines and discuss better terms, if they would send their workers back. The family held a conference (in which they were clearly enjoying the chaos they had wreaked), then agreed, on the condition that they be consulted before any future fines or changes were imposed. The airline accepted.

Although the Tans' story is quite different from Beth's, they both express outrage over perceived unfairness in the negotiating process. The Tans felt browbeaten every time they negotiated with the airline. Beth, on the other hand, found her interview to be warm and respectful, her future boss asking her many questions and showing a keen interest in her ideas and work preferences, which only increased her sense of having been duped. She cringed with embarrassment in recalling how her boss had intentionally misled her: the long, calculated pause after she had stated her payment terms, while he seemed to weigh whether he could afford it. How could she have fallen for such an old ruse? Both Beth and the Tans recalled their negotiations as humiliating experiences—and both ultimately walked out as a result.

Process fairness is necessary not only for building a lasting deal. It's also central to creating value. People tend to clam up when they feel they are being ignored. We dig in our heels when we feel we are being coerced. And we lose creativity when our ideas are dismissed. None of these is conducive to achieving a deal that enhances value.

To return to the Tans' case, rather than belittling their concerns about the feasibility of cleaning a plane in fifteen minutes with a reduced team, the airline's contract manager could have created a much better outcome for his company, its customers, and its reputation had he inquired about the problems they foresaw and listened to their suggestions about how to solve them. If the airline's goal was to maintain top service levels within budget constraints, a "both/and" approach (exploring how to *both* reduce costs *and* maintain service levels) would have served its interests far better than the age-old "either/or" or "take it or leave it" approach it chose. The discussion would at the very least have made the Tans feel that the airline listened to their concerns. By working together, the parties might even have come up with better ways of deploying workers or taking advantage of work-saving technology.

The keys to process fairness are

- Open, respectful, and honest communication

- Active listening by all parties

- Empathetic consideration of both sides' concerns

- Giving sufficient time for the other side to question and understand

- Comprehensive explanations of the reasons behind your positions

- Openness to new ideas for resolving issues

- Offering a choice rather than forcing an outcome

There is a significant difference between an agreement negotiated with respect and a deal that is forced. The former is far more likely to be honored. In fact, the same study that reported that employees were five times more likely to steal from an employer who cut their pay without fair process found that there was *no significant increase* in theft among employees whose pay was cut similarly but who felt the process had been fair, because they had been given an opportunity to ask questions and raise their concerns, had received full explanations, and were satisfied that the management had openly explored various means for resolving the problem before making its decision. The difference between the two groups, therefore, was not the result of the pay cut (which was the same in both cases) but of the process: the manner in which the issue was communicated and the extent to which they felt they had a voice in the matter.

A common error among negotiators is that they feel that in order to establish their negotiating power they need to start off by acting as if they are confronting public enemy number one. They scowl, posture, interrupt, and lie, and they openly insult their counterpart. Or they push their agenda so hard that the other party can't get a word in edgewise. Or they smile and say "win-win" while they make one-sided demands or hoard all but the most basic information as if it were their life savings. Then they are bemused when they get no deal—or a very bad deal—or their counterparts publicly announce that they will never do business with them again.

Yet how could they possibly think that they will "win" a negotiation by openly seeking an unfair advantage? Do they think that it will inspire the other side to want to work with them or help them make money?

Would it inspire you?

Equity

This is a hard pill for many negotiators to swallow, but here it comes: if one side is seen to profit disproportionately from the deal, the other side will look for an excuse to break it.

There are dozens of highly publicized cases of this, especially in cross-border contracts. One of the most famous is Enron's Dabhol Power fiasco, which dragged on for a decade from 1992 to 2001. The bare bones of the case are these: In 1992 the Indian state of Maharashtra, whose capital is Mumbai, was desperate to bring in foreign investors to develop its increasingly inadequate power grid. However, because India had a history of nationalizing foreign companies, virtually no international energy company was willing to touch the deal. Enron, always ready to take gambles for potentially big profits, was the sole exception.

As the only company willing to take on the Dabhol Power Plant project, Enron International enjoyed—and exercised—disproportionate muscle in the negotiations. In a series of closed-door negotiations marked by threats, walkouts, and total disregard for normal rules of the competitive bidding process, Enron's negotiators pushed through what (on paper) looked like an incredible deal. Enron International and its consortium would build, own, and operate the Dabhol Power Company (DPC), a 2,000- 2,400-megawatt power plant near Mumbai. Instead of using coal, which was cheaply available in the region, the DPC plant would run on liquefied natural gas (LNG). Although this would more than double the price of energy for the consumer, it had a distinct advantage to Enron, since the fuel would be bought from an LNG facility Enron International was then developing in Qatar. Win-win, Enron-style: we win, then we win again. In fact, it was even more heavily weighted in Enron's favor, since the deal was made virtually risk-free. The Maharashtra State Electricity Board was contractually obligated to buy the electrical power produced by the plant, regardless of actual consumer use, and the DPC was even exempted from paying tax on the earnings.[4]

Realizing that the lopsidedness of the deal created some potential for political risk (the World Bank had openly condemned the plant's production capacity as excessive, forcing the residents of Maharashtra to pay for far more kilowatts of electricity than they could possibly consume), Enron International sought to protect itself from any future lack of cooperation on the Indian side by sealing the agreement within a "water-tight" contract. Enron International's spokesman crowed that the contract they drafted and pushed through had it all: "a strong security structure, for instance, letter of credit, an escrow mechanism, a Maharashtra-government guarantee for the entire project and a partial government of

India guarantee."[5] Specifically, the twenty-year contract included a guarantee by the Maharashtra State Electricity Board to purchase a minimum of 90 percent of the plant's monthly output (which exceeded actual demand by nearly 50 percent), backed up by a 100 percent payment guarantee from the Maharashtra state government and a counter-guarantee (in case both the electricity board *and* the state should default) from the central Indian government.

The only problem was that once the electricity plant was up and running, no one—not the citizens of Mumbai, the state of Maharashtra, or the Indian government—was willing to pay the high prices the DPC was charging.

It didn't matter that everyone originally had agreed to the terms. The Indian under-secretary of economic affairs admitted so openly: "When we read the fine print of the power purchase agreement, we realized that perhaps the mistake was on our side as to why did we agree to such exorbitant tariff rates." But regardless of where the initial blame lay, he said, the bottom line was that the price and other terms were unreasonable.[6] From the minute the contract terms were announced, the unfairness had begun to stick in the losing side's craw, manifesting itself in charges of corruption and backroom dealing. Price riots followed. Once a new government was elected in Maharashtra state (on the platform of throwing Enron into the sea), the deal was dead in the water.

Enron sued, of course. Maharashtra state countersued. Calling on the dispute resolution mechanisms in the contract, Enron International initiated arbitration proceedings in London. Maharashtra refused to show up. Eventually, beaten by the sheer force of Indian resistance, Enron conceded more generous terms, but by then it was too late. Just months after the power plant finally became operational, in 2000, the Indians defaulted on the deal. In a last bid to make something out of its $3 billion investment, Enron got the White House involved. As luck would have it, the day before President George Bush was to speak with Indian prime minister

Vajpayee on Enron's behalf, the company collapsed under the weight of its greed.

After the debacle, the Enron spokesman, who had earlier gloated over the perfect contract, reported that he had learned a valuable lesson. Contracts, he said, needed *even stronger* security mechanisms and more-binding remedial clauses. As usual, the powers at Enron had missed the point. The problem wasn't that the contract was less than perfect (no contract is perfect, as any good litigator will tell you) but that the agreement was patently unfair.

We see smaller cases of this "fairness restoration" impulse every day—especially in times of economic stress. I am not arguing that people shouldn't honor agreements they deem to be unfair. My point is merely a warning. People who feel, in retrospect, that they didn't get a fair deal very often don't keep their promises—regardless of the fact that they signed a contract. If that happens to you, then all of your hard bargaining has gone to waste. It just doesn't pay to be seen as coming out too far ahead.

So what can negotiators do to avoid this outcome? Some, like the infamous used-car salesman, will try to paper over bad deals with small giveaways at the end. However, it is far more effective in longer-term deals to control your desire to take your future business partner to the cleaners, keep your eyes on the ultimate goal, and give clear and convincing reasons for everything you ask for and all perceived imbalances *from the outset*. Explanations made after you have been "caught" are never as effective.

Thus, an employer who starts a new hire at a lower salary than his or her predecessor would be better off not disguising the fact but rather explaining the reasons for the salary offered, such as that the new hire is coming in with fewer specific skills or weaker overall experience than the norm. The airline negotiators could have explained to the Tans that they do not like cutting costs but that they are being forced to by rising fuel prices and an increasingly competitive airline market, thanks to the large influx of discount airlines; and they could have asked the Tans for their ideas on how to manage costs. Enron International could have followed due process and had open dialogue with the relevant Indian interest groups to explain (and modify) their position before throwing billions into building a power plant that would never earn them a penny.

Remember that fairness cuts both ways. One of the most effective tools for deflecting demands for special favors is to explain that you treat all customers (or all who fall within a certain category) equally, and that for you to give preferential treatment to one would be unfair to the others. It's a difficult argument to resist. Few of us like to say we oppose fairness. More practically, even though your counterparts may not care in the least whether *others* are treated fairly, they have a strong interest in ensuring that *they* are, so they would have a hard time pressing you to become less transparent, which could come back to bite them next time.

Here is a final personal story to illustrate this point. Years ago I coached a Thai business school team that took part in an international business case competition. To everyone's delight, they qualified for the finals. Then the problem hit: there were insufficient funds to attend the weeklong championship rounds to be held in Montreal. Never quitters, the students scrambled for money, coming up with a corporate donation system with three categories of funding—donor (below $1,000), silver circle ($1,000–1,999), and gold circle ($2,000 and above)—each with an increasing set of advertising and public relations benefits. The students did an amazing job of publicizing their cause and pulling in donations. By the time the competition was just a week away, they had raised nearly all they needed, short by only $1,500 or so. They had resigned themselves to paying the remainder out of their own pockets, when the fateful call came in. A local company had read in the newspaper about the students' success and wanted to make a donation of $1,000. The students were elated. Problem solved! Well, problem almost solved. The only condition was that the company wanted to be listed as a gold-circle donor. New problem.

Knowing that I might be killing the goose that was about to give us a silver egg, I patiently explained to the woman on the phone that only companies who contributed $2,000 or more qualified for the gold circle. "The other companies in the gold circle each gave at least $2,000," I said. "It would be unfair if, after requiring that level of donation from them, we then let in another company that contributed only half that amount. It is important to us to respect all of our donors—and to keep all of our promises."

"But we are helping you out by bringing you money late in the day, when you desperately need it," the woman replied.

"That's true," I said, "and we're extremely grateful for whatever you can donate. We do understand that you've missed out on some publicity by helping us at this late stage, so we're happy to give you additional benefits beyond the usual silver-circle category to make up for it, such as a special PR event. We're open to any suggestions you might have. That said, we simply cannot break our word to the gold-circle donors who were there for us from the start by changing the rules they had to honor. I hope you will understand."

The caller said she would have to discuss this with her boss and hung up. I then faced some very annoyed students. They might lose the donation because of my insistence on fairness, they grumbled. "Perhaps," I replied, "but why should that happen? We have welcomed their help, been fully transparent, and offered them other options. They will see us as fair and trustworthy. At the least, even if we lose this donor, we will ensure the loyalty of our current donors if we need to call on them in subsequent years."

Half an hour later the phone rang. "My boss has decided to donate $2,000," the voice said. That is the power of fairness.

Conclusion

Fairness doesn't require a Marxist society in which each gives according to his ability and collects according to his needs. Nor does it mean giving up on your goals or giving away the store.

It merely means being open, honest, and reasonable; offering explanations, legitimacy, and objective evidence; behaving in a way that is justifiable; and understanding your own value as well as the value that other parties bring to the table. It means considering the relationship over time, not just how much you can squeeze out of the immediate transaction.

It is quite straightforward, really. A fair employer negotiates a pay package with his or her employees according to a set scale or their personal contribution to the company. A fair business partner seeks a deal that balances risk and creates reasonable (not necessarily equal) profit for both sides. A fair negotiator listens, explains, and responds insofar as possible to the concerns of the other side. And the result is an agreement that not only looks good on paper but keeps looking good in practice.

KEY LESSONS FROM THIS CHAPTER

- The need for fairness is hardwired into our brains.
- A sense of unfairness leads to uncooperativeness, even revenge.
- If one side is seen to profit disproportionately from a deal, the other side will find an excuse to break it.
- The three key aspects of fairness are
  - Process — how reasonably you treat people during the negotiation
  - Equity — the justice of the final result
  - Conduct — how faithfully agreements are kept

Chapter 3

THE POWER OF US

In addition to helping you avoid the potentially devastating pitfalls of post-deal resentment and retribution, relationship-based negotiation brings a wealth of positive benefits. Through working together to solve problems and create synergy, negotiation beyond dealmaking becomes a platform for generating immediate and lasting gains for all parties by

- Increasing understanding

- Building trust

- Maximizing value

- Reducing resistance and gaining acceptance

Whatever your job—be it salesman, buyer, service provider, business owner, manager, team-worker, consultant, or home-maker—you will find that negotiation goes more smoothly and you get better results by moving from forceful opposition to collaborative problem-solving, from dealmaking to relationship-building.

Let's look more closely at these benefits by exploring a few real examples.

Increasing Understanding

As the final assignment in my MBA negotiation courses, I always require my students to prepare and conduct a negotiation. The subject of the negotiation can be anything, as long as it involves a genuine and serious issue. Students in past classes have negotiated everything from selling a business to buying a car; from resolving a long-standing property line dispute with a neighbor to reaching a reasonable accommodation with a boss who strongly opposed the company's flextime policy. I have read hundreds of these papers describing and analyzing personal negotiations. Although their grade is based solely on the planning and analysis, not on the outcome of the negotiation, nearly all of the students have reported successful outcomes, often startlingly so to those who had taken on problems they originally felt were intractable.

In the last section of their papers, the students assess the key factors that helped them reach (or prevented them from achieving) agreement. By far, the most common positive factor they list is understanding. In case after case they report that they were able to resolve differences that had once seemed insurmountable, largely because they had gone from positional fighting ("I want X") to putting in the effort to achieve genuine mutual understanding ("What are your concerns? Let me explain mine. How can we fashion a solution that will respect them both insofar as possible?").

One of my favorite negotiations was conducted by a midcareer student, Nick. He and his wife, Susan, were a working couple in their early thirties. Their marriage had been happy and dynamic until about seven months earlier, when two longed-for blessings upended their lives in unanticipated ways: Susan gave birth to their first child, and Nick was accepted into an executive MBA program. By mutual decision, Susan left her job and put her career on hold to take care of the baby for its first eighteen months. Meanwhile, Nick became the family's sole breadwinner, holding down his full-time logistics job while also attending MBA classes Thursday nights and all day Saturdays. Since then, the combination of Susan's isolation and Nick's heavy outside commitments had taken a toll on their nerves and on their marriage.

One long-simmering issue that had become a serious dispute was Nick's desire to play basketball with his old group of regulars on Sunday afternoons. Nick felt as if all he had done since starting the MBA program was work, eat, and stress out. He felt sluggish and out of sorts most of the time. He worried about the weight he had begun to put on. He strongly needed a regular, vigorous workout, he said, as well as the camaraderie of old friends, to get back into mental and physical shape. Yet, whenever he broached the subject with Susan, she reacted with hurt and anger, pointing out that Sunday was the only day of the week he could spend with her and the baby. She was alone every day, she reminded him, as well as many nights when he was at school, working late in the office, or doing homework with his teammates. How could he even think of spending Sundays playing with his buddies? She openly questioned his commitment to his family and even began to wonder aloud whether she might not do just as well on her own. Alarmed by Susan's response and feeling guilty for appearing not to care about her or the baby, Nick backed off. But he remained sluggish and stressed—and secretly resented being denied something that, to him, seemed both reasonable and important.

Nick admitted that he was worried about taking on this topic for his negotiation and feared that raising the issue with Susan again could jeopardize their tenuous peace. But he also realized that this unresolved dispute and his resentment were damaging their relationship, so he decided it was worth one more try.

He began by planning the negotiation using the GRASP method laid out in Chapters Seven through Eleven. From the start, he later reported, he began to see things in a new light. He had always looked at this issue only from his own point of view: *he* was stressed out; *he* was gaining weight; *he* needed a break; *he* missed his friends; *he* was only asking for a few hours a week. Now he realized that he was only half of the picture. As he began to list Susan's goals, his perspective broadened and deepened.

Susan wasn't a harridan who sought to control his life and deny him any personal outlets, as he had begun to imagine when he saw her only in opposition to his own desires. She had desires and concerns of her own. She was used to spending her days in an office, with a position, projects that could be accomplished, and co-workers to talk to; now she was home alone with a preverbal baby, doing repetitive tasks with no clear conclusion, undoubtedly worried about losing her skills and sacrificing her future career. She felt unrecognized by Nick, who prioritized his job, studies, and now even *basketball* over her. Like him, she was stressed out, needed time away, and missed her friends. She may also have felt jealous of Nick's many colleagues and MBA classmates, with whom he spent most of his time.

After thinking about how Susan saw the situation, Nick understood how his request to spend Sunday afternoons with his basketball buddies because he "needed a break" must have sounded to her. This thought process, before he even spoke to her, markedly increased his understanding and commitment to finding a win-win solution.

This time, when Nick approached Susan, he spoke in a way she had never before heard from him. Instead of pressing to play basketball, he started by talking about what a rough time she had had and the sacrifices she had made since the baby was born and he had started his MBA course. He told her honestly how much he appreciated that she had carried much of the domestic load for them so that he could concentrate on his studies. He asked her about how she saw her present life, and they talked about her professional goals and their future once the baby was old enough to go to preschool. Only then did he share his concerns with her.

"Life hasn't been easy for either of us for the past seven months," he said. "We both feel that all we do is work. We're both stressed out by responsibility. We both miss our old friends and activities. On top of that, as you've pointed out a few times, I'm getting fat!" This time she could smile with empathy. No longer on the defensive, she began to listen to his explanation and to understand that Nick had valid concerns as well. Perhaps he wasn't the selfish, immature chauvinist she had begun to fear she'd married.

Having moved from opposition to mutual understanding, Susan was able to open her mind when Nick proposed a solution. He suggested that she choose one night of the week (except Thursdays) to be her night off. On that night, he promised to be home by 6:00 at the latest; no excuses, no exceptions. She would be free to do anything she wanted—see friends, take a class, go to the spa, sit with him and talk for hours, whatever she felt like—while he watched the baby. This would give her a needed break and a chance to regain some of her lost independence. In exchange, he would play basketball Sundays from 3:00 to 5:00 and she was welcome to bring the baby and watch the game or not, as she chose.

Within minutes, they settled a dispute that had caused increasing tension in their marriage for the past seven months. Even better, Nick related, they came away with a stronger relationship. Why? Because they had stopped fighting and had started understanding.

No doubt many of you are thinking right now that while understanding may be important within a marriage, it is unnecessary in the competitive world of business negotiation. On the contrary: understanding is a cornerstone of compliance in *any* relationship. A KPMG study of why well over half of all mergers and acquisitions (and more than three-quarters of international alliances) broke up in the first three years found that companies that focused their negotiations primarily on financial and legal issues had a failure rate that was 15 percent higher than average. Conversely, negotiators who worked to gain a thorough understanding of the other party, and how they could generate value together, had a 28 percent higher than average *success* rate.[1]

Numerous studies have found that people across the spectrum assume very little responsibility for agreements they don't understand. This is why it is vital to the success of the agreement that you question everything you don't understand in a contract and keep questioning until any ambiguity is resolved. Just as important, you need to make sure that your negotiation counterparts fully understand everything they agree to, as well as the reasons behind an agreement, because a failure to fully understand it will become an excuse to violate it—and will lead to a destructive blame game.

Let's say you object to the wording of a clause in a contract. If you believe you have enough power, you could use force, insisting on your own wording. Or if you feel you have very little power, you could give way and leave the clause as worded, despite your misgivings. Neither solution will lead to dependable implementation. In the first instance, you ignore the interests of the other party, making your counterpart feel he or she has lost a battle with you; in the second, you make an agreement that ignores your own interests and that you will feel less than fully committed to.

The third—by far the best—way is to seek an honest understanding among all parties. You ask your counterpart what the clause is designed to accomplish or avoid, explain your own concerns about the way it is written, and work together toward a mutually acceptable solution that takes *both* parties' concerns into consideration. By increasing understanding, you can move from "either/or" (fighting for domination) to "both/and" (working together to find the optimal solution), greatly increasing your ability to work together beyond the deal.

What if the other party doesn't want a fair deal? Undoubtedly, there are short-term players who are only out for their own gain and don't care a fig for explaining themselves. When you encounter such transactional thinkers, it is tempting to dismiss any effort to reach a deeper understanding as a waste of time. In fact, these are the times when it is most important to be persistent in asking questions until you clarify their attitudes and goals. Their response will give you an important forecast of the problems that will likely arise in any future relationship. If your negotiation counterpart refuses to share information, shows no concern for your interests, doesn't listen to your arguments, and behaves in a domineering and high-handed manner across the negotiation table, you should not expect the relationship to be any different once the ink on the contract is dry.

Having said that, I assure you that in the vast number of cases, once you get beyond positions and start sharing concerns, you will find that what seemed initially to be a win-lose face-off can be resolved in a mutually productive way. Moreover, the deepening understanding that results will lead to smoother and more reliable implementation and, as an added bonus, the growth of trust.

Building Trust

Trust is an essential feature of successful relationships of any type. It is also a necessary part of doing business. Psychologists tell us that a foundation of trust is a precondition to people's willingness to contribute time and attention to pursuing common goals, to reveal useful and frank information, and to exercise "responsible restraint in sharing resources" (as opposed to grabbing everything for themselves).[2] When there is no trust within a negotiation, your counterpart will misinterpret your statements, dismiss your explanations, view your offers suspiciously, and generally question your motives. When problems arise, as they inevitably do, the lack of trust will merely validate the other side's conviction that you had bad intentions all along.

Moreover, if you are going to rely *solely* on the enforcement power of a contract to ensure that I deliver the product I promised at the quality I promised and on the schedule I promised, then you'd better be prepared to spend a lot of time, money, and emotional energy taking me to court. Wouldn't it be much more effective and straightforward if I were to do it willingly, because you and I had built up a basis of mutual trust? This is especially important if you are in Milwaukee and I'm in Mumbai, Manila, or Managua, where the likelihood you'll get positive results through the courts is very slim indeed. When it comes to cross-border deals, if the parties are not committed to carrying out the agreement, the grim reality is that any contract we sign will be at best difficult, and in many places virtually impossible, to enforce.

Even within the same legal system, if you need to rely on my fulfilling my promises without going to all the expense and effort of getting a judge to force me to comply, then we need to develop a store of trust in each other's intentions and ability to follow through. In fact, alliance managers interviewed by KPMG overwhelmingly singled out the development of a trust-based relationship before entering the partnership as their key success factor.[3]

Naturally, it will never be complete trust. Even the closest family relationships require reasonable limits and responsible oversight. (You may trust your teenager overall but still have a curfew and keep watch to ensure it's honored.) Nor should trust be handed over immediately. Trust needs to grow step-by-step over time, as each side proves through its actions that it has earned trust. Despite these limitations, however, we always benefit by seeking to build trust.

A contract does not and cannot replace a relationship. It can never be wholly unambiguous or anticipate all problems that might arise. Worse, the very attempt to put onto paper all the potential evils that might occur can poison the relationship. Many people around the world find long contracts full of detailed obligations and enforcement clauses to be offensive, in the same way that a long prenuptial contract setting out the penalty to be imposed every time a spouse is late taking out the garbage would be deemed an offensive start to a marriage. In most cultures, a degree of personal trust is prerequisite, not just to loyalty but to honest communication.

In a survey of three thousand American and European business executives engaged in manufacturer-retailer relationships (ranging from pharmaceuticals to apparel), London Business School professor Nirmalya Kumar found that dealers who said they had a trusting relationship with their supplier generated 78 percent more sales than those who felt they were just selling its products. Kumar found that in the long run trust was a far stronger force than raw power. "Partners that trust each other generate greater profits, serve customers better and are more adaptable," he concluded. By working as partners rather than hiding information, the manufacturers and retailers were able to provide the greatest value to customers and to significantly reduce costs.[4]

On a smaller scale, a survey of 187 project managers published in *Project Management Journal* listed trust as the single most important factor in successful completion of projects that involve multiple partners with diverse interests.[5] Building trusting relationships is at the core of creating successful professional service firms or in dealing harmoniously and productively with internal clients, colleagues, and employees.

The difficulty with trust is that it is so easy to destroy through short-term thinking by bending the truth or making promises that can't be fulfilled, in the confidence that the real picture won't be discovered until after the contract has been signed and the negotiator has safely left the scene. How many deals have fallen apart over the negotiator implying certain interpretations or understandings that the contract implementer later claims to know nothing about? How many long-sighted negotiators have then moved in to fill the vacuum of that broken trust and to reap the benefits their more transactional predecessors squandered?

In 1989 Dr. Kim Yong-Ho was working for General Dynamics, hoping to persuade the South Korean government to buy a fleet of 120 F-16 fighter jets. Although he worked hard to create strong relationships with the Korean government and military and to show the advantages of the F-16, he was disappointed to learn in December that the government had signed a purchase and sales agreement for the McDonnell Douglas F-18.

Despite the setback, neither Kim nor his boss on the F-16 project was ready to throw in the towel. "I view business as a long-term relationship," Kim told me nearly twenty years later. "Sure, I was disappointed, but you can't focus on each deal as a separate venture that's done and over once the ink is dry. Business is a continuum. The best way for me to achieve General Dynamics' long-term goals was to keep working to understand the customer and to develop their trust." Over the next months, Kim maintained regular contact with his Korean government counterparts and continued to share information and ideas with them.

That put him in an excellent position when the McDonnell Douglas deal started to fall apart the next year. The price of the F-18 had skyrocketed, from an estimated $4.2 billion at the time of the purchase agreement to $6.2 billion a year later. Additionally, the Korean government was unhappy with the new people McDonnell Douglas had sent in to implement the deal after it was negotiated.

"One problem in a lot of businesses is that they care less about the customer once they get the contract," Kim explained. "Before winning the contract, the business development guys are in charge. They make all kinds of assurances to get the deal. Then, once it goes into implementation, it's passed over to a wholly new team in the program office, and they say, 'Oh, they shouldn't have promised that.' So frustrating for the customer! That's how you lose trust."

Kim promised the Korean officials that if they withdrew the purchase from McDonnell Douglas and opted instead for the General Dynamics F-16, there would be total continuity between the business development and program office teams, ensuring no surprises or memory lapses. He promised personally to move from Fort Worth to Seoul to oversee the contract from beginning to end. That and assuring a firm (no bait and switch) $5 billion price tag for the F-16 swung the deal. In March 1991, the South Korean government announced that it was dropping the F-18 and would instead buy 120 F-16s from General Dynamics. When Lockheed Martin, coproducer of the F-16, acquired the General Dynamics division in 1993, Kim kept his promise to remain in Korea to manage the project, moving to Lockheed Martin to become senior vice president for South Korea.

By looking beyond the deal and keeping their promises, Kim and Lockheed Martin moved from outsider to partner with the Korean government, earning the company tens of billions of dollars. The F-16 was only the first project. In the years following that first deal, Lockheed Martin entered into a license agreement with the Korean government to produce a local version of the F-16 and a coproduction arrangement to jointly develop the T-50 Golden Eagle. The company now sells Korea maritime patrol craft, combat systems, early warning radars, air traffic control systems, and communication satellites and is negotiating to help produce the KF-X stealth fighter. Meanwhile, crushed under heavy debt, McDonnell Douglas was absorbed by Boeing in 1997.

"If you want to survive in this competitive world, you have to get out of the mentality of thinking only about the written agreement," advises Kim. No idealistic dreamer, he bases his philosophy on his experience of what succeeds and what fails in the real world of international business. "Foreign companies will never be loved. That means you have to work hard to be trusted more than others, many of whom are hated. We make every effort to understand and align with the customer's goals. We help the Korean government bring up their aerospace development program as much as they can. That way they come to trust us and appreciate our contribution. Each program then leads into the next. But it has to start from being open and fair, listening, and always keeping your word."[6]

Maximizing Value

When parties to a negotiation lengthen their perspective from the deal to the relationship, they are able to look beyond particular terms to the potential impact their agreement will have on their business or personal goals.

America's largest natural food retailer, Whole Foods Market, places "creating ongoing win-win partnerships with our suppliers" among its core values. The company deals directly with local farmers and manufacturers to get just-in-time delivery of organic produce in order to reduce the consistent problem of short shelf life that plagues the standard global purchase and warehousing system. It works with vendors to develop new products and reduce production and distribution costs; educates them on how to become "greener"; and provides advice and assistance in packaging, marketing, and media relations. Whole Foods' philosophy is to treat its suppliers with "respect, fairness and integrity at all times and expect the same in return."

The management recounts with pride how those strong supplier partnerships saved its flagship store from ruin in its earliest days. Eight months after opening its doors, on Memorial Day, 1981, the first Whole Foods store was badly flooded, wiping out its entire inventory and damaging much of the building and equipment. The company at that time was uninsured, a surefire trigger for a raft of lawsuits. Instead, the retailer's creditors and vendors worked with the store management to help it reopen just four weeks later. Today Whole Foods has grown from that single store in Austin, Texas, in 1980 to 270 outlets across North America and the United Kingdom.

It never pays to assume that you're too powerful to need allies—or that you are so efficient on your own that you don't need the knowledge synergies that allies bring. That lesson was learned most painfully by the Port of Singapore in August 2000 when its single biggest customer, Maersk Sealand, announced that it was moving all of its operations from Singapore to the Malaysian Port of Tanjung Pelepas (PTP), an overnight loss of 10 percent of Singapore's harbor terminal business.

The world's busiest port with no competitors in the vicinity, the Port of Singapore accounted for around 3.5 percent of the city-state's GNP. The port's management arm, PSA, held a virtual lock on the regional shipping market, so it could call the shots, paying little attention to the requests of the shipping lines that used its berths. PSA pursued a single-minded policy of providing facilities that were among the most high-tech and efficient—and therefore most expensive—in the world. That wasn't a bad policy in and of itself. It's just that it wasn't what the customer wanted in the wake of the Asian financial crisis.

Faced with a severe economic slowdown, the shipping lines complained that PSA's high prices were draining away their already reduced profits. They were willing to sacrifice premium service, they said, if it would lower the price. Dismissing their appeals, the port authority held firm to its high-quality–high-cost policy. Occupying an effective monopoly position in the region, PSA was not troubled by the shippers' accusations of "inflexibility" and "heavy-handed" negotiation approach.[7] Nor did its executives lose any sleep in October 1999 when Malaysia announced that it was opening its own port just across the narrow strait. PSA was confident that Tanjung Pelepas would not be able to match the Port of Singapore's size, quality, or value-added services.

Maersk, on the other hand, saw the challenge posed by the PTP as an opportunity to get in on the ground floor and develop a mutually beneficial relationship with a more customized port. While PSA rested secure in its position, Maersk management experts and engineers set to work with PTP's planners to develop the facilities and service menu the shipping line wanted. In exchange for a 30 percent equity stake in PTP, Maersk negotiated the right to dedicated berths so that it would no longer lose money waiting offshore for the next available slot (a request that PSA had consistently refused in order to maximize use of its terminal resources), as well as the right to manage its own terminal operations and to employ its own procedures and systems. The new arrangements reduced Maersk's costs by 30–40 percent.

PTP's willingness to look beyond the deal and negotiate a mutually profitable relationship with Maersk enabled the upstart David to beat Goliath and walk away with the prize. By problem-solving rather than fighting, Maersk saved time and money for years to come, while PTP not only got Maersk's business but also benefited from the shipping line's expertise and ideas for improving the port facilities, boosting productivity, and reducing costs. The knowledge and skills PTP gained from this partnership attracted other customers. In 2002 Evergreen Lines, the world's second-largest shipper, followed in Maersk's wake, moving its operations from Singapore to Malaysia as well—another 5 percent loss to PSA's business. Yet, as big a coup as that was, it was not the most surprising moment. That came in 2006 when PTP beat Singapore for the coveted Lloyd's List Asia award as "Container Terminal of the Year," recognized for having the highest recorded productivity among global ports as well as for its value, customer service, facilities, and overall efficiency.

Of course, maximizing value doesn't have to take place on such a large scale. It can be a part of your everyday life once you move away from positional thinking. Years ago I took part in an outing with my husband's extended family to visit some ancestral sites in Korea. We rented what seemed to be an excessively large bus, which soon proved to be just that. The bus made it over a narrow wooden bridge into a tiny village where an ancient Yun scholar had once lived. But when we got back after viewing the site, we found the bus driver in a shouting match with the villagers. The bus was stuck. There wasn't space to turn around, and given the angle, the driver couldn't maneuver the enormous vehicle backward across the bridge. Everyone was accusing the other of being at fault for "having such a ridiculously small bridge" or "coming here in such a ridiculously big bus."

At some point, however, one of the frustrated disputants pointed out that all parties shared the same goal of getting the bus out of the village and on its way. It was as if a bell had gone off. Fighting stopped, as everyone started throwing out ideas as to how to get the bus over the bridge. Soon everyone was working together, actually tearing down a fence and hauling in boards to widen the on-ramp to the bridge, then guiding the reversing bus across. Amazingly, the whole thing was accomplished in just over an hour. In our heartfelt gratitude, the bus occupants collected a generous "tip" to thank the local work team for their efforts, which was much appreciated by the poor, rural farmers. Everyone left feeling like a winner. Now that's creating value!

Reducing Resistance and Gaining Acceptance

The brilliant innovation that made Tupperware a product found in millions of homes around the world was not molded polyethylene or even Earl Tupper's patented "burp" seal. When Tupperware was introduced in stores in 1946 it had both of these qualities, but sales were stagnant. What made the difference was the "Tupperware party," a sales concept developed by Florida saleswoman Brownie Wise. Begun in 1948, Wise's housewife sales concept proved so successful that within two years it became the company's sole sales outlet. Why were the parties so successful? Earl Tupper believed it was because people needed demonstrations to understand how the airtight seal worked. That may have been true in the early years, but why are these parties still going strong sixty years later? The answer—and the reason it is relevant to a book on negotiation—is that Brownie Wise understood that we like to say yes to people we like and with whom we feel a sense of kinship.

This was not a wholly new idea, of course. In 1936 Dale Carnegie published *How to Win Friends and Influence People*, the best-selling self-help book that has now sold over fifteen million copies.[8] Carnegie's insight was that building positive relationships—by such steps as showing a personal interest, being respectful, letting the other party talk, and not arguing—went hand in hand with reducing resistance and gaining acceptance.

While Carnegie's may have been a new way of thinking to many in the United States, it has been a standard business assumption for centuries in much of the rest of the world. When Geert Hofstede interviewed over one hundred thousand IBM employees in fifty countries, he found that 60 percent of cultures (consisting of all societies outside of Europe and the Anglo-Saxon countries) put higher priority on honoring relationships than on achieving tasks.[9] So the question is, why do so many people still not get it?

I was called in to advise a government agency that was having tremendous difficulties working with a partner agency whose permission it needed to launch any new initiative. Unfortunately, after years of minor turf wars, the relationship had become toxic. Nearly every issue turned into a fight, even down to who would be the first to come on the phone line when the secretary of one of them called the other. The irony of the situation was that the two organizations and their staffs had many similarities, faced many of the same issues, and operated under similar constraints. What they lacked were friendly, personal connections. I advised them to get to know their counterparts in the other agency in order to build up a store of goodwill and empathy that would reduce the level of resistance. "Why not invite them out for lunch sometime," I suggested, "or at least chat a bit before and after meetings?"

One woman on the team, Caroline, shook her head in disgust. "How can I act friendly toward someone who is so rude and sarcastic?" she asked. As Caroline explained it, the last time she had called her counterpart in the other agency, her contact had answered the phone by asking, "Am I speaking to the complaints department?" In some confusion, Caroline repeated who she was, then asked why the other woman would think it was the complaints department. "Because whenever you call, it's to complain about something," she replied. Caroline was miffed, yet when I asked her if she ever called her counterpart for any other reason than to raise a problem, she snapped back, "No, why would I? She's obnoxious!"

In this case, business communication had devolved into a vicious cycle of personal sniping. I worked with the staff to make them aware of their part in perpetuating the cycle and of how, by doing so, they had made their jobs significantly harder and their work lives more stressful. To help them change the dynamic, I set them some tasks to start creating more positive connections with their counterparts. They were skeptical of my assurance that it only takes one side to break a cycle, but they eventually agreed to give it a try. When I checked back with the agency head a few months later, he told me that things had indeed improved considerably. "They are beginning to understand our point of view," he said. "There's more give-and-take, and we're able to reach quicker agreements."

Swiss psychologist Carl Jung showed in 1921 that about half of all people base their decisions on feelings more than on rational calculations and that everyone combines the two to some degree. In other words, any decision is based on a combination of emotional benefits (Do I enjoy doing business with you?) and tangible benefits (What will I gain materially from this relationship?). It's vital to remember that people look to receive the emotional benefits first, as any tangible profit will be realized only after the negotiation is concluded. Moreover, even if the potential profits are high, if you feel emotionally accosted, you'll become so defensive and inflexible you may never reach agreement. If, on the other hand, you feel emotionally secure, your defensive mechanisms will come down, allowing you to get back to the business at hand.

Many times I have seen a skilled negotiator step into a seemingly intractable dispute over certain terms and break the impasse in just a few moments, simply by being warm, empathetic, open-minded, and seriously interested in understanding the other party's concerns. This has the almost immediate effect of allowing the other antagonist to step away from the corner he or she had felt trapped in. When people feel cornered or attacked, they are simply too engaged in defending their position to consider solutions. However, once they recognize that you are not trying to take advantage of them—even though you may have different interests or perspectives from their own—their minds relax, their creativity flows, and they are once again able to concentrate on maximizing value.

Even in disputes, you need to make it clear to other parties that you don't dislike them personally, that you respect their right to hold their own point of view, and when appropriate, that you regret the actions or misunderstandings that led to the impasse. Though you may disagree on how best to resolve the problem and move forward, you will stand a far greater chance of reaching a favorable resolution if you always give other parties the benefit of the "3 A's":

- *Admiration*—treating them and speaking of their company or group with respect, as opposed to putting them down or taking a superior tone

- *Affiliation*—approaching them as business partners with whom you want to work cooperatively, or even as fellow victims, as opposed to enemies or cheats

- *Acknowledgment*—appreciating the merit of their thoughts, feelings, and actions (or at least their right to have them), as opposed to dismissing or demeaning them

Creating a positive connection is particularly important because people are subject to emotional contagion: an automatic, subconscious response to another's voice, facial expressions, and body language that causes us to mimic those actions or emotions. We feel heartache when a child cries over a dead pet in a movie; we yawn when we see or hear another person yawn. In a negotiation context, we reflexively mirror the attitudes we observe in other parties. If they appear sour, we also begin to feel sour; if they sound upbeat, we too feel upbeat. In other words, the way we say things is just as important, if not more, than the content of our message.

A short time ago, I was working with a group of internal auditors to help them reduce resistance and build rapport with their clients.

At the end of a day of training, the auditors took part in a paired role play in which they were to discuss with a "client" the problems they had uncovered, then agree on a jointly developed plan for fixing it. Most teams handled the task well. However, one pair still hadn't reached an agreement forty-five minutes later and showed no signs that it was likely to reach one. When I asked them what the problem was, the client said that the auditor had been hostile and demeaning throughout the meeting, so that he simply didn't want to work with him. The auditor seemed genuinely confused and slightly annoyed by the client's negative attitude to what he felt had been his fair and collaborative approach. Indeed, when the auditor summarized what he had said, his words sounded reasonable. Puzzled, I asked them to role-play their discussion again while I observed them. Immediately the problem became apparent. Although his sentiments were positive, the auditor wore a grim-faced expression and spoke throughout in a flat, downbeat tone. The client picked up the negative body language and tone, interpreted them as connoting a sense of coercive superiority, and began to mirror that behavior. The mirrored feeling was so palpable that the role-players remained genuinely upset well after the conclusion of the exercise.

On the other hand, people are able to deal quite positively with disagreements when they are approached in a respectful, friendly, and problem-solving manner, especially when the other party acknowledges the difficulties or frustrations they have faced. All negotiators would be wise to recall the words of William James, the father of American psychology: "The deepest principle in human nature is the craving to be appreciated."[10] Admiration, affiliation, and acknowledgment cost the giver nothing, but they pay extraordinary returns. They may even be the "concessions" that break through a heretofore intractable conflict.

I experienced the power of the 3 A's in a dispute-resolution negotiation I conducted on behalf of a young financial analyst. Rich had accepted a job offer from a midsized bank for a position that required highly specialized knowledge. As he was working at the time for another company, Rich asked for a three-month delay before starting, so that he could complete his current project then take a vacation before beginning the new job. In light of the specialized nature of the position and Rich's excellent qualifications, the vice president who ran the section agreed to the delay. Rich signed a contract promising to start in three months' time.

About a month before he was to start the new job, though, Rich got a call from a search firm offering him a position at a larger, international bank at a base salary nearly 40 percent higher than that of the job he had already accepted. It was an offer he couldn't refuse. He contacted the first bank to let them know that he wouldn't be coming after all.

Naturally, they were furious, particularly the vice president, who had been waiting for Rich for over two months and was now convinced that he had used her offer in a calculated scheme to get a better-paying job. She sent him an official warning that if he failed to show up for work on the agreed date, the bank would sue him $27,000 for breach of contract. He pleaded for mercy, but the vice president was unmoved. He argued that a lawsuit would be expensive and time-consuming. She replied that as they were a bank, they had money and their own legal department, so it was no problem. Clearly, the trust between Rich and the bank had been shattered. But that didn't mean that another person couldn't step in to create a warmer relationship that would open the door to a resolution.

When I walked into the meeting with the vice president and the HR manager to try to resolve the dispute, the mood was icy. I smiled as I introduced myself and shook hands but got only dour faces and stiff arms back. The head of HR started the conversation with, "I don't know why we're wasting our time on this meeting. Your client is a liar and a cheat!"

Had I mirrored this mood or gotten defensive, I would have walked out with no deal, perhaps even heightening the animosity between Rich and the bank. Therefore, I set out to create positive emotional contagion. My first step was to show the two bank officers admiration, affiliation, and acknowledgment, first by thanking them for meeting with me when I knew they had many other demands on their time, then acknowledging their anger: "I really appreciate your agreeing to talk with me about what I know has been an unpleasant situation for you. I understand that Rich has caused you considerable problems. Even he knows it—and he honestly regrets how this happened. When you are ready to hear it, I'd like to explain exactly what took place, so that you can understand that he didn't intentionally set out to take advantage of you. But if you don't want to go there yet, that's okay. For now, let's just focus on how we can clear up this mess so that you can forget about this guy."

With those few words, the mood began to change. By the middle of the meeting, we were making jokes as we worked together to come up with a reasonable settlement. And at the end, we had reached an amicable agreement that was far better than Rich had hoped for.

Looking Beyond the Deal

Although being respectful and affirmative is essential, of course, negotiation based on the relationship is not just about saying nice words. It requires sincerity—and being "in it for the long haul." It means creating deals that are fair and that will be carried out as agreed. It's about approaching negotiation as the foundation for working together productively, not as a game in which one party sees how much it can trick or squeeze out of the other.

As we have seen, focusing on problem-solving rather than fighting or blaming makes negotiation far more likely to end in a value-maximizing agreement. Even more important, it carries the relationship beyond the deal into and through implementation, which brings you strong and lasting returns:

- Ensuring reliable and complete carrying out of agreements

- Creating more productive, cooperative, and sustainable working relationships

- Building loyalty

- Reducing conflict and the high costs associated with conflict resolution

- Paving the way to future agreements

The next chapters will introduce the practical skills you will need in order to negotiate beyond the deal, starting with setting the stage.

KEY LESSONS FROM THIS CHAPTER

- Relationship-based negotiation creates better outcomes through
  - Increasing understanding
  - Building trust
  - Maximizing value
  - Reducing resistance
- Understanding is the cornerstone of compliance.
- Trust is an essential feature of every successful business and social relationship, but
  - It should be tempered by reasonable limits and oversight
  - It needs to develop step-by-step over time

- You are never too powerful to need allies.
- People say yes to people they like.
- You will have greater success in your negotiations if you give your counterpart
    - Admiration
    - Affiliation
    - Acknowledgment

Part 2

THE MIND OF THE

NEGOTIATOR

Chapter 4

THE FOUR PILLARS OF
RELATIONSHIP
NEGOTIATION

The first step in becoming a successful negotiator over the long run is to understand precisely what negotiation is—and what it is not. Let's start with a definition of what it is:

Negotiation is communication between two or more willing parties with conflicting goals in order to achieve mutual gain.

That eighteen-word sentence contains a lot of powerful ideas, so let's break it down phrase by phrase.

Negotiation is communication—It's a forum for exchanging thoughts, messages, and information. It's not a sport or a battle or a magic act. It doesn't require any special tricks or even oratorical genius. It is simply an attempt at connection.

. . . between two or more—The key word here is "more." Even when only two people are in the room, on the phone, or exchanging e-mails, there are usually more than two parties involved in the negotiation at some level. These invisible

participants might include the boss who has to approve the deal, business partners who have to accept it, or family members who are able to influence the outcome—which is why force, by and large, is an ineffective negotiating technique. You might be able to force a timid negotiator to accede to unreasonably one-sided terms, but when that negotiator takes that deal back to the influencers for feedback or to decision makers for approval, it stands a high chance of getting tossed out. Therefore, it's vital always to give the other party not just a fair deal but good reasons the party can take back to demonstrate *why* it's a fair deal.

... *willing parties*—Unlike intimidation, unsolicited sales pitches, or courtroom trials, negotiation requires the voluntary participation of all parties. Everyone enters the process through his or her own free will. If someone is unwilling to negotiate, whether because of mistrust, long-standing enmity, or mere lack of interest, that person cannot be forced. What is more, everyone has the right to walk away at any time in the negotiation if he or she is dissatisfied with the process or the terms being offered. Without all parties being on board, there can be no resolution.

... *with conflicting goals*—Here's the rub. The reason so many people say they dislike or even fear negotiation is because it entails facing up to conflict. If there is no open conflict—for example, we both want to go out for Chinese food tonight (or you secretly don't want to, but say you do)—we simply have a conversation. Only when one of us directly raises a point of conflict—I want Chinese food and you want Italian—does a conversation become a negotiation. However, it is imperative to keep in mind that negotiation doesn't *create* the conflict. The disagreement already exists. Indeed, if such disagreements are never addressed, they can build up a store of resentment that can destroy relationships. Negotiation, done properly, is the tool that enables us to resolve the conflict and put the relationship back on course so that it can move forward profitably, productively, and happily.

. . . to achieve mutual gain—This is what separates negotiation from simple persuasion. Although persuasion is an intrinsic part of negotiation, negotiation isn't just talking another party into giving you what you want. Rather, all parties must acknowledge that everyone at the table has the right to gain *something*. I am not talking about an equal division. Who gets what will be determined by many factors, from power to competition to market conditions to the value each party brings to the deal. But there must be an understanding that everyone has to win something.

Even police hostage negotiators are willing to let the robbers holed up inside of a bank have something, although it will be far less than they demand. New York Police Department's chief hostage negotiator, Dominick Misino, explained in an interview in *Harvard Business Review*, "Before the bad guy demands anything, I always ask him if he needs something. Obviously I'm not going to get him a car. I'm not going to let him go. But it makes excellent sense to be sensitive to the other guy's needs. When you give somebody a little something, he feels obligated to give you something back. That's just good common sense."[1]

For me, it is this quest for mutual gain that makes negotiation exciting and rewarding, despite the occasional discomfort along the way. All the parties at the table have entered into the process in the belief that if the right terms could be worked out, they would be better off working together than not. We need to keep this in mind during the heat of the negotiation, when we naturally tend to focus on areas of disagreement and forget that all parties have actively chosen to invest time in talking to one another in the hopes that they will benefit by settling their differences.

The Four Pillars

Relationship-based negotiation differs from the standard definition of negotiation in that it sets a more ambitious target. Instead of aiming solely for mutual gain in the terms of a deal, it aspires as well to develop the mutual trust, reliability, and future cooperation that will create value stretching far beyond the deal. Such a strong and enduring edifice is constructed on four central pillars: a focus on relationships, outcomes, solutions, and fairness, as shown in Figure 4.1.

First Pillar: Build a Productive Relationship

The aim of every negotiation is to find a way to collaborate with others so as to benefit yourself now, throughout the life of the agreement, and possibly into the next agreement, even when the situation changes or problems arise. To create effective collaboration you must start by inspiring cooperation. As we saw in the

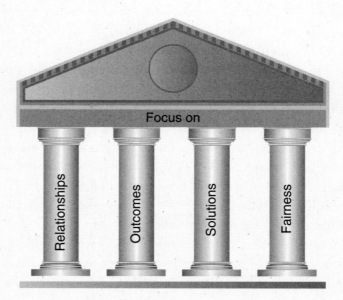

Figure 4.1. The Four Pillars of Negotiation

preceding chapters, cooperation is far more dependable and easier to achieve when others like you, trust you, and feel that you have their interests at heart (and not just your own). In the end, they must feel that they too are benefiting from collaborating with you.

While negotiation will always involve an element of conflict, it rarely furthers your goals to turn that conflict into personal animosity. Berating, accusing, snubbing, or generally insulting others is not likely to win them to your point of view. Behaving secretively or mistrustfully merely makes *them* more secretive and mistrustful. Even when your differences in outlook are extreme (such as between the police hostage negotiator and the bank robbers), you gain nothing by vilifying or preaching at your negotiation counterparts.

In most of the world outside of northern Europe, North America, and Australia, a respectful and comfortable personal relationship has to precede any serious business negotiation. This may feel terribly time-consuming if you come from one of the more individualistic societies, but it is necessary, period. If you try to force the process to get straight into dealmaking, you will most likely end up with nothing. Even in the rare instance that you do get an agreement, it will not be reliable.

Wherever you negotiate, you will benefit by first trying to understand the other party's concerns and build empathy, then working together from that positive foundation to resolve the issues dividing you. Otherwise you will just butt heads. Let me share a story that was certainly a valuable life lesson for me in not letting different perspectives turn into attacks on people.

When my son, Matt, turned twelve years old, he quite naturally began to grow much more independent and argumentative. The sweet, pliant little boy was replaced by a budding teenager whose personal motto was "every rule is made to be resisted." While I understood intellectually that this was a normal stage kids go through, in my self-centered core I felt that Matt was being obstinate for the sheer joy of torturing me.

One frequent argument was about what time he was supposed to go to bed. Because he had to catch a school bus at 7:00 each morning, his designated bedtime was 10:00 P.M. Yet more and more often this bedtime rule was becoming a struggle, with Matt pressing to stay up later to watch some TV program or pretending not to hear when his father or I reminded him of the time.

One night my husband was out of town and I had been working late with a client. I came home tired and short-tempered. My son and I had a late dinner, and at 10:00 I told him it was time for bed. After the usual protests and arguments, he reluctantly headed off. Around 11:00, however, as I walked past his room on my way to bed, I saw that his light was still on. I admit it: I snapped. I banged open his door and attacked: "Why do you always defy me? Why can't you follow rules? Why do you have to make everything so difficult?" I shouted.

Somehow in the middle of this harangue a small, rational voice in my head spoke up: "Melanie, you just spent all day with a client telling them to attack problems, not people. What are you doing now?" In that moment I saw myself as my son must have seen me—and it wasn't pretty. I saw the fear and resentment in his face, and I knew that my behavior had created those feelings. I saw that my scolding words were creating, not reducing, his defiance. To my shame I realized that I had become so upset over a point of disagreement that I had lost sight of my greater goals. Yes, I wanted him to get enough sleep, but I also very much wanted to have a warm and communicative relationship. Moreover, I wanted Matt to obey the rules voluntarily, not have a fight every night.

After taking a deep breath, I spoke again, this time in a calm voice. I told Matt I was sorry that I'd shouted at him. I was very tired, I explained, but that was no excuse for taking it out on someone else. When I saw that he was opening up a bit, I stopped talking and asked him what was going on. Why was he still up an hour past his bedtime?

Reaching under his blanket, he slowly pulled out a book. "Because I'm at this really exciting place in my book and I just couldn't stop." His response stunned me. I had been convinced that his only goal was to defy me, and it had nothing to do with me! More important, he wasn't playing video games or watching TV; he was reading, something I very much wanted to encourage.

Nevertheless, we still needed to address my concern over his getting enough sleep. I explained to him why I felt it was important for him to go to bed at 10:00. "You have to get up by 6:30 to get ready for school in time to catch the bus. Lately, you've been complaining of headaches. I believe it's because you're not getting enough sleep. At your age sleep is important so that you'll be healthy, grow strong, and do well in school. Besides, I don't like seeing you feel bad. I love you." To my chagrin, I saw that Matt had the same stunned look on his face that I had had a moment before. "She loves me?" I could imagine him thinking. "I thought her only pleasure in life came from yelling at me."

I then asked him what he thought we should do to resolve the problem. He proposed that he would read until the end of the chapter, then stop. Thumbing through the book, I saw that the chapter went on for quite a few pages more. "I don't think that will work to resolve the headache problem. It will take you another twenty minutes at least to read all of that. What if you just read to here?" I suggested, pointing to a breaking point a page and a half ahead. He agreed. I left the room. Five minutes later his light went out.

We never fought about that issue again.

Second Pillar: Pursue Outcomes, Not Points

Have you ever had a conversation with someone who was fixated on getting you to agree to *her* point? It's pretty irritating, isn't it? What about when someone tallies up your weaknesses or failings? Does it make you more cooperative? If negotiation is not a game, then what's the purpose in racking up all these points?

Sadly, most negotiators come in with a shopping list of points they believe they must win. "These are our standard terms." "Payment must be within ten days." "Drop your price by 20 percent, or there's no deal." "We're not even going to consider flextime." Even as embarrassing as it is to admit, "Bedtime is 10:00; no arguments!"

The problem with all of these approaches is that they are focused on specific points (terms a party hopes to secure) rather than on the outcome parties want to achieve from the negotiation. Only by broadening your perspective to consider the outcomes that might result from those terms, or from the methods you use to obtain them, will you be able to connect the dots to see the bigger picture. Before forcing down the price on a tender to rock bottom, for example, you need to consider the potential impact on the quality of materials or after-sales service. Before demanding a sky-high corporate room rate, you should think about the likely impact on the customer's willingness to book your hotel if they have other options. Before issuing a "take it or leave it" threat, you would be wise to assess the consequences of the other side actually walking away.

As we saw in Chapter Two, Enron International secured virtually all of the terms it wanted in the Dabhol deal, but the resulting outcome was a price that set off riots and resulted in a multibillion-dollar loss that helped send Enron into bankruptcy. The exporter in Chapter One who sold beef to Choi during the Asian financial crisis was 100 percent correct that Choi had failed to honor the purchasing schedule in the contract; but in pressing that point so stridently, the company lost Choi's long-term business. In my own case, while it was true that I wanted my son to get enough sleep, I also wanted him to take better care of himself without my having to nag him, to become more self-reliant and responsible, and for all of us to have a happy family life. By getting stuck on the point of the 10:00 bedtime rule, I was able more or less to achieve the first outcome but was miserably failing in all the others.

It is imperative that you look hard to see whether the specific terms you are pursuing will lead to the outcome you desire. Fundamental questions to ask include

1. Why do I want this term? What will it help me achieve?
2. Does it conflict with or imperil any of my other goals?
3. Are these terms implementable?
4. If the terms were to become public, what negative repercussions might they set off?

Several years ago, U.N. delegates from around the world gathered to give official approval to a "plan of action" on population issues. Approving any U.N. accord is a major undertaking. All the parties have to agree to every word in the document, requiring round after round of minute negotiation. Then every government has to sign off on the final version. This particular action plan was especially problematic because the policies it promoted had been negotiated during the pro-choice Clinton administration, but it was now up for ratification during the pro-life Bush administration.

To the shock of nearly all the gathered delegates, who had arrived for what they had expected to be a pro forma endorsement of a document that had already received every government's approval, the American delegation, drawn from the leading right-to-life organizations, announced that they wanted to renegotiate a number of the terms. They then produced a list of changes they were demanding, all aimed at specifying that the paper was sanctioning neither abortion nor a number of forms of birth control.

A delegate to the conference told me what happened next:

> Of course everyone was horrified. It was crazy. International agreements are intentionally vague. There was literally nothing in the document that supported abortion. How could we

have gotten the approval of the Muslim or Catholic countries if the document had promoted abortion or unlimited birth control? Moreover, it had taken years to get all of the member governments to sign off on the existing document. There was no way to reopen what had been accepted by all. To make matters worse, there was considerable resentment of the United States, since the initial draft had been pretty much written by Washington under the Clinton administration. Now the American delegation was refusing to endorse the agreement that their own government had drafted!

The conference was scheduled to last for three days. At the end of the second day it was clear that we had reached a dead-lock. Delegates were really angry. That was a serious problem since it's a policy of this committee that every decision should be made by unanimous consensus. That night, though, I had an inspiration. If the U.S. delegation was worried that certain terms in the document, such as "unrestricted access to medical care," could be read to signify support for abortion, instead of rewriting every single ambiguous clause, we could just put an asterisk at the bottom of the first page saying, "Nothing in this document should be read as either promoting or approving abortion or unrestricted access to birth control." I ran the idea by several delegates and even those in the hard-line anti-American bloc agreed it would work. At least then we could get the document approved and go home.

But the American delegation would have none of it. They insisted on holding firm to every item on their shopping list. No compromises. By then everyone else was fed up. Finally, the chairman warned us all that if we couldn't reach a consensus by the end of the day, he would have to put the issue to a vote. It would be the first time in the committee's history that we passed a plan of action without everyone's approval. The Americans still refused to budge. So it went to a vote. The paper passed with every national delegation voting in favor except two: the United States and, are you ready? Iran. Like I said, crazy.

That evening I ran into the American delegation in the hotel bar. They were so excited. "We made our point!" they crowed. "We refused to back down. By standing up for our principles we won the moral victory!" All I could think was that they had failed in everything they had set out to do. The action plan had passed by near unanimous vote in the form they did not like. They had exercised no influence over the outcome. And by forcing a vote that they lost so roundly, they had marginalized the U.S. in a way that could have a grave impact on its influence in future international agreements. Ten, twenty, fifty years from now, that document will still be here. Who will remember the loser's "moral victory"?

The American delegates had become so fixated on winning their points that they let the outcome they desired slip out of their grip. They heedlessly rejected a compromise that would have answered their concerns and retained their influence. By their single-mindedness they lost the support of even their staunchest allies and found themselves alone in a corner with Iran. Perhaps when you are as mighty as the U.S. government (or as isolated as Iran) you can afford such losses. Most of us, however, cannot.

Third Pillar: Search for Solutions, Not Victory

Point-winning contests don't just divert our attention from our desired outcomes. As the above example shows, they also mire us in conflict that, as it grows more heated, blinds us to creative and effective solutions. We blame the other party for being unreasonable and dig in even further. Negotiation becomes a private battle for victory.

This can happen so easily. Imagine that you and I are in a room having a meeting. As we are talking, I walk over and casually open the door, then return to my seat. If you don't want the door open, you will feel annoyed. Not only does the open door bother you (there was, after all, a reason you had initially closed it), but you feel that I have behaved discourteously by pursuing my personal desires with no consideration for your opinion. You take my actions as evidence that I am self-interested and pushy. Of course, you may be entirely wrong. I may have responded automatically to a physical stimulus, such as feeling uncomfortably warm, while my mind was elsewhere. But unless we have a good enough relationship for you to give me the benefit of the doubt, you'll probably opt for the unfavorable interpretation.

What would happen if you were to act on your negative feelings by mirroring my behavior and walking over and closing the door? It would surely set off a reciprocal negative reaction in me. In the resulting battle for dominance—open door/closed door—one of us would have to win and the other to lose. All that door banging certainly wouldn't leave a lot of room for a mutually satisfying solution.

Does that mean that you should just sit there and stew in your juices while I dictate the terms? Of course not. The answer is to put your energy into understanding and problem-solving rather than into jumping to conclusions and fighting. Instead of immediately responding to my action with your counteraction (or my demand with your opposite demand), you would start by asking me why I wanted the door open. Was there a problem? My reply might be that I found the room so stuffy that it was hard for me to concentrate on what you were saying. From that single question and answer we would already have reached a higher level of rapport, since you appreciate what stuffiness feels like (you may even agree that the room is stuffy) and you have now learned that I have an interest in hearing what you're saying. That puts things in a different light, doesn't it?

That understanding might be enough to end things there. Or if not, you might explain to me why you wanted the door closed: perhaps people are chatting in the hallway just outside the door who are distracting you when the door is open. On seeing things from your perspective, I would feel the same surge of empathy. Your reasons make sense. More important, we realize that we both have the same larger goal; we just have different problems to be solved. You are more bothered by noise in the hallway and I by the lack of air in the room, but we both want to have a productive meeting. Now it's no longer open door/closed door—I win or you win. It has become a simple problem: how do we get more air in the room without raising the noise level? This one is solvable.

Problem-solving is the skilled negotiator's greatest asset. By getting away from positional fighting to win an "either/or" battle and instead focusing our problem-solving skills on achieving "both/and," myriads of possible solutions present themselves. We could open a window, ask the noisy people to be quiet, turn on the air-conditioning, move rooms; the list goes on. Once we put our minds to problem-solving, we are able to work out our differences in a fraction of the time and energy we would have spent fighting over who was going to win the battle of the door.

EXERCISE: How Do You Deal with Opposition?

Are you a natural problem-solver, or is that a skill you need to develop? Take this self-assessment to see how you tend to approach opposition. Afterward, read the description "Approaches to Negotiation" to see the pluses and minuses of your style and get some tips on how to adjust your approach to get better results.

Instructions: Think back on how you have handled negotiations with customers, buyers, colleagues, family, or friends. Try to remember a few situations when your point of view was in conflict with another's. Once you have those instances firmly in mind, read the following statements in light of how you *normally* behave (not how you think you *should* behave).

No one behaves exactly the same in every instance. However, if the statement sounds like your attitude or approach most of the time, check the box. If it is generally unlike you, leave it blank and move on to the next statement. When you are finished, score the test according to the chart below.

❏ 1. I see nothing to be gained in adding fuel to a disagreement. I prefer to remain neutral if possible.

❏ 2. Nothing will ever satisfy everyone, so I believe everyone should give in enough that we can move on and get things done.

❏ 3. Disagreements are natural and should be dealt with openly and objectively rather than suppressed.

❏ 4. I will fight hard to win my point, even if a few feathers get ruffled.

❏ 5. I put first priority on keeping people happy. I normally will go along with what others want, even if it means I hold my feelings inside.

❏ 6. I believe that everyone's thoughts and opinions should have equal weight.

❏ 7. I am very uncomfortable when there is conflict, so I try to avoid it or keep a low profile in those situations.

❏ 8. I believe that maintaining harmony is more important than standing up for one's individual beliefs.

❏ 9. In my opinion, "win-win" is a naïve aspiration; in reality, if you want to win, then someone else has to lose.

❏10. When two sides can't agree, I think the best solution is to hold a vote.

❏11. Consensus is great when you can get it, but sometimes you simply have to force agreement or nothing will ever get done.

❏12. Long arguments are painful and destructive. I will state my opinion, but if it becomes a protracted disagreement, I will usually back off.

❏13. I am willing to spend quite a bit of time, effort, and emotional energy to get to the root of a problem and reach a consensus agreement.

❏14. The quickest and best solution to a dispute is to settle on the halfway point. That way both sides win something.

Calculating Your Score

Step 1: Count the number of statements you checked: _____ **(N)**

Step 2: Enter your scores for the statements you checked, based on the point chart below. (For example, if you checked statement 2, enter 3 points in the P row and 7 points in the G row.) Then add up the points you have entered in each row to get a total score for P and G.

Statement	1	2	3	4	5	6	7	8	9	10	11	12	13	14
P score	1	3	9	1	9	7	1	9	1	5	3	7	9	5
G score	1	7	9	9	1	3	1	1	9	5	7	3	9	5

P score: ___+___+___+___+___+___+___+___ +___+___+___+___+___+___ = ___ **(P)**

G score: ___+___+___+___+___+___+___+___ +___+___+___+___+___+___ = ___ **(G)**

Step 3: Divide (P) by (N), then (G) by (N):

____ ÷ ____ = ____
(P)   (N)   **People Orientation**

____ ÷ ____ = ____
(G)   (N)   **Goal Orientation**

Step 4: Plot your score on the chart below (with your P score on the vertical axis and G score on the horizontal axis) to see your style of approaching conflict.

Negotiation Styles

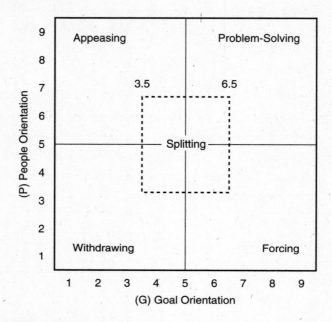

My negotiating style is: _____

_____

Approaches to Negotiation

There are five basic strategies for dealing with disagreement: splitting, forcing, appeasing, withdrawing, and problem-solving. Here is a brief description of each style, with its pluses and minuses, as well as some tips on how to be more effective in dealing with opposition.

Splitting is a popular negotiation approach because it requires little mental effort and everyone comes away with something. Unfortunately, it produces poor results because the discussion stays on the positional surface. No effort is made to uncover or satisfy underlying interests, to get at the root of problems, or to build value. Splitters therefore walk away grudgingly aware of what they gave up as opposed to what they gained by working together. Most harmfully, splitting encourages the parties to make extreme demands, since they know they're going to settle on the halfway point.

Tips for Splitters: Control your desire to get a quick, easy solution. Instead of accepting the initial terms the other side lays on the table as the starting point of the negotiation, ask your counterpart to explain the basis of those terms. Even if you end up settling on a midpoint, you'd be better off starting from justifiable valuations rather than basing the midpoint on arbitrary numbers plucked out of the air in hopes of skewing the results. Moreover, in the process of uncovering the other side's reasoning and explaining your own, you may find better ways of solving the problem.

Forcing uses hard-sell techniques — from vigorous persuasion to threats — to pressure the other party to agree to whatever favors the forcer's interests. While an ultimatum can sometimes "unstick" paralyzed negotiations, as an overall strategy forcing results in one-sided outcomes; it creates a deep sense of resentment on the part of the losing side, and can even escalate a dispute. It is also the most likely approach to end in a "no deal." If an agreement is reached through forcing, it is far more likely than others to be broken during the implementation phase.

Tips for Forcers: Think long term. Set aside at least twice as much time for the negotiation as you feel you need. Ask questions and listen patiently. You are goal-oriented and that is fine. Just remember that in order to achieve your goals, you need others' active cooperation after the negotiation. Once you understand others' viewpoints, you can apply your native problem-solving skills to craft a workable solution that will optimize all parties' goals.

Appeasing also produces a win-lose deal, but this time with you being the loser. The appeaser sacrifices his or her long-term goals in hopes of immediately calming the other side. While this may be an effective way to lower the heat when it threatens to derail a negotiation, it becomes self-destructive if it entails giving in on key interests. When one party consistently appeases a more aggressive party — as, famously, with British prime minister Neville Chamberlain and Adolph Hitler — the appeaser encourages greater demands and more aggressive behavior. The appeaser then suffers from bottled-up resentment over having given in. When *both* sides are appeasers, outcomes are depressed to minimal levels. That said, appeasing is a good way to close negotiations when you've gotten what you want, only minor points remain, and you want the other party to walk away happy.

Tips for Appeasers: Don't imagine that you will improve relationships by always putting others' well-being above your own. Instead, they will see it as an entitlement. If you find it difficult to push for what you personally want, remember that most negotiations affect others. Is it fair that your team, your organization, your family must make do with less than others? Use your high people orientation to think of those you are supporting and negotiate on their behalf. Then call on your strong people skills to keep negotiation on a positive footing by asking questions, giving complete explanations, and using empathetic phrases such as "Help me to understand" or "What if we tried this?" If the other party gets hot under the collar, don't get flustered; just call a break, and resume when tempers have cooled.

Withdrawing is the least productive negotiation style overall, since it doesn't deal with the issues. A toothache won't get better by ignoring it. However, withdrawing can be useful as a temporary strategy when emotions get too high or a team needs to regroup.

Tips for Withdrawers: Consider whether you're really doing yourself a favor to allow problems to go unresolved. Will they resurface again and again, magnifying your stress? If you find it difficult to face conflict directly, try putting your thoughts into an e-mail or asking for the help of an ally who can express your position more effectively for you.

Problem-solving yields the best outcomes. This method seeks to reconcile the parties' interests and maximize their joint gain by digging below the surface to unearth fundamental objectives and concerns. By promoting open communication and mutual gain, problem-solving improves the parties' relationship and produces outcomes that are of higher value and more sustainable. Although this approach is time-consuming, especially when one or more of the parties is resistant or mistrustful, the investment of time early in a relationship will pay off in much smoother and more productive negotiations in the future.

Tips for Problem-Solvers: Don't rush in too quickly to try to come up with a solution. Allow all parties to state their positions and get their feelings off their chest first. People need to feel heard before they will listen to your ideas. And don't feel frustrated if the other party doesn't initially respond to your problem-solving approach. It may take a good deal of patient resolve and lots of open questions to overcome entrenched win-lose habits.

While the example of the door may seem a bit trite, it's actually the way even the most complex negotiations work at the fundamental level. You and I each have a set of goals. Where those goals don't align, we have a clear choice in how we deal with the conflict. Option one is that we could fight hard to see who emerges victorious. Frankly, if neither of us explains our reasons or makes an effort to understand the other's needs, that's the only option we have. But if we take option two—explaining our reasons, listening to one another, then working together to find a solution—we will create at least the possibility that we can both come away satisfied. Moving from fighting to problem-solving is critical because all parties have to feel that they benefit from the deal in order to work together cooperatively and productively.

Let's look at a business example. A midsized retail chain owned a warehouse in an industrial estate. Over a period of several weeks, cracks began appearing in the warehouse walls. The facilities supervisor was certain that the cause could be traced to the pile driving that was taking place at a nearby construction site. She wrote an angry letter to the owners of the new building, accusing their construction team of causing the damage and demanding that they pay compensation. How much cooperation do you think she generated from the owners of the other building?

This much: they sent over their chief engineer, who looked at the cracks, denied any possible connection to their construction project, and left.

Frustrated by the construction site manager's stonewalling, the facilities supervisor issued a series of letters with escalating demands over the ensuing weeks: the first demanding compensation; then compensation plus an admission of responsibility for known as well as any possible unknown damage; and finally, compensation plus an admission of responsibility, plus an apology. The first two letters received denials of any liability; the third got no response.

Seeing no end to the dispute, the warehouse manager took the matter into his own hands. First, he took a hard look at his goals. The biggest concern for the company was that it was planning to put the warehouse up for sale and wanted the facility to appear in tip-top shape so that it could get the highest price. In other words, it wanted the cracks repaired. That was it! The facilities supervisor had demanded compensation, an admission of liability, and an apology, but the company's real interest was to get the building on the market as quickly as possible.

Putting himself in the new building owners' shoes, the warehouse manager could appreciate that they would fiercely resist any apology or admission of liability for possible unknown damage—which could open a legal can of worms—and would stand firm against what they viewed as exorbitant compensation claims. However, they probably wanted the problem to go away as much as his company did. And they had a whole site full of construction workers and materials that might provide an easy solution.

With those thoughts in mind, the warehouse manager sent a letter to the owners of the construction site setting out the situation. It began by apologizing for the sharp tone of previous letters. Such acrimony among neighbors never benefited anyone, he wrote. He then explained the problem and the chain of events leading up to it—cracks in the walls of his company's warehouse had formed shortly after the pile driving had begun—but he did not insist that there was an absolute connection between the two. He neither cast blame nor demanded money. Instead, he asked the owners of the other building if as a gesture of neighborly goodwill they would send over some of their crew to repair the cracks.

Two days later, the site manager of the construction project called to set up a time for his crew to make the repairs. They fixed the cracks that weekend. They even repainted the exterior. Both sides were happy to resolve the issue and get back to business. (For those who ask, skeptically, "But what if there was additional damage to the foundation they didn't know about?" I would point out that nothing in this settlement would prevent the company from taking action over any problems they discovered down the road.)

Although engaging in arguments over who's right and who's wrong may have a hallowed tradition in the courtroom (and the playground), it's counterproductive at the negotiating table, where we are seeking to build mutual cooperation. Let me assure you, you can *never* build cooperation by forcing another party to admit to being wrong. It is much more advantageous to all to focus on how you are going to work together to solve the problem. That's genuine victory.

Fourth Pillar: Focus on Fairness

As we saw in Chapter Two, fairness involves creating a sense of equity. In a nutshell, not only do effective negotiators have to be able to set out clear reasons for everything they ask for, concede, or agree to, but those reasons have to be *reasonable*. Moreover—and this is crucial—the arbiter of what is or is not reasonable isn't the person making the offer, explanation, or request; it's the one receiving it. In other words, I have to offer a reason that *you* will find fair and reasonable.

For example, I may think that "This is our standard contract" is a perfectly reasonable explanation for why I am not willing to change the language in a certain clause. But chances are that you won't find it either reasonable or fair. Why should your concerns be swept aside because my company likes to use its own template?

The Singapore Port Authority undoubtedly felt that increasing rates was perfectly reasonable given its mission of providing the most high-tech facilities. But neither Maersk nor Evergreen Lines had signed on to PSA's mission. Facing an economic slump, they put a far lower priority on technology than on price. They found it unreasonable to pay to support PSA's internal decisions.

A skilled negotiator needs to be able to step back and imagine what the other side would feel is fair, to develop a measure of objectivity. I find it extremely helpful to ask myself (and sometimes the other party), "How would an impartial observer see this? Would they find this position or supporting argument reasonable?"

The ability to speak in neutral terms—not strongly biased toward your own side—will win you far more of what you want in the negotiation and far more cooperation afterward than all the rationalizations you can make for why your view is the right view. Which of the following approaches would be the most likely to get you on my side in a project management negotiation?

> "We need to revise the project's division of responsibilities. All the biggest jobs have been dumped on my team. It's unfair that we have to write the manual as well. I need your team to pull more weight."

or

> "Can we discuss revising the project division of responsibilities? Since half of my team has been seconded to another project, we're really stretched. I'm worried that as it stands, we may not make the deadline. Would it be possible for your team to take over production of the manual?"

The first statement may accurately reflect my point of view. I may have good cause to feel that my team has been given an unreasonable proportion of the work on the project. However, even if you could see that in a calmer light, my biased approach and accusing words would have put you on the defensive. "You don't have *all* the biggest jobs," you are thinking. "We do x, y, z. And what about the last project when you guys practically got a free ride? Don't lecture me on my team pulling its weight!"

The second statement gives you explanations that *you* are likely to find reasonable. I am not blaming you; I am explaining the situation factually. Additionally, I am showing you why you should care: if we don't redistribute responsibilities, both of us may fail to meet the project deadline. Finally, I am suggesting a solution but not imposing it on you. As a result, you will be far more likely to feel that what I am asking for is fair.

A fair approach leads to an optimal outcome because it reduces mistrust and animosity, allowing parties to focus on their common interests. While it requires patience to see things from the other side's perspective and to provide arguments that they would find reasonable, the payoff in results is well worth the investment.

KEY LESSONS FROM THIS CHAPTER

- Negotiation is communication between two or more willing parties with conflicting goals in order to achieve mutual gain.
- Relationship negotiation rests on four pillars:
  - Building a productive relationship
  - The pursuit of outcomes, not points
  - The search for solutions, not victory
  - Focusing on fairness

- The aim of negotiation is to find a way to collaborate with others so as to benefit yourself.
- A problem-solving approach produces consistently better results than forcing, appeasing, withdrawing, or splitting the difference.
- The reasons you give have to sound reasonable to others.

Chapter 5

DON'T FEED THE BEARS!

When you look beyond the deal, managing the behavior of the parties becomes far more important than it is in a short-term transaction. In a transactional negotiation your focus is on getting an agreement, after which you move on, letting someone else worry about implementation. As a result, if you encounter aggressive and demanding negotiators on the other side, it can be tempting to give in to their demands in order to get the deal or just to make them go away. In relationship negotiation, however, every action sets the terms of the subsequent relationship.

One of the most dangerous snares that transactional negotiators fall into is what I call "the bear trap." By this I don't mean those mechanical iron jaws used to capture bears but rather the powerful, finger-length claws bears are endowed with for capturing their prey and destroying anything that gets in their way. If you have been to Yellowstone National Park in Wyoming, you have seen signs warning visitors not to feed the bears. Why is it so important? Quite simply because once you feed bears, they will learn that you are a source of food. And since they have enormous appetites, they will come back for more. Gratitude and moderation are not qualities bears understand.

In negotiation, "bears" are those people who press you for unjustified discounts, one-sided concessions, or undue favors. They want something for nothing. Their sole objective is for *you* to satisfy *them*. Giving in to their demands merely whets their appetites.

Even if they accept what you offer this time, they will demand more the next time you negotiate. Worse, they'll actually come to resent you—as your willingness to give in plays into their mistrust, convincing them that you were inflating your terms to begin with and may still be cheating them now. So they push harder and demand more. Be assured, human bears are no more grateful or restrained than their four-legged cousins. That's why "Don't feed the bears!" is one of the most valuable messages all negotiators should keep in mind.

Lesson One: Feeding Bears Is Self-Destructive

I have seen proof of this maxim countless times as clients have called for help in getting out of bear traps they negotiated their way into. One typical example was a European transport company that was seeking to expand its operations throughout Southeast Asia. The regional representative, Jack, had been told to get the necessary permits to set up operations. When he flew in to meet with the local transport licensing agency, however, he got disappointing news. The director told him that he would very much like to help him, but his office was terribly backed up in all of its work, so he couldn't predict how long it would take to process the permits. However, the director said, if Jack helped out by buying them a few late-model mobile phones, the permits could be moved onto the fast track and be ready in a matter of days.

Jack later admitted that he had been a little uncomfortable giving in to an up-front demand for no specific return. But as he was under considerable pressure to get the new offices set up on schedule, he reasoned that the cost of a few "gifts" was a small price to pay for getting the permits quickly—and would boost his career in the process. To show his goodwill, Jack didn't wait for spending authorization from headquarters (which might get sticky). Instead, he bought the phones from his own travel allowance and gave them to the agency head. The agency head seemed delightfully surprised at Jack's quick response. They parted warmly, with assurances that the permits would be ready in two weeks. Assuming he had resolved the impasse, Jack flew off to the next location confident that he would have the permits in hand on his return.

Instead, two weeks later he was told that the licensing agency had found a few "problems" with the application. "Nothing to worry about," the director assured him, but it would mean a delay while they cut through red tape higher up. The director advised Jack to exercise more patience.

Jack grew nervous. "How long of a delay?" he asked.

"That is very hard to say," the director replied. "Sadly, we are so slow here. We don't have up-to-date computers like the one you are carrying there." He paused and looked meaningfully at Jack's computer bag. "Now if we had a nice laptop computer like yours, that would certainly make our work go considerably faster." Jack said he would see what he could do.

While Jack was naturally annoyed at being shaken down yet again, his irritation was offset by his panic over what to do next. If he were to refuse the latest request, he would be back at square one. Worse, he had told his boss that he was on top of things and that the approvals were just around the corner—and his boss had made similar assurances to the head office. How could he now go back and say he had been tricked, especially when that involved a gift he had never disclosed? Not knowing any way out of this bind, he jumped even further into the trap, compounding his error by giving away *even more* in the hope that this would finally win him the deal. Swallowing hard, he agreed to buy them a computer. The meeting ended with more assurances. Jack smiled weakly, praying that in a short time all would be settled.

Another month went by without any sign of the permits. By this time Jack's boss had grown concerned about the delays in meeting the head office's timetable for expansion, so he had flown down himself to find out what was holding things up. The meeting at the licensing agency was a disaster. There had been no progress whatever on the approvals. When the boss demanded to know what was holding things up, the agency head replied resentfully, "You foreign businesspeople expect everything to move so quickly. Well, of course you do, since you have all the latest technology in your office. I bet you even have one of those new multimedia conferencing systems, don't you?" He showed them a picture he had cut from a magazine. "Now, if we had a system like that, I am certain we could process your application much more quickly."

Jack and his boss walked out in shock. Jack was forced to confess all. A few days later they called my office for help. "When will they stop shaking us down and just give us the permits?" Jack moaned.

The more interesting question was why Jack thought the agency head's behavior would ever change as long as Jack continued to reinforce it. Ethics aside, the man was behaving logically. Every time he demanded something, Jack delivered it. So why should he either give Jack the permits (which would bring an end to the gift flow) or stop making demands (since so far it had gotten him everything he asked for)?

Jack, in short, had been feeding a bear. Although he thought he was appeasing the bear's greed by doing this, Jack was in fact emboldening him. In the painfully ironic words of American journalist Heywood Broun on the eve of World War II, "Appeasers believe that if you keep throwing steaks to a tiger, the tiger will become a vegetarian."[1] If the agency head could get ever-larger gifts from Jack in exchange for nothing, why should he satisfy Jack's needs and give him a reason to stop giving?

That's clear enough, but it leaves open the question of why the agency head had actually grown less friendly and more aggressive with each new request. To answer that, you have to look at Jack through the bear's eyes. From the bear's perspective, Jack wasn't warm and openhanded; he hadn't volunteered anything. Rather, he had had his tight fist forced open. They had stared each other down, and the bear had won. Moreover, the fact that Jack gave in so easily every time the agency head pushed convinced him that

Jack had a generous spending allowance, which he would only dip into when forced. Who knew how deep those pockets were? Yet, thought the bear resentfully, Jack had initially tried to buy him off with a few paltry telephones. Each time Jack gave in to a new demand, the bear's conviction grew that Jack must be making huge profits on the agency's back.

Jack's mistake was to be submissive in hopes it would make the other party more generous. But a strong relationship cannot rest on such unequal foundations. Dominance feeds on weakness, and submission sets up a destructive pattern of expectation.

You may have personally encountered people who were extremely demanding, even abusive. Perhaps, feeling intimidated, you gave in to their threatening behavior in the hope that it would calm them down. In the short term, it may even have had a positive effect. But, like Jack, you would have learned quickly that feeding a bear brings only momentary peace at the price of reinforcing a bully who will expect more and more while returning as little as he or she can get away with.

Lesson Two: Bear-Feeding Damages the Relationship on Both Sides

People are naturally mistrustful. This mistrust grows exponentially if the parties

- Are strangers, especially if they look different (race, dress, and so on)

- Come from other countries or speak different languages

- Represent social, economic, cultural, or ethnic groups who have a history of conflict (such as unions and management)

- Are already in a dispute

The most effective antidotes to mistrust, as we have seen, are openness, sincerity, and the slow building of credibility. Giving in to one-sided demands has no place on that list. When, as Jack did, you give gifts or discounts for no other reason than that your negotiation counterpart has demanded it, it confirms the other party's suspicion that you had originally inflated your terms in an attempt to take advantage of him—and only his forceful response has protected him.

Let's imagine a situation in which there is no basis for trust.

You are in a bazaar in a foreign country. An intricately designed ceramic pot catches your eye. You ask the woman at the stall how much it is, and she replies, "Two hundred dollars." You like the pot and are certain that you couldn't find one of the same quality at home for that price, but you're also a bit leery, since a number of your fellow tourists have warned you of the dangers of being ripped off by the locals. You could easily pay $200, but you strongly suspect that that isn't her "real" price. In fact, price isn't really the issue here. It's mistrust. You fear that she is overcharging you and will spend the rest of the day laughing about how she took the stupid tourist for a ride. So you say, "No, that's too much. Give me a better price."

She replies, "Okay, okay. For you, my friend, only $170."

Are you satisfied? Do you now feel you're getting a fair deal? If you are like most of us, the answer to both questions is no. By giving in to your demand so easily, she has set off every alarm bell in your brain, specifically in the prefrontal lobe, which regulates trust and social behavior. The bear within you roars, "If she can drop the price that quickly, who knows what her real price is? The first number was surely bogus. She must really think I'm a chump! Well, I'll show her what I'm made of!" And the haggling begins.

What if you do end up buying that pot for $170, $150, or even $100? Do you have warm feelings toward the seller? Would you recommend her to other tourists in your group as an honest merchant who dealt fairly with you? Of course not! Your natural instinct is to see her as someone who sought to cheat you, who was foiled only by your quick wits and great bargaining skills.

This presumption of guilt has nothing to do with reality. In fact, she may have sold you the pot at a loss. Perhaps it had been a bad day for business, and she was desperate to make enough to bring food home to her family that night. You actually don't know one way or the other—but your gut reaction will always leap to the more negative interpretation. Why? Because her willingness to drop the price, for no other spoken reason than that you had asked her to, convinces you that her first price was a lie.

This doesn't only apply to buying and selling. A few years ago, a multinational company hired me to help develop a negotiation strategy for its contract talks with the labor union of a recent acquisition. In the decade prior to being bought out, the local company had been through a couple of different owners; wages had been frozen for several years. Naturally, the union was mistrustful of management and full of pent-up demands. Although the new owner was planning to give a substantial 30 percent raise to workers to bring them back up to the industry standard, the management anticipated a fierce fight with the union.

In my first meeting with the HR team, which would be conducting the negotiation, I asked their chief negotiator how he intended to approach the union. "We'll offer 10 percent to start, then work our way up from there," he said.

"Why would you offer only 10 percent if you are planning to give 30 percent?" I asked.

"To give ourselves room to maneuver!" he practically shouted in exasperation, amazed at my inability to grasp the fundamentals of negotiation strategy. "They'll make a ruckus, naturally. Probably walk out. But in the next round we'll come up a bit, which will make them feel they're winning something. Then there'll be the usual back-and-forth, and we'll be positioned to settle on 30 percent in the final round. If we start any higher, they're sure to call a strike, since we won't have enough to give away in the later rounds."

"But if you offer them such a low figure, won't that encourage more radical demands?" I asked. "Why not begin with a reasonable offer, close to the amount you're actually hoping to settle on? You'll earn their trust, which you can build by sharing the economics behind the offer as well as your financial constraints, while making it clear that you're willing to work with them within those constraints. You can then focus the negotiation on trading off basic wages with performance pay, retirement, and medical benefits to come up with a package that the union feels best meets its members' needs without you substantially raising the overall price tag."

The company negotiator looked stunned. "There's no point bothering with trust and offering explanations! These aren't our friends. The union is like a bunch of demanding children whose method is to shout, threaten, and strike until they get what they want. If we start with a reasonable offer, they'll demand something totally unreasonable. That's the way it works here."

His strategy was not an uncommon one. Nevertheless, I suggested to him that there may be a link between the negotiation strategy and the subsequent hostility. He was treating the union as a bear (or a spoiled child), goading it to roar, feeding it generously when it did, then wondering why it kept roaring.

Let's again look at the issue from the bear's point of view. The union and its members would be unaware that the 10 percent the company negotiator initially put on the table was merely an appetizer and that the owners were fully prepared to deliver up the full dinner after a little game-playing. The negotiator would lead them to believe that that first crumb was all management would willingly part with—in short, that the company was intending to exploit them. Enraged, the union would demand an equally unreasonable number, say 50 percent, gaining wide adherence among the rank and file for defending their well-being. They may even go out on strike. Facing the union's fury, the company would unaccountably find that it had a greater ability to pay, offering more with neither justification nor explanation for this change in circumstances other than that it was responding to union demands.

In turn, the workers would learn that their ability to earn more is directly linked to radical behavior.

Even were they to settle at 30 percent, the employees wouldn't feel grateful to the company for the significant raise but would credit their union leaders and their own militant action for winning the increase, which they would believe management had tried to deny them. They would now be poised for the next fight. By creating and feeding a bear, management would have worsened labor-management relations and fed mutual mistrust.

With this argument, I finally convinced the company to treat the union as a long-term partner in the company's success, starting with an offer of a 27 percent raise (a number that could be justified on financial calculations and industry comparisons). That was close enough to the 30 percent figure the company felt it could reasonably afford in order to appear generous to the workers, but it left room to give the union a small but visible victory, if needed.

The chief negotiator was uneasy heading into the first meeting with labor. "What do I do to bring them back when they walk out of the negotiation, since I can't offer them more money?" he asked grumpily.

"Let's concentrate on keeping them from walking out in the first place," I replied. "Show your sincerity by making it clear that you're trying to give them a fair deal—not playing games. Show them the figures. Let them suggest other ways of apportioning the money. Listen. Have an open mind. Be accommodating. But don't feed bears!"

He was dubious as he departed for the meeting with the union reps, but when he called back that night, he was a convert. It was the first time in his many years as a management negotiator that the union team had *not* walked out. "They are now acting more like the company's allies," he told me. There was still the rank and file to contend with, and a lot of feelings of injustice and mistrust that could only be conquered over time and through credible follow-through, but the foundation had been laid to turn bears back into working partners. In fact, two weeks later they signed an agreement that both sides were happy with.

Feeding bears happens whenever you appear to give up something for no other reason than that the other party demands it. (If the company had initially offered 10 percent, its ultimate rise to 30 percent would have *appeared* to have been a surrender to pressure—regardless of the fact that it had been part of the company's secret strategy all along.) The key phrase here is "for no other reason." Giving in to unjustified demands is quite different from offering something of your own free will, seeking to create a sense of reciprocity by conferring trust in order to receive the same, making an investment in a potential partnership, or simply doing someone a favor. If you *willingly* give someone some leeway on terms or a price reduction because you feel it could win you an advantage in building future business, that's a calculated commercial risk. Feeding the bears is when you *unwillingly* give in to force—and when both sides understand that you have done just that.

Once, after I had spoken to a company's sales and marketing team about the dangers of feeding bears, a salesman asked me, "But what do I say to important customers who, when I quote them a price, reply by asking me to give them my best price?"

I will give you the same two options I gave him. You could say,

"Oh, you didn't like the inflated price I just gave you?" and then quote him something lower; or

"The price I quoted is my best price, under the terms we've been discussing. However, we could reduce it if we . . ."

Which do you think would lead to a stronger working relationship and less painful future negotiations?

Lesson Three: Feeding Bears Creates Bigger Bears

This brings us to our final lesson about bears: every time you feed a bear, you train a bear. A few months ago on an intercontinental flight I heard a mother arguing with her daughter in the row behind mine. The little girl apparently had wiggled out of her seat and was sitting on the floor. "Get up off the floor; you'll get your nice dress all dirty," the mother said sharply.

No response.

"The seat belt light is on; get back into your seat now!"

No response.

"All right, that's it! I'm counting to ten," the mother warned. "Six ... seven ... eight ... nine ... ten! ... Please! I'll give you some candy."

Having earned her reward, the bear cub promptly hopped back up.

One of the first things a good negotiator learns is that people of all ages are trainable. Every interaction is a lesson. It makes little sense to think you can create good behavior through rewarding bad behavior. For the little girl, the lesson she already knew by heart was that by refusing to obey her mother she would get something she wanted. Similarly, if your business associate sees that she will get a better deal by bullying you, she will begin mentally rehearsing her list of threats every time she enters the negotiation room. I once observed a negotiation in which one side, a diminutive woman, started by saying to her very large male counterpart in a timid voice, "I don't want to fight. Please don't shout at me." I could practically see the bear's teeth grow as he grinned back. The outcome was as predictable as it was painful to watch.

How to Handle Bears

While it is not uncommon for people to behave aggressively, their antagonism is more often motivated by mistrust than by gratuitous hostility. They are reacting to things another person has done or said to trigger that mistrust. However, if they are approached in the right way, they will hold their belligerence in check. Put simply, the best way to avoid falling victim to bears is not to create them in the first place. The principal tools for keeping the negotiation moving in a profitable direction are honesty, credibility, and communication.

1. *Start from a defensible position.* While you naturally want to get the most out of any deal, the terms you offer must be sincere, reasonable, and respectful. A relationship-centered negotiator fully recognizes and communicates the value of what he or she brings to the table but never offers terms that are so extreme or one-sided as to demean the value of the other side. As we saw in the case of the labor negotiation, taking an unreasonable position makes *you* appear to be a bear, which sets off a reciprocal response in the other party. Newton's third law of motion applies equally to negotiation: for every action, there is an equal and opposite reaction.

2. *Communicate valid arguments for every position you take.* This topic will be dealt with in much greater detail in Chapter Nine, but let's look at it briefly here. Assuming that the initial terms you offer in a negotiation are supportable, if the other side responds by asking for a reduction of those terms, you mustn't simply comply. As we have seen, groundless backtracking sets off bears—and you will be doomed to a cycle of ever-increasing demands. On the other hand, you should not flatly refuse, a sure way to come across as a bear yourself. Instead, you must sincerely ask the negotiators on the other side to explain the basis of their request. Then do one or more of the following:

   • If they tell you, for example, that the price you are proposing is beyond their budget, suggest ways to change the terms of the package (such as by reducing the size of the order, lengthening the payment terms, or finding a way to cut costs) so that all sides maximize their value without sacrificing fairness.

   • If they say they've received lower bids elsewhere, ask them about their goals in more detail, then show how your product or service does a better job of satisfying those goals than the competitors do. As a prepared negotiator you should know in advance where the competition stands and where you stand in comparison. (We'll look at preparedness in Chapter Six and at setting goals in Chapter Seven.)

- If they can come up with no reason beyond their feeling that your price is not genuine, you need to put in more effort to gain their trust, for example, by providing additional, preferably written, evidence showing that the terms you quoted were honest and reasonable.

3. *Convey a valid reason for every concession you make.* It is insufficient to have even the best of reasons if it remains hidden in the depths of your own mind. Only through sending the explicit and consistent message that you are looking for ways to craft a deal that is fair to both sides will you overcome the bear. When you provide a credible reason every time you "give," the process becomes less a game of intimidation or a battle of nerves and more a cooperative exercise in problem-solving. Valid reasons can come in the form of

- A trade-off (either current or in the form of a future commitment)

- Adjustment of the terms

- New information that changes your assessment of the situation

- A compelling argument that changes your perception of the situation

- A voluntary and clearly articulated favor

Let's see how this works by returning to the case of the $200 pot in the bazaar. If instead of just dropping the price the shopkeeper had said, "Actually, all of these prices are fixed, but I do have one pot over here with a small flaw that I can sell you for $170," would you have experienced the same bear-like reaction as when she just dropped the price for no reason? If you are like most people, the answer is no. They not only would be more comfortable paying the offered price but would actually walk away more willing to recommend the merchant. Explanations signal honesty and respect. Both create positive feelings.

Handling Grizzly Bears

While the bear-like behavior of the great majority of negotiators stems from mistrust, from time to time you may encounter those who simply get a thrill out of dominating others and whose goal is to win by any means. They don't want fairness; they want to triumph. They don't listen to your arguments or suggestions. They withhold or misrepresent key information. They seem to go out of their way to intimidate you with loud, menacing, and abusive language. What can you do when you encounter a grizzly bear?

1. *Never base your decisions on the decibel level of the other party*. If you believe that the terms you offered were fair and reasonable, you should change them *only* for the valid reasons mentioned above. Insults ("You're out of your mind!") or threats ("There's no way we'll ever agree to that!") are not valid reasons. The best way to respond to grizzly attacks is to demonstrate your legitimacy calmly and ask the attacker to explain the basis of his objections. The more collected you remain, the quicker he will realize that (a) aggression isn't shaking you and (b) he's the only one shouting, which leaves him looking rather foolish. He will soon give it up.

2. *Never negotiate against yourself*. One common trick played by bears is to get you to make repeated concessions, by professing

dissatisfaction with every offer you make. For example, you offer a price. The negotiator on the other side replies, "No, that's too high." So you come in with a lower price. "Actually," says the other, "we were looking for something better than that." You keep offering better terms, without any movement on the other side. It's as if you are at an auction and the price is going up, only you're the only one bidding. It's a surprisingly easy trap to fall into, even if you are scrupulous about justifying your concessions. The way to guard against this is to insist on a two-way exchange. If the other negotiator tells you that your initial offer is too high or too low, instead of automatically adjusting your terms, ask her what price or other terms she is looking for. This gives you something to respond to and takes the negotiation away from mind reading and bear-feeding and into justification and problem-solving.

3. *Be willing to walk away.* Your decision whether or not to accept certain terms must not be based on what the other negotiator wants, regardless of how forcefully he presses his case or what she may do if you say no. Rather, it's a question of whether the offered terms achieve your basic needs and are better than any other current or potential offer on the table. If a deal brings you no value, or less value than you could obtain elsewhere, you are better off walking away. Chapter Ten will show you how to identify substitutes and build a Walk-Away Line, or WAL. They are powerful tools. Just knowing that you have other options will create an invincible fortification against bears. Being able to convey that message confidently will stop them in their tracks.

4. *Think beyond the deal.* A negotiation sets the stage for a future relationship and offers a glimpse into how that relationship will function. Therefore, a dysfunctional negotiation process is a vital warning signal, which should lead you to question

whether this is the party you truly want to work with. A negotiation with a major purchaser, vendor, or business partner that is characterized by power plays and take-it-or-leave-it ploys will likely lead to a working relationship characterized by ever-increasing demands and little concern for your needs. A negotiator who lies or misleads you to get a deal will likely take advantage of or cheat you during the implementation of the deal. If you feel from the negotiation that this is not a person or a company you could work with beyond the deal, you need to reassess whether you really want to enter into this relationship. If not, you are better off walking away.

Watch Out for Honey Bears

A final category of bears to watch out for is the honey bear. These seemingly pleasant creatures are more likely to flatter or cajole than to growl or attack. "Help me out." "I depend on you." "Be a friend." Their method is manipulation rather than assault, but like all bears they still want you to do something that benefits them at your expense.

A honey bear is the boss who tells you that she can't give you the promotion and transfer you are entitled to, because she depends on you too much to lose you. Or the buyer who constantly wheedles you for unwarranted discounts. Or the contract negotiator who asks you to do him a favor and sign off on the terms quickly, because he has another meeting in an hour.

I am not suggesting that you shouldn't do people favors. Favors are the food of relationships. However, there are three qualifiers. For favors to be constructive, they must be *reasonable, reciprocal,* and based on *honest* information. Absent any of these qualities, they are merely sugar-coated exploitation. Whenever requests for favors appear unreasonable, one-sided, or dubious, they should be resisted in the same way you would resist any bear trap.

Conclusion

By using these techniques, will you be able to turn every bear into a fair-minded negotiating partner? That's too much to ask. There will always be a small number who are addicted to power or games or who have built up such implacable mistrust over time that it cannot be subdued. But the overwhelming majority of aggressive negotiators—motivated to push one-sided demands because of inexperience, mistrust, fear, habit, or even an urge to win—will change course when confronted with firm resistance. Even if they carry through with their threats and walk away, at the very least you will have protected yourself from becoming their next victim.

KEY LESSONS FROM THIS CHAPTER

- Giving in without reason to one-sided demands
  - Creates larger demands
  - Damages the relationship on both sides by creating mistrust
  - Sets up a negative pattern of behavior
- To avoid creating mistrust and aggressive self-protection
  - Start from a defensible position
  - Communicate valid arguments for every position you take
  - Convey a valid reason for every concession you make
- If you encounter a demanding, hardball negotiator
  - Don't base your decisions on the decibel level of the other party
  - Never negotiate against yourself
  - Be willing to walk away
  - Think beyond the deal
- Not all bears growl; watch out for those who use manipulation for their advantage.

Chapter 6

BE PREPARED

Whether your negotiation challenge involves taming bears or the more enjoyable task of collaborating to look for maximum value, the cornerstone of success is preparation. To approach negotiation as a spontaneous transaction, like haggling over an item that catches your eye in a yard sale, may win you a prize now and then, but far more often will net you poor results and the remorse that inevitably follows.

I have heard countless tales of woe from people who went into a negotiation blindly, imagining that all they needed was quick wits. "I figured that if I could get the other guy to reveal what he wanted, then I could knock him down from there," explained one humiliated company rep who had been sent for negotiation coaching. Unfortunately, as he had found out the hard way, there are a couple of fundamental problems with this approach.

First, how can you get a good deal, much less create a value-enhancing relationship, if you don't know whom you're dealing with, what they're looking for, where their problems lie, and why they are better off working with you than not? At minimum, if you don't know the competitive environment in which you're negotiating, how can you prevent yourself from becoming the victim of those who would seek to gain bargaining advantage by feeding you false or misleading information?

By following a reactive strategy (basing everything on what the other party says), the unprepared negotiator loses his or her ability to guide the negotiation in a positive direction. Additionally, it becomes impossible to gauge the truthfulness of others' claims or the sincerity of their declarations. The unprepared negotiator is left helplessly wondering, as one client plaintively asked me, "What do you do if your customer tells you that your prices are higher than the competition's?"

The answer, of course, is that you need to know where you stand before you walk into the negotiation. Put another way, you have to understand the sense of what you're saying before you start talking. How else can you justify your terms or build trust? Neither solid relationships nor fair outcomes are built on blind faith.

Successful negotiation doesn't start with hello. Rather, it takes place in three stages, two of which begin well before opening words are spoken:

1. *Understanding*—learning everything you can about the parties and issues involved
2. *Anticipating*—developing approaches, imagining likely reactions, and preparing appropriate responses
3. *Connecting*—communicating in the most effective manner; building the relationship

The first two stages—understanding and anticipating—will normally take up anywhere from two-thirds to three-quarters of the negotiator's time. Most of that time will be spent in advance of the first meeting, but not all of it. For while the stages of negotiation begin in a defined order (starting with understanding, then drawing on that knowledge to begin anticipating, and finally, using the information and planning to connect more effectively with the other party), none of the stages has a clear end point. Indeed, the connecting stage, when the negotiators are meeting and actively exchanging information about themselves, is a prime opportunity for clarifying your understanding of the other party (which until then had been partly guesswork) and correcting erroneous assumptions.

The dynamic of the three stages, therefore, can be represented as a helix in which the shade (representing understanding) grows ever deeper as each new stage adds depth to, but does not replace, the previous one:

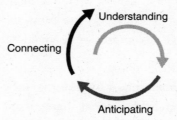

The Three Stages of Negotiation

Let's look at these stages one by one.

<u>Understanding</u>

To be an expert negotiator, the first thing you should do, well before meeting the other side or presenting a proposal, is examine everything of relevance you can about

- *Yourself or your organization.* What is your current situation? What are your goals in this relationship? What particular strengths do you bring to the table? What weaknesses, if any, do you need to diminish?

- *The people or organization you will be negotiating with.* Who are they? What about them most attracts or concerns you? How do they stand apart from others? What kind of reputation do they have? What is their current situation? Historical baggage? Future ambitions? How are they likely to view you or your organization?

- *Your competitors.* Whom are you likely to be competing with or compared to? How do you set yourself apart from them? What advantages do you offer? What advantages do they have over you? What terms do you expect the competitors to offer? How can you justify the difference between their and your terms?

- *Their competitors.* Who or what else might be able to satisfy your goals? What do you know about them? What possible advantages or disadvantages do they offer?

- *External environment.* What external factors (such as economic trends or political change) will have an impact on the parties, the issues, or the negotiation terms?

This examination does take time, but the results it yields are invaluable. The expression "knowledge is power" is not an empty cliché. The benefit that knowledge delivers in *confidence* alone is more than worth the effort. Confidence plays a major role in any negotiation. Studies in every field of endeavor have shown that you are more likely to succeed at something if you believe it is within your ability to do so. Confident people also spend less time worrying and second-guessing everything, so they can dedicate more of their mental energy to creative problem-solving. And they project a more trustworthy and competent demeanor. People are more willing to go along with someone who comes across as secure and knowledgeable.

On the other hand, when you lack knowledge and the confidence it gives you, the negotiation can come to feel so punishing that you just want to get it over with. A negotiator from a well-known appliance manufacturer told me of his miserable experience once when negotiating the acquisition of a smaller company, which had a more prepared team. "I came in with nothing but a target price in my mind, prepared to listen to what the other side had to offer. They came in carrying this enormous stack of information on our company, their company, economic trends, you name it. As soon as I heard the sound of those books landing on the table—THUD!—I knew I didn't have a chance of getting the terms I'd hoped for. They began peppering me with questions, half of which I couldn't answer. I actually found myself agreeing to their terms just to end the humiliation. It was a disaster."

Another beneficial result of understanding is that it enables you to build *trust*. Genuine trust must be based on solid understanding, not blind faith. By understanding the landscape before entering into the negotiation, you will be able to test the honesty of the other side and to challenge dubious assertions. Knowing the facts in advance will enable you to judge when your negotiation partner is being reliably honest, in turn creating a firm foundation from which to take your relationship to a higher level of openness and cooperation. It's next to impossible to build trust and openness if there is no basis for knowing whether what you are being told is true or not.

The more you understand others, the better you will be able to *connect* with them. Generalizations are useful, but at the heart of every negotiation—just as of every relationship—are individual needs, wants, fears, and preferences. When you view your negotiation counterparts as stereotypes (your basic car salesman, a typical big company, and so on), you make it impossible for them to see anything special in you. Connections are by nature particular.

One of the first corporate negotiation training programs I ever conducted was the result of finding that connection. I was living in Bangkok when I was approached by the director of a large American multinational. He was looking for someone to train the company's Thai sales staff, who he felt were getting low-value deals and allowing themselves to be run over by their biggest customer. He had heard that I was teaching negotiation at the local business school, so he asked what I could offer them.

Instead of responding with a proposal for a standard negotiation training program, I invited him to lunch in order to understand his situation and hear his perspective on what his team needed. Over the meal I asked a lot of questions about the particular situations his salespeople faced: who their big customer was, how it approached negotiations, what specific problems he saw in various team members, what kinds of changes he would like to see, and so on. From the length of the lunch, it was clear that he enjoyed sharing his thoughts. Who wouldn't like talking to someone who was so interested in understanding his problems and listening to his views?

Toward the end of the lunch I asked him if he was looking at any other training providers. By then we had built enough trust that he openly confessed that in fact his head office had recommended that he use a well-known overseas training firm and that he had initially approached me only to fulfill their competitive-bidding vendor requirement. However, he said, as a result of our conversation, he very much wanted me to put in a serious proposal.

I put a lot of thought into what I had learned from our conversation. My deeper understanding of the company's problems and personalities allowed me to find a number of points of connection where I could offer value that I believed the overseas company could not. The preferred firm certainly had impressive credentials and slicker materials, but I understood from the manager that what he really wanted was someone who could help Thai salespeople better negotiate within a distinctively Thai environment. The manager didn't want generic negotiation training, no matter how professionally packaged. He wanted someone who would help his specific team negotiate more effectively with a specific customer.

Based on the knowledge I had gathered, I included in my proposal my experience living in Thailand, working in a Thai university with Thai MBAs, and my understanding of the local business culture and its challenges. Knowing that the manager was concerned about the behavior of particular employees, I offered to interview the sales team prior to the course in order to customize the program, to develop materials specific to their situation, and to prepare a brief post-training assessment. Most important, I suggested that the final day of the class be a genuine planning session to prepare the team for the next big negotiation, which he had told me would be coming up in just over a month.

Are you surprised that I got the contract? I admit that I was at the time, since the manager had to go against the recommendations of his head office in order to award it to me. Then again, I had made it easy for him to justify his decision, by showing a deep understanding of his situation and, based on that knowledge, pointing out which of his concerns I would be able to satisfy better than the competition either could or would be able or willing to invest the time to do. How great do you think the likelihood of my winning the contract would have been if I had submitted a generic proposal?

Anticipating

Once you have a good understanding of the situation as well as the goals and personalities of the people you'll be negotiating with, it's time to consider the best approach to get maximum value from your negotiation. I prefer the term "anticipating" to "planning" because it is unrealistic to imagine that you can plan out the step-by-step flow of a negotiation. There will *always* be surprises.

However, even though you can't plan out every step in advance, you will still be far ahead in the negotiation if you spend some time considering the best approach to take and anticipating what is likely to occur thereafter. Anticipating

- Allows you to hit the right note at the start and gives you a rough idea of where you'd like to take the negotiation from there

- Helps you prepare responses for questions or objections that are most likely to arise

- Insulates you against the power of those who use emotional or aggressive tactics

The one thing you can plan with precision is your opening statement, which is vital for setting the direction of the ensuing talks. The opening statement establishes the overall tone of the negotiation, gives a sense of the kind of relationship you are hoping to build, provides an opportunity for you to demonstrate your confidence and knowledge and to alleviate any negative feelings, and outlines the general outcomes you're aiming to achieve.

Considerable thought must go into the opening statement. Based on the understanding you acquired in the first stage, consider the kind of approach that will resonate most positively with the other negotiator. What image do you want to present? What should the overall atmosphere be like? In most negotiations, you are seeking to send out the positive yet assertive message that you

- Have done your homework

- Are confident of your strengths

- Would very much like to work with the other party, if a reasonable agreement can be reached

- Put a high probability on your reaching that agreement

In some cases, such as when the negotiation involves a dispute, the opening statement is also an opportunity to calm strong emotions that might otherwise obstruct the process. Anticipating includes considering how the other party is likely to react to you (or, in multiparty negotiations, to one another). If you anticipate a high level of animosity, for example, instead of ignoring it and plunging ahead with your demands (which usually ends up with a fight bursting out across the negotiating table), you will get much better results if you address those negative feelings at the outset. For example, you might open with the words, "In the past we've exchanged some harsh words over this issue. I understand that you're angry and that we've sometimes given you cause to be. But I hope we can put the anger aside today, and find a way for both of us to move on productively." By anticipating and dealing with personal feelings at the start, you stand a much better chance of reducing them to a workable pitch, enabling the two sides to cooperate long enough to solve the problem.

Although you have less control over the negotiation after the opening statement, there is no less need for preparation for the give-and-take that will follow. In fact, anticipation is critical to ensuring that the negotiation stays on a constructive and profitable track. A relationship negotiator imagines in advance how the other party is likely to respond to his or her opening statement and to the terms initially proposed, then prepares explanations, rebuttals, questions, or even written evidence to allay those expected concerns and challenges.

If you are raising your price, for example, you can rationally anticipate that the buyers are going to want to know why. If you've prepared a response and they don't ask, you've lost nothing but a few minutes' time. However, if they do ask (a far more likely scenario), you will be much more persuasive by being ready with a good reason and convincing evidence supporting your decision. Conversely, in a falling market, you can safely anticipate that the buyers will push for price reductions. Instead of being caught off guard and then caving in, by predicting their concerns you may be able to come up with trade-offs they would value enough to allow you to hold your price as high as possible.

Anticipation works both ways. In addition to anticipating the challenges you are likely to receive from other parties you need to spend some time before the negotiation imagining the positions they will likely take as well as the arguments they are likely to make. Then you can plan the questions you will ask to challenge those positions, in order to ensure that the final agreement benefits you fairly.

I think of this process as the "IQ" of negotiation. IQ refers to intelligence, of course, but it also serves as a reminder that intelligence in negotiation is a combination of the *information* you provide to earn the other party's trust and agreement, followed by the *questions* you must ask to ensure that the other side provides you with the level of information you need in order to achieve a confident and high-value agreement.

This IQ process benefits from brainstorming and practice to prepare for likely challenges. Especially if the negotiation is an important one or if you've had difficulties with a particular negotiator in the past, it's valuable to sit down with a colleague or family member to role-play the upcoming negotiation. First, you imagine every question the other side might ask or objection they might raise, then your colleague plays that role while you practice your response. Those who have gone through this process invariably report back improved results, saying that they retained much better control of the negotiation than they had in the past.

This role-play exercise is particularly useful if you are the type of person who has difficulty thinking on your feet or who is prone to get flustered when directly challenged. By anticipating, you won't have to come up with a quick answer, because you will have an answer ready. Anticipating also helps to take away the shock factor. If you know in advance that you will be dealing with someone who uses aggressive tactics or emotional blackmail, role playing ahead of time makes those behaviors predictable and therefore less alarming. Once you accept that you're dealing with a screamer, the noise won't rattle you as it would if it came out of the blue—in the same way that you jump when someone sneaks up from behind and shouts "Boo!" but are unaffected when you know it's coming.

Connecting

Finally, it's time to talk! Though much of the art of connecting will be covered in Chapter Eleven, let's spend a few minutes here on what you can think about in advance to start the relationship on the right foot when you finally meet, whether physically, by phone, or by e-mail.

Most important, remember that you are negotiating in the hope of reaching an agreement. It can be easy to lose sight of that basic goal in the heat of the negotiation. We all fall prey to the thrill of competition now and then. Often we will fall into the trap of speaking only about what *we* want, forgetting that we are trying to get another party to cooperate with us. Then we wonder why the negotiation isn't going anywhere.

How much more effective we would be if, before plunging ahead with our positions and arguments, we spent a few minutes thinking about the other party, their likely preconceptions or concerns about us, and what we could do to help put them into a cooperative, rather than a defensive, frame of mind. Things you should consider include

- *Style*—What, if anything, do you know about the manner of the individuals you will be negotiating with? How have they approached past negotiations, either with you or with someone you know? Do they like to chat a bit or get straight to business? Do they like lots of detail and evidence, or do they prefer bullet points and big-picture summaries? Do they like to take their time mulling things over, or do they move quickly? How can you modify your own style to enable you to work most effectively together?

- *Knowledge*—How much is the other party likely to know about the topic under negotiation? What information should you be ready to share to fill in the blanks or give them a more balanced understanding?

- *Values*—What are the guiding principles of the other negotiator or organization (for example, as evidenced in past encounters or on their website)? How will those values potentially come into play in this negotiation? How can you speak to those values?

- *Authority*—Does the other negotiator have the power to say yes, or is he merely a gatekeeper? How can you work with him to move the negotiation to a decision-making level? Do any obstacles stand in the way of his authority to agree? What can you do to help remove those obstacles?

- *Perceptions*—How is the other party likely to view you and your organization? What potentially negative preconceptions should you seek to counter? What image do you wish to project?

- *Receptivity*—How open and welcoming is the other negotiator likely to be to you or your message? Why should she care about this issue? What obstacles (such as age, status, or cultural difference) might block her receptivity to you? What steps could you take to generate more comfort and openness?

This is a long list, and you probably won't have answers to all of the questions on it. But any amount of time spent in advance, thinking of your counterparts, how they might perceive you, and most important, what they care about, will give you a great advantage going into the negotiation. Finding ways to connect from the moment you walk in the room will spare you from the misguided start that can painfully prolong or even doom a negotiation.

If nothing else, remember this: Your counterparts are not interested in hearing what *you* want. They want to know why *they* should care, how *they* benefit, and why *they* should agree. It's hard to provide answers to those questions unless you've spent some time looking at the world from their perspective.

In the next part of the book, we will put all of these lessons together into the five-step GRASP negotiation process, which generates value-maximizing and sustainable agreements through understanding, anticipating, and connecting.

KEY LESSONS FROM THIS CHAPTER

- The cornerstone of a winning negotiation strategy is preparation.
- A reactive strategy removes your control over the direction the negotiation takes.
- The three stages of negotiation are
  - Understanding
    - Yourself or your organization
    - The people or organization you will be negotiating with
    - Your competitors
    - Their competitors
    - The external environment
  - Anticipating
    - Your opening statement
    - Your counterparts' likely questions and objections
    - Positions they will likely take and arguments they will make
    - Your responses and challenges to those positions, arguments, questions, and objections
  - Connecting. Being aware of the other side's
    - Communication and decision-making style
    - Level of knowledge
    - Values
    - Level of authority
    - Perceptions
    - Receptivity
- Confidence is a prerequisite to successful negotiation.
- The "IQ" of negotiation is the *information* you share and the *questions* you ask.

Part 3

FIVE STEPS TO SUCCESS

Chapter 7

GOALS — WHAT YOU

REALLY WANT

Now that we have explored why relationships matter and examined the values and practices of the successful negotiator, it's time to learn the step-by-step negotiation process. Negotiating well is a process of following five simple steps: Goals, Routes, Arguments, Substitutes, and Persuasion. The first letter of each step combines to spell the word "grasp," which means both to understand and to hold on tightly. The acronym GRASP is not merely a mnemonic device: by following the GRASP method, you will actually create a sustainable agreement (to which the parties hold on tightly) because it is based on mutual understanding (see Figure 7.1).

This and the next four chapters will take you through the GRASP method one step at a time.

The First Step

As with any process, the first step is to develop a clear vision of where you're aiming to go: your *Goals*. What, at bottom, do you hope to achieve through this negotiation? What risks or negative outcomes do you want to avoid? Where would you like this agreement to lead beyond the immediate deal? Which of these

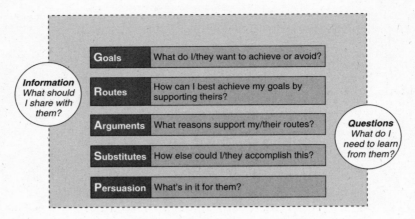

Figure 7.1. The GRASP Negotiation Method

goals are most important to you and which are merely "nice to haves"?

It is vital, if not always easy, to resist the impulse to leap over this stage in a rush to compile a shopping list of specific terms you will push for, because only by first focusing on the big picture—that is, everything you're trying to achieve through the negotiation—can you correctly identify what terms would most help you to reach those goals. Otherwise, you may find yourself going off course, pushing for terms that are of no immediate value and that may even get in the way of achieving a mutually advantageous agreement. Or you might come across as being pointlessly demanding and selfish and damage the working relationship you are trying to build by asking for things that you can't explain or justify. The way to avoid this pitfall is to understand the full range of your goals and to keep your attention relentlessly on them by continually asking yourself "Why?"

Why, for example, do you want a specific clause in a contract? The only sensible answer is that it will help you achieve one or more of your goals (either bringing positive benefits or reducing the likelihood of problems arising that might materially harm you later). Yet, how many times have you heard negotiators explain that they want this or that because "those are our standard terms"? This can be translated as, "I have no idea why I'm demanding it or if it serves any purpose whatever, but I insist on it because it makes my life easier or I want to win this point." Admittedly, the "standard terms" approach has the advantage of being easy—a genuine no-brainer—but it is not likely to lead to honest acceptance, much less a value-creating negotiation or a positive relationship. The *only* way to achieve sincere agreement on the inclusion of the clause, or if the language is unacceptable to the other party, to amend it in a way that preserves your interests, is for you to know and be able to explain why it is important to you.

Keeping your eye on your goals also allows you to find solutions where others see only impasse. Let's look at a simple illustration. Suppose that you order four cases of fifty white binders from your regular stationery supplier. You tell the supplier you need the binders delivered by Monday. He replies that unfortunately he can't get them to you until Friday. If you are fixated on getting *your* terms, you will keep demanding a Monday delivery. You might cajole or plead, but if the supplier truly doesn't have two hundred white binders in stock, you will eventually be forced to accept defeat. You could take a harder line, threatening to find a new vendor and withdraw your business if he's not more forthcoming. But do you really want to spend time sourcing out another stationery supplier? You might settle for a "split down the middle" agreement: delivery on Wednesday. Unfortunately, you need the covers on Monday—and the stationer knows full well that he can't get them to you on Wednesday anyway, despite what you've pressured him into saying.

This is a standard win-lose problem, which is caused by confusing positions (the terms you ask for) with goals (why you want them). The impasse can be broken profitably only by going back to your goals. Why do you want four cases of white binders delivered by Monday? The answer might be that you need covers for the materials to be used in a series of internal training sessions you are running. The first session, for eighteen people, will be on Tuesday. In the past you've used white covers for your in-house training, and you'd like to keep a consistent look. Finally, you want four cases so that you have stock on hand for future trainings and also because you get a 15 percent discount when you order a single delivery above a certain volume.

If you were to prioritize these goals, they would be

1. To get eighteen binders delivered by Monday
2. To receive the 15 percent volume discount
3. To have 182 additional covers on hand for future trainings
4. Preferably for the covers to be white

By thinking of goals as opposed to positions and by considering which are top priorities and which are of less value to you, you can begin to devise a mutually workable solution. The stationer might have eighteen white binders in stock now and could deliver the remainder of the four cases on Friday. You could negotiate to get the volume discount even though you are splitting the delivery. If you would rather get everything at once, he might be able to supply you immediately with four cases of binders in off-white or another acceptable color. Every one of these outcomes would satisfy your priorities, as well as meeting the stationer's goal of keeping your business. But if you remain stuck on your original terms ("I need four cases of white binders delivered Monday"), there is no good solution.

Goals Give Clarity

In training negotiators, I am struck by how many, when preparing for a negotiation, throw together a list of perfunctory demands, then put all of their remaining energy into devising feints and strategies in hopes of outmaneuvering the other side, rather than into focusing on what they need and want to get out of the deal, how their goals might dovetail with their counterpart's, and what kind of relationship, if any, they hope to develop moving forward. Invariably, once these negotiators are in the thick of the negotiation, they become overwhelmed and confused, miss critical opportunities to create gains, and may even kill an otherwise advantageous deal by getting into a battle or going to the brink over a matter of little real importance. Rather than keeping their eye on their goals, they get trapped in a game of blindman's bluff. No wonder most people find negotiation so stressful!

To show how easy it is to lose sight of goals, I often have participants in my MBA classes and executive training programs play a decision-making game. In the game, the players are told that they have been cast away in a dangerous and unfamiliar setting—a forest, jungle, or desert—and have only a dozen or so scavenged items at their disposal. Their task, first as individuals and then in groups of four or five, is to rank each item according to its importance to their survival. The players are given only five minutes to make their initial, individual rankings—and are hectored throughout that time to "hurry up; don't worry so much; just put something down." (My hidden goal in pushing them to go faster is to have them make impulsive, relatively thoughtless choices.)

Once their initial lists are made, the participants are divided into groups of four or five and are given forty-five minutes to come up with a single consensus list. Logically speaking, they would enter this second phase with relatively open minds, considering the choices carefully now that they have more time and a broader knowledge base. Their first question should be "What are our goals?" followed by "What will most help us achieve those goals?" But that is almost never what happens. In the hundreds of these games I have observed over the years, nearly all players approach the group decision-making process in a mad rush, clinging to their initial lists as if they were the Ten Commandments and always starting with the same question: "What did you put as number one?"

Once the various teams confront the inevitable problem that their members have ranked the items differently, most immediately launch into bartering, leading into one of three traps.

Splitting the Difference

Some will take the easiest way out, numerical averaging: "I listed this item as twelfth most important, and you put it as second, so let's settle on seventh." These teams invariably get the worst scores in the game, because their choices are based solely on numbers rather than reasons. While this approach satisfies the members' overriding goal of reaching an agreement as quickly and painlessly as possible, the problem is that the result doesn't make any sense. While there was some rationale, even if shallow, why one player listed a certain item as twelfth (of very little value to the group's survival) and another reason behind another player's deciding it was second (extremely important), there is no reason whatever behind their ranking it together as seventh.

It's as if a pair of cheetahs hunting gazelles couldn't agree on whether they should pursue the oldest or the youngest member of the herd (both reasonable choices given that the goal is to go after the weakest target), so they split the difference and settled on one in the prime of life. It's a compromise intended solely to get a quick and easy agreement, regardless of the practical consequences, in order to minimize the immediate conflict between the negotiators. The result is a rock-bottom score that in the survival game translates into "death," and in real life translates into an arbitrary, meager deal that satisfies no one. This is a pretty high long-term price to pay for avoiding a few minutes of brain work.

Forcing and Appeasing

Also largely unsuccessful are the teams dominated by players who ram through their own rankings by outtalking or bullying their teammates, silencing all other opinions or counterarguments. The other players give in, not because they agree but simply to buy peace. Because dominators seek to "win" by forcing through their views, they aren't willing to reconsider their original choices, so the discussion stays on the most superficial level of justifying a list that had been drawn up in under five minutes. As a result, unless the forcer was truly knowledgeable about the hypothetical terrain, his or her personal victory usually results in the whole team losing. Interestingly, once the team finds that the forcer has led it into defeat, the appeasers' pent-up anger at having been bullied usually results in quite genuine retribution. The blame and scorn they heap on the dominator will often continue far beyond the role play and perhaps throughout the entire training.

Missing the Forest for the Trees

This group will carefully go through the resource list item by item, discussing how each object could be used and what its potential value might be in various situations. With their more open, problem-solving approach, they are more successful than the two previous types as a rule. However, they too will lose the game. Their flaw is that they have become so diverted by the details that they have lost sight of their overall goal. The right question isn't "What are all the possible merits of this item?" but rather "What will most help us achieve our goals?"

The Winning Approach

The sole way to win in the survival game is for the team members to let go of their original randomly compiled lists and agree instead on a set of encompassing goals. In this case, it would be to (1) make it out alive (2) as quickly, (3) securely, and (4) in as good shape as possible. Only by focusing on their goals can the players begin realistically selecting and prioritizing the items that would provide the most reliable means of escape, nourishment, protection, and so on.

While what I have described is a game, the same problematic mind-sets are evident in most real negotiations. The negotiators begin by setting out a list of demands without any serious thought of what they're hoping to achieve overall or how those demands will or will not help them reach their goals. Since they have no precise idea of what they are seeking to win, when they are confronted with opposition they are unable to negotiate a win-win solution. Instead, they aimlessly haggle over each item, fall into mechanical patterns of splitting the difference, force their way with threats or power plays that create resistance and damage the relationship, give in to create momentary harmony, and in the end get a list of terms that doesn't add up to a value-maximizing agreement.

Why Do You Want This?

Let's look at a real example. Lynne wanted to negotiate a partnership agreement. For the past few years she had been giving occasional weekend classes for a project-management training company that was solely owned and operated by the original content developer. Now she felt that she would like to make a career move into conducting trainings full-time and taking an ownership role in the business. So she decided to approach the owner to negotiate a partnership in the company. She sought my help in setting out the terms she would ask for and preparing a strategy for persuading the developer to accept the deal.

Instead of starting with the terms, however, I asked Lynne what her underlying goals were. Why did she want this partnership? What was she hoping to achieve through it?

Lynne explained that she had been working for the past ten years as a project manager for an aerospace company. Recently, though, she had had a baby and had grown tired of the demanding hours, industrial environment, heavy responsibility, and high pressure of her regular job. She found she enjoyed training and the friendly, easy interaction with students; she liked "having fun" at work. She also wanted a job that gave her more personal control over what she did and when she did it. Most of all, she wanted a sense of ownership. After managing projects for others for a decade, she wanted to run her own shop, to be responsible for her own future, and to see what she was capable of achieving without the constraints of having to wait for a boss's okay.

Next I asked her to tell me about Paulo, the training company's developer and owner, the man she would be negotiating with and, more important, who would be her business partner if she succeeded. What was he like? How did he run the business? What were his goals? At this point, worry lines crossed Lynne's face. It was complicated, she said. On the one hand, she truly admired Paulo and the training program, software, and materials he had developed. On the other, she felt he was a domineering and temperamental "control freak." Although he had spoken highly of her training ability and had even footed the bill for her to take an advanced trainer's course, he had refused to let her into any other part of the business. He had waved off her earlier offers to help with marketing or attend conferences on the company's behalf, and he would not share any information with her beyond what he felt she needed to do her training job. When she had pressed him to give her more responsibility, he had grown visibly angry, telling her that the company was "his baby," he had developed the concepts and software, and he would decide how the business was to be run. Later he had apologized for his outburst, but he made no mention of her concerns.

After this recitation, Lynne conceded that she knew it was going to be a difficult sell. But, she insisted, all she needed was a strategy to overcome his objections. That was why she had come to me for professional help, she said. She wanted me to help her come up with the best terms, to give her the arguments to support those positions, and persuade Paulo that her vision was the right one.

It was becoming increasingly clear that Lynne had missed the forest for the trees. Instead of taking a hard look at her goals and what would best help her achieve them, she had concentrated all of her attention on specific contract terms and negotiation strategies. Yet there were a number of serious problems with the partnership idea. If the only stumbling block had been Paulo's reluctance to share his business, that could possibly be negotiated away through offering him incentives or guarantees. But the larger truth was that even if he said yes to Lynne's offer, she still would achieve almost none of her other goals.

Lynne had prioritized her goals:

1. To own her own business
2. To run that business as she chose
3. Personal independence and self-reliance
4. A happy work environment
5. Control over her own responsibilities and work hours
6. To become a professional trainer
7. Not to be constrained by a boss

Lynne's stated negotiation objective—forming a partnership with a secretive and hot-tempered control freak who saw the company as his "baby"—flopped in virtually every category. The only exception was that it would allow her to work full-time as a trainer, which she could easily do without the partnership: Paulo was quite open to her extending her training responsibilities within their current employment arrangement. As for her other goals, there were also ways of achieving those, but a partnership was neither a satisfactory nor a sustainable option.

It was hard for Lynne to let go of her original assumption that a partnership was the way to go. But doing so opened her thinking to a possible solution that would fulfill her top-priority goals while also benefiting Paulo. After much consideration of both parties' goals, Lynne came up with and successfully negotiated a franchise-type plan, in which she would own the rights to market and run the training business exclusively in the aviation industry. For Paulo, this was attractive because it expanded his company's reach into an industry he knew little about and was unable to penetrate on his own, yet it didn't impinge on his overall ownership or control over intellectual property development. Meanwhile, Lynne got the autonomy, the work, and the sense of ownership that she sought, entirely supported by the developer's software, training materials, and methodology, while sparing herself the headache of having to work on a daily basis with a temperamental and controlling partner. Win-win.

It seems an obvious solution in retrospect. But it begs the question of why, when there were far better ways of achieving her goals, had Lynne initially been so determined to negotiate a partnership? The answer is that once she came up with the idea of partnering she gave all her attention to how she would convince Paulo to agree. Like so many negotiators, Lynne had focused on *how* to persuade the other side to accept her positions rather than on *what* she was trying to achieve and *why* that was important to her.

What Do *You* Really Want?

Lynne's approach to negotiation is not unusual. Around half of those who have come to me for help in negotiating a sale, a new position, or the resolution to a dispute have started off by insisting, "My only goal is to get the highest price" (or some variation on that theme).

This was essentially what I was told by a CEO who had founded and built his IT company into a multimillion-dollar enterprise and now said he wanted to sell it to whoever would offer the most money. "So," I confirmed, "you're saying that if Buyer A is willing to pay $1 more for your business than Buyer B, even though Buyer A's intention is to shut down your company and sell off the assets, you still want to sell to Buyer A?"

"No, no, no, no," he urgently reconsidered. "I want a buyer who will manage the company responsibly and build on what I have developed." After widening his vision, he was then able to identify quite a few other goals he felt were important, and we had the beginnings of a negotiation strategy.

Then there are those whose only conscious goal is to "get the deal." Never mind the cost or price; they've just got to get the contract. Frankly, such people might just as well wear a sign around their necks that reads, "I'm desperate. Name your terms." As should be clear by now, a deal or a sale or a contract are *means to an end*, not ends in themselves. Their value lies only in what they will bring you once they are implemented.

Therefore, the key starting point is to bring the full range of your goals into the forefront of your mind by repeatedly examining what you want and why you want it. What do you feel you must get out of the agreement? Why do you need or want that? What additionally would you like to achieve? Immediately? Down the road? What outcomes do you want to avoid? Do any of your desires potentially conflict with your concerns? In that case, which is more important to you?

You need to keep asking questions and challenging your assumptions until you have a full understanding of your objectives. Perhaps your reason for wanting to get the deal at all costs is that your boss told you to get it—and your goals are to please your boss, protect your job, and ideally get a bonus or raise. Fair enough. But if those are your goals, you'd better find out your boss's objectives for the deal, because it's a safe bet that it won't please the boss or earn you a raise if you come back with a lousy deal that hurts the business or makes your boss look bad to his or her boss.

Three Types of Goals

In coming up with your list of goals, it helps to consider three categories:

- *Needs:* The terms you *must* get for the deal to be minimally acceptable

- *Desires:* What additionally you would *like* to achieve or prevent through this negotiation

- *Aspirations:* Your aims beyond the immediate transaction

Needs

Needs are the few minimum requirements that the agreement must satisfy to be worthwhile: for example, a price that exceeds costs, delivery by a required date, or a minimum quality level. Although you may occasionally have trouble separating your needs from what you merely would like (in these examples, a higher price, faster delivery date, superior quality), the key difference is that needs, unlike desires, are nonnegotiable. That's why it's so important to know your genuine needs before you negotiate—because they must not be traded away. If you need to buy a car for your family of four, for example, no amount of tantalizing bells and whistles should make you settle instead for a motorcycle. Similarly, a high-volume deal at a price that doesn't cover your costs will merely drive you into bankruptcy.

Desires

These will be far more abundant and ambitious than needs. They are everything you ideally hope to achieve from the negotiation as well as the pitfalls you want to avoid. While a level of realism is obviously required (we are all bound by the laws of supply and demand), you shouldn't limit your goals only to those terms you think the other side will accept. Naturally, there will be differences of opinion between the parties over what constitutes the most desirable terms, but in many instances your counterpart might just surprise you by agreeing. On the whole, inexperienced negotiators tend to be overly pessimistic, assuming that the other side will want the opposite of everything they desire and therefore, anticipating rejection, not even daring to ask. How many times have you heard or been guilty of making defeatist statements (such as, "I'd lose my customer if I charged for that service" or "My boss would never approve a raise") based on nothing but the fear that they might say no?

Even if these assumptions were true (which they are far less often than you imagine), why say no for somebody else? How does not asking for something for fear of being refused put you in any stronger position than actually being refused? It doesn't. In fact, it puts you in a weaker position. At the very least, you will have created nothing to trade off. More important, by not revealing the full extent of your desires, you give your counterparts the false impression that they have satisfied you more than they have and that you are more content with the outcome than you are. If after reaching an initial agreement you later try to raise what you previously left unmentioned, your counterpart may well feel manipulated or even deceived.

In addition to specific terms, desires might include building a trusting relationship with the other party, understanding its business better so that you can improve synergy, resolving mis-understandings, ameliorating hurt feelings, or just growing more comfortable with one another. These affiliative goals may not be essential to achieving a workable agreement. Two long-term enemies can certainly reach a nonaggression pact with minimum trust and little mutual understanding; two strangers can complete a successful transaction over the sale of a house without knowing anything about the other. But in most instances, you will have greater success if you include relationship-enhancing goals within your list of desires.

Aspirations

Aspirations look beyond the terms of the immediate deal. They are the ultimate goals toward which the current negotiation is only a step. "*I am selling my company because I want to . . .*" or "*My long-term business goal is to . . .*" While the majority of negotiators tend to ignore all but the most immediate terms of the deal, they do so at the cost of reducing both their negotiating power and their ability to gain a high-value agreement. Sharing aspirations widens the focus of the negotiation beyond the "now," greatly enhancing the potential appeal of doing business together and correspondingly leading to more flexibility on terms. People are willing to take more of a gamble on a deal or relent on a point if they feel that it will lead to larger joint gains in the future.

In Lynne's case, for example, she enhanced the attractiveness of her franchise proposal and was able to extract more favorable terms from Paulo by sharing her aspiration of developing her arm of the business across the global aviation industry and backing it up with her business plan, industry growth trends, and other evidence that she had a serious chance at success. Now Paolo began to view Lynne's offer as bringing him something valuable in the coming years, not taking away from what he currently had. Had she focused only on the terms of the immediate agreement—profit split, shared responsibilities, and so on—he would have seen much less value in the arrangement and would surely have been less generous with what he was willing to offer in return.

What Do *They* Really Want?

Of course, negotiation isn't just about achieving your own goals. Sustainable relationships hinge on all parties feeling that they have benefited from the arrangement enough that they will be willing to carry it out as agreed. In order to achieve that willing cooperation, you have to consider not only what you want but also what you can offer the other parties that will attract and satisfy them.

Try to imagine the world from their perspective. Given their situation, what are their likely goals? What do they need and want from this negotiation? What are they likely to be worried about?

Unfortunately, we think of the other side's goals all too rarely. We are so busy thinking about what we want and how we plan to get it that we have little time left to consider our counterpart's perspective. When it comes to the other side, it is so much quicker and easier just to plop them into a random stereotype:

- *The miser:* A single-minded cheapskate
- *The enemy:* Will fight you to the death on every point
- *The clone:* The exact reproduction of everyone else in that category

Let's deal with the *miser* myth first. I cannot tell you the number of people—even those sitting in richly appointed offices behind six-foot mahogany desks—who have told me with a straight face, "My customers care only about price." It simply defies common sense. Let me assure you, if your customers cared only about price, then you wouldn't have any customers. They would be doing their own investing, sewing their own clothes, buying street-corner watches, and riding the bus instead of buying a car. Your suppliers wouldn't care about winning your long-term business. Does that sound like the world you actually live in?

Your negotiation counterparts may *think* they care only about price, but that's simply a lack of reflection. What they want is value. It's your job to help them uncover and try to satisfy their additional desires in a way that maximizes the value they feel they get from the arrangement without cutting away from your own.

The *enemy* myth is that the person sitting across the negotiating table opposes you on every count. Again, common sense makes you wonder, if the other party is your nemesis, why are you trying to negotiate a working relationship with him or her? The fact is that negotiators are rarely so clearly opposed. Instead, virtually every negotiation includes a mixture of

- *Common* goals (the reasons you and the other party want to work together)
- *Opposing* goals (the differences you need to resolve in order to work together)

- *Distinct* goals (the individual interests held by one side but not the other)

Even in negotiations dominated by tough rhetoric, you wouldn't be sitting down to talk with the other party unless you shared common goals. It's just that the inevitable conflict over opposing goals can sometimes blind us to those commonalities. However, if you buy into that illusion of total opposition, the negotiation will all too easily turn into a sparring match rather than a problem-solving exercise. The rising hostility will lead the parties to hide information or even intentionally misinform one another. Mistrust shuts down each party's willingness to explore distinct goals from which they could begin to generate synergy and create mutual value. If enmity grows strong enough, it may close the door to any deal at all. It is far more effective to go into a negotiation in the belief that, opposing goals aside, you can establish enough common ground to share ideas and create a productive working relationship.

It's only slightly less dangerous to see all people with whom you negotiate as utterly alike. While a *clone* is certainly a less negative image than a miser or an enemy, it is equally unreal. Given that human beings are unique—from culture to personality to tastes—how could we possibly all be motivated by the same desires? Yet time and again I have heard negotiators insist that "All customers want the same thing" or "That's how you've got to treat vendors."

Just like you, the people with whom you are negotiating have individual needs, desires, aspirations, and priorities. The more you can learn about their goals—either before or during the negotiation—the better able you will be to craft an agreement that satisfies them at relatively low cost to you. The keys are in

- Understanding enough about their goals to come up with high-value trade-offs

- Showing, through your words and offers, that you recognize and respect those goals

- Tapping into their aspirations (long-term desires that
  may not initially be part of the negotiation but that, if
  realized, could create greater benefits for all
  parties)

How can we find out the goals of the other side in a negotiation?
As we saw in the previous chapter, research is tremendously useful.
But the simplest and most effective method is the commonsense
approach: you ask.

Hotel Rate Case Study

Over this and the following four chapters, I will focus on a contract
negotiation I took part in several years ago to show you how each
negotiation step can be put into practice. The general manager
of a five-star hotel in Singapore, which for confidentiality I'll call
the "Empire Hotel," wanted to secure a 32 percent increase in the
hotel's most preferred corporate room rates. The management had
very good grounds for wanting a rate increase. Three years earlier
the SARS epidemic had swept through the region, causing hotel
occupancy to plunge and hotels to drop their rates in response. Like
most of its competitors, the Empire Hotel had reduced its rates,
in its case by nearly 20 percent. However, while its competitors
inched back up at an average of 10 percent a year, the Empire had
kept the same low price for three years as the management focused
on getting occupancy back to its former level.

Now a price increase was very much needed. Occupancy was
running above 80 percent. The hotel had undergone a significant
renovation, rebranding, and staff retraining project. The management needed to find a way to pay for all of that upgrading, to get
operations out of the red, and just as important, to position their
pricing back into the five-star band. (Their discount price, low even
compared to four-star hotels, was beginning to degrade their image
in the market.) The 32 percent increase would undoubtedly shock

their customers, used to the competition's average 8–10 percent yearly raise, but it would still leave them at the very bottom of the five-star range.

While normally the hotel's account executives would handle contract negotiations without outside assistance, the sales director was quite nervous about the two largest accounts because, in her previous position at another hotel in the chain, she had lost one of those same corporate customers over a price increase. She was now torn between her honest conviction that the hotel needed to raise its rates and her equally heartfelt fear that if she lost either of those two customers this time, it would seriously damage her career. Nervously, she wondered whether the two customers would accept the new rate.

The answer, unfortunately, is never so clear-cut. While the 32 percent increase was undoubtedly justified from a cost stand-point, whether or not either of the customers would accept the higher price would depend on whether they felt they were getting sufficient value in return. To predict that with any confidence, we needed to know what each of the hotel's major customers *individually* valued. We needed a more specific understanding of their situation, needs, desires, aspirations, and how they viewed the hotel. Only when we had a clear picture of our counterparts' goals could we develop an approach for successfully negotiating the price increases without losing their loyalty. I suggested that we schedule appointments with the procurement heads of the two companies to learn more about what qualities they most wanted from a hotel.

Initially the general manager resisted. He said that they already knew their customers. Both were multinational Fortune 100 companies in the consumer products business. Both booked over a thousand room-nights a year, and also used three or four other hotels in the city. Their employees came on business, rarely bringing their families, and usually stayed two to five nights. Their big concern in every negotiation was price. "Isn't that enough to go on?" he asked.

Not enough to build a winning negotiation strategy. If we hoped to prevent "sticker shock" and convince these companies that the hotel's services were worth 32 percent more than they cost currently, we needed to understand what the buyers individually needed, wanted, and dreamed of that, if satisfied, would make them willing to pay the higher price.

The general manager remained leery. He was worried that it might offend his customers to be asked what they wanted. "Don't you think they would feel that, since they are our top customers, we should already know them?"

His concern was as familiar as it was misplaced. Who would be insulted to have a business partner sincerely seek to understand your desires and aspirations in order to give you better and more individualized service? It is far more normal for customers to feel insulted because their vendors commoditize them, making no effort to satisfy their particular needs. Although we all get irritated by generic, mass-market surveys, it's rare to meet people who don't appreciate being asked about themselves, their opinions, preferences, and desires, especially when the questioner's purpose is to fulfill those desires. Persuaded, the general manager finally approved the customer meetings. Not surprisingly, those conversations immediately revealed strong differences between the two companies in their goals and styles.

The procurement head at Company A was warm and forthcoming. "We are very happy with the Empire Hotel and its service," he said. "No complaints at all." While that was nice to hear, "no complaints" at the hotel's current price did not translate into "and we would have no complaints if you increased the price by one-third." We needed to find a way to make the procurement head feel that the hotel was worth significantly more than its current rate, so that he would willingly accept the increase.

Our questions then became more focused. What would make your employees' stays less stressful and more pleasing? What do you personally look for when you travel on business? What irritates you? What do other hotels offer that you can't find here?

With some prodding, the procurement head began to come up with some tangible goals. All centered on speed and convenience. One goal was having instant internet access on arrival, which was still uncommon in those days. "Our people fly here from all over the world. Often they have been in the air for twenty hours or more, so they're pretty tired by the time they check into the hotel. They want to go straight to their rooms and turn on the computers, check their e-mail, and contact their families. One thing they do complain about is the rigmarole of having to buy an internet card, ask for a cable, wait for the technician to set it up, etc. If they could just have the internet installed and ready to go when they arrive, that would really be great." He added a few other "great to haves," which we dutifully jotted down.

We now had enough understanding of Company A's goals to lay the groundwork for a good negotiation plan: they valued convenience, ease, and efficiency. Would that mean that Company B shared these same goals? Not necessarily. The only way to know would be to ask Company B.

In fact, Company B, despite its outward resemblance to Company A, had a very different corporate culture and entirely different goals. Known for its hardball, take-no-prisoners negotiating style, this was the company that had earlier canceled its contract with the Empire Hotel in another city over a price increase. True to form, the procurement head of Company B initially came across as hostile. "What do I think of your hotel? I think the price is too high!" she growled.

We asked her why she felt the price was too high. Did the company feel it wasn't getting sufficient value for its money? Was there anything the hotel could do to improve its service in her eyes? "No," she said. "There's nothing particular about your hotel, your value, or your service. It's simply that your price is too high." This was not an auspicious beginning, seeing as the hotel management intended to announce a 32 percent rate increase in the next round of contract negotiations.

As we were getting nowhere asking Company B's procurement head what she found objectionable or lacking in the Empire, we tried a different approach. (If you can't get an answer by knocking on the front door, don't give up. Try the back.) "You work with many hotels and clearly have acquired broad knowledge and high standards. Would you be willing to share an example of a hotel you really like?"

Instantly, she dropped her scowl and grew wistful. "I like the _____," she sighed. "They treat you like a queen." She went on to catalog all the wonderful things the other hotel did to make her feel special, from the doorman who greeted her by name to the handwritten thank-you note the manager sent after each inspection visit. When it was pointed out to her that the hotel she was describing charged $60 a night more than the Empire, she was unmoved. "True," replied the woman, who only minutes before had insisted that the only factor that mattered in her decision making was price, "but it's worth it."

Her response may have seemed contradictory, possibly even a bit silly, but it was neither. In a few short words she had made it clear that although the Empire Hotel may have had much to recommend itself, the management and staff had made this important client feel that she was nothing special to them, a generic customer. Therefore, she had accepted the commodity shopper role, haggling over room rates as if they were cabbages in the market. The other hotel, meanwhile, had treated her like an honored patron—a "queen"—and she had responded with warm, personal feelings, among which price became a far less important priority. This was a problem we needed to fix.

Given the markedly different goals in—and relationships with—Companies A and B, it would be necessary to develop a separate negotiating approach for each customer. Company A, with which the hotel had an open and comfortable relationship, had prioritized convenience and efficiency for its end users as its goals. Company B, on the other hand, put a higher value on having its booking agents treated with honor and appreciation. (The hotel also needed to expend some extra effort to repair the cold relationship that had developed with Company B over the years.)

Despite the obvious differences between the two customers, in both cases we had uncovered distinct goals that opened the door to mutually gainful trade-offs. In-room internet and royal treatment could both be provided at little or no cost to the hotel. We hoped that if we could satisfy these goals, both Companies A and B would be more willing to bear the increased room rate. In the following chapters we will see how that approach worked out.

Conclusion

When I watch participants in training programs prepare for a negotiation role play, I can normally predict who will come out with a more profitable agreement even before the two sides meet. The people who spend their preparation time establishing clear goals and priorities for themselves, then thinking about the goals of the other party, will almost always emerge with better results than their counterparts who focus on negotiation power and developing stratagems and tactics to dislodge the other side. Indeed, the latter often create such resistance that they get no deal at all.

There's much misguided advice out there on how to "win" negotiations through tricks, fakes, and performance artistry. No doubt, such techniques do sometimes work. I am reminded of how, as a child, I once amazed my family while we were fishing in the ocean by reeling in a large crab that had grabbed on to my line. Clearly, that technique can work now and then as well, but it's not a very reliable way to run a profitable crabbing business.

Negotiation is in fact quite straightforward. It's an effort to find a profitable basis for two or more parties to work together to accomplish what they each want insofar as possible. Therefore, the most effective approach is equally straightforward: start by clearly understanding what it is that everyone at the table wants. In the next chapter, we will look at how you find the most profitable Routes for reaching your Goals.

Key Lessons from This Chapter

- Know your goals (needs, desires, and aspirations).
- Understand why those goals are important (what you are trying to achieve).
- Separate your needs (must-haves) from your desires (good-to-haves).
- Prioritize desires and aspirations so that you know which are most important and which you can let go of, if necessary.
- Learn as much as you can about the other side's goals (put yourself in their shoes).
- Look at both sides' goals for commonalities and also for distinct goals that can open the door to possible trade-offs.
- Focusing on goals rather than on terms promotes problem-solving.

Chapter 8

ROUTES — HOW TO GET THERE

Once you understand the various goals you and your negotiation counterparts are aiming for, the next step in your planning process is to think of possible *Routes* that will get you there. Routes are sets of terms or trade-offs that will achieve as many of your objectives as possible while also satisfying the other party.

This stage of the negotiation process requires the most creativity and flexibility. It's easy to come up with a shopping list of things you'd love to have. But relationship-based negotiation requires that you also recognize the needs, desires, and aspirations of the other party as well. It's through thinking of various mutually rewarding routes that you steer the negotiation away from head-butting toward working together.

Coming up with mutually rewarding packages is commonly practiced in sales, in which it has long been understood that customer satisfaction is good business. The phone company offers a variety of monthly plans to suit the preferences of diverse customers. Airlines offer different pricing options depending on a range of factors from legroom to the flexibility passengers need in booking flight dates. I'm pretty sure that the management at Amazon doesn't feel that it's making a wrenching concession by giving free shipping to customers who order over $25 worth of books, and that Nordstrom doesn't feel that it's losing by offering shoppers easy merchandise returns. These companies understand that such gestures, made voluntarily and enthusiastically, contribute both to customers' loyalty and their willingness to spend.

Why, then, do so many negotiators hold on to an antiquated hard-sell mentality, bent more on persuading the other side to give them what they alone want than on achieving mutual satisfaction? How does it make sense for negotiators to cling to a win-lose mind-set in which every concession is seen as a personal defeat? The simple answer is that it doesn't.

For example, in the case described in Chapter Four of the company whose warehouse's walls cracked after a nearby building site had begun construction, the facilities' supervisor's demand that the owners of the new building admit to causing the damage and pay to have it repaired offered no upside whatever to the other side. Had the company continued to insist on it's win-lose position, both parties would likely have ended up in court. However, when the warehouse manager came up with a less adversarial but equally effective route—to have the new building's construction crew repair the damage on a "good neighbor" basis, with the benefit being that no one need bear any blame—the problem was quickly solved without making neighbors into permanent enemies.

Similarly, in the previous chapter, Lynne initially thought that convincing Paulo to agree to a partnership was the way to achieve her goal of running her own business, regardless of Paulo's firm conviction that the company was his personal creation as well as his expressed goal of keeping it under his sole control. By ignoring his concern that a partnership would only take away from what he had, Lynne had created a one-sided strategy bound to fail. But by coming up with a different route—building up an independent segment of the business Paulo would otherwise have no access to, thereby *adding* to what he had—she was able to satisfy even more of her own goals while not encroaching on Paulo's ownership concerns.

Rather than sticking to a rigid, obviously self-interested shopping list, the relationship-building negotiator comes up with a flexible package of terms and ideas that aim, insofar as possible, to realize both parties' goals, enabling everyone to come away feeling like a winner. The trick is to constantly try to move from "either/or" to "both/and." For example, instead of thinking, "Either we include clause 13, which you want, or we delete clause 13, which I would prefer," you ask yourself, "How can we modify clause 13 so that it satisfies both your and my concerns?" Similarly, rather than thinking only of the highest price you can get, you consider what trade-offs you would accept (based on your other goals) in exchange for a price reduction, as well as what extras you would be willing to throw in (based on their goals) to make that high price more palatable.

When coming up with negotiation routes, you should be guided by three powerful ideas practiced by leading companies to maximize their sales revenues and increase customer loyalty:

- Get more of what you want by helping others get what they want.

- Trading off beats marking down.

- Always seek to expand the pie.

Get More of What You Want by Helping Others Get What They Want

In Chapter Three we looked at Nick, the overstretched MBA student, who successfully ended the dispute with his wife over his playing basketball on Sundays by offering to give her a night off once a week in exchange. You may recall that this agreement was reached quickly and harmoniously after a number of failed attempts, which had created growing discord between the couple. What had changed? Nick had gone from thinking in terms of *either/or* (either I get my way and play basketball, or you get your way and I stay at home) to *both/and* (I can both play basketball on Sunday, giving me the break I want, and take care of the baby one night a week, giving you the break you want). He had finally understood that his wife would be more open to his desires if he also was open to hers.

Would Nick have been more of a winner if he had simply pressured his wife to give him free rein to do what he wanted on Sundays without taking on additional family responsibilities of his own? Perhaps on certain weekday nights, when he faced a crying baby and a looming homework assignment, he might have felt that that would have been the case. But looking at the big picture, it's hard to see how he would have been better off. By giving his wife something she needed—a night away to recuperate and reconnect with friends—he not only achieved his top priority (Sunday basketball) but also had a happier wife to come home to each night, a closer bond with his child, and a stronger marriage.

While the benefits to be gained from helping others get what they want may be obvious in a personal relationship, those benefits may be less readily apparent in a professional setting. Nevertheless, the same formula applies. Let's look at the case of Jamie, an attorney in a community "storefront" law firm, who was wondering how she could successfully negotiate with the firm's senior partner to reduce her work hours.

Jamie enjoyed her work and relied on the income, but as the single mother of a special-needs child who required frequent visits to the doctor, she was finding it increasingly difficult to juggle both responsibilities. She had calculated her expenses and found that with the child support payments she got from her ex-husband, she could get by if she cut her hours down to twenty a week (the minimum load to retain her medical insurance and other benefits). The problem—a serious problem—was that the idea of part-time work was not accepted among her legal colleagues, who had to be ready to handle major cases as they came in and to go to trial at any time. Part-time work had never been approved at her firm.

Anticipating considerable resistance, Jamie knew that she would have to come up with more than a personal appeal to back up her request. Therefore, she considered what the partners of the law firm might want that she could offer them or what problems they faced that she might be able to solve. Jamie understood that she would have to give up the status and excitement of handling the big cases if she reduced her hours, but she was comfortable with trading off work challenges temporarily for the even greater challenges she faced at home. Maybe the answer lay in taking on the important but less prestigious work that the other attorneys consistently grumbled about. Chief among these was the after-hours walk-in desk.

As a neighborhood firm, the law office stayed open for walk-in clients until 9:00 every night plus 10:00 to 6:00 on Saturdays. From 9:00 to 6:00 on weekdays, a secretary monitored the walk-in desk and referred each new client to a lawyer. However, after 6:00 P.M. Monday to Friday and all day Saturday, the lawyers had to take turns manning the desk, an assignment that caused loud complaints across the firm. Removing this source of chronic discontent, Jamie realized, might very well be something the law firm's partners wanted that in turn could help her get what she wanted.

As Jamie had suspected, when she met with the firm's senior partner to negotiate her new contract, he initially denied her request to reduce her hours, for all the reasons she had anticipated. From his point of view, having a lawyer who wasn't in the office when the work needed to get done would only create problems, with no benefit for himself or the firm. However, instead of taking no for an answer, she was ready with a route designed to solve one of *their* problems. What if she were to handle the walk-in desk from 6:00 to 9:00 four nights a week and all day Saturday? She could personally deal with any cases that came in that didn't require court work (wills, contracts, legal advice, and so on) and pass on the litigation cases to the full-time lawyers after doing the preliminary interviews and collection of documents. That way, she said, the firm would have dedicated coverage for the walk-in desk, faster turnover of the small cases, and most important, increased morale among the lawyers.

Jamie hadn't come up with this idea on the spur of the moment. She had asked her colleagues what dissatisfied them with the current setup and had thought long and hard about the partners' concerns and the possible trade-offs she could offer to alleviate them. She'd talked to a neighbor to ensure that she would be willing to be on call to manage any emergencies the regular caregiver couldn't cope with. She'd even planned how she was going to present the idea: simply setting out the facts and her proposed solution, careful to avoid the extremes of coming across as a supplicant, on the one hand, or a pushy salesperson, on the other.

Although she was confident going into the meeting, Jamie was still surprised at how quickly the senior partner responded to her idea. After a short discussion of how the system she proposed would work, he made the counterproposal that she instead work five nights a week and only half a day Saturday, since the partners had been thinking of reducing the weekend walk-in hours. As this gave her the same number of total hours (her primary goal), she was prepared to be flexible. Although the boss was not willing to make an immediate commitment, explaining that he would have to sound out the idea with the other partners first, it was clear he was ready to back her plan. By the end of the week, Jamie learned that she was to become her law firm's very first part-time lawyer.

Finding a win-win solution doesn't always call for routes as creative as Nick's or Jamie's, of course. Some negotiations, such as selling your car, are limited in scope and involve little or no onward relationship. Nevertheless, even in onetime price negotiations with immediate implementation, there are at least a dozen ways you can give people more of what they want. You will gain tremendously in any negotiation by

- Being friendly and courteous
- Treating other parties (and their product, company, and so on) with respect

- Listening actively to what they say

- Answering their questions fully and patiently

- Asking them questions to show your interest in them

- Providing information

- Explaining why you take the positions you do

- Addressing, rather than belittling, their concerns

- Agreeing to small requests that cost you little or nothing

- Probing for possible trade-offs

- Allowing them time to think and question

- Giving them a sense of control over the outcome

Some skeptics have objected that people expect negotiators to come across as tough. My reply is that to give something pleasing unexpectedly makes it even more appealing. In response to those who have asked me whether this doesn't make one seem weak, I ask when was the last time that you felt someone was weak because they were courteous, knowledgeable, and open?

Trading Off Beats Marking Down

This is another concept that has long been appreciated in the better-developed sales field but has not yet achieved the same level of awareness among negotiators, to their disadvantage. Faced with opposition, negotiators tend to settle for less: offering discounts, giving up demands, compromising their goals. Salespeople, in contrast, have mastered the art of reducing resistance by offering more.

Even the most prosaic sales pitches now include inducements designed to respond to a range of customer desires, aspirations, and concerns. To overcome your resistance to purchasing a product you have never seen or touched, for example, you are given a "free" set of Ginsu knives when you buy a set of pans from the TV shopping network. If you charge $200 on a certain credit card over the next month, you are told that you will be entered into a lottery that might win you a free vacation in the Bahamas. A health insurance company offers to throw in a year's gym membership if you sign up with their plan. The idea is that vendors gain less from price-cutting than they do from maintaining their profit margins by offering an incentive that is attractive to customers but of lower value to the vendors. The same practice can be applied by negotiators to maximize the value of their relationships. The difference—and the challenge—is that whereas the sales team has been provided with a set of prearranged mass-market offers, negotiators have to base each route and trade-off on the other side's specific interests. There is no generic negotiation.

Fortunately, this isn't as daunting as it sounds. By taking time ahead of the negotiation to imagine the other side's goals, putting in the effort to verify or modify that picture within the negotiation process, and doing a little creative thinking, you can nearly always find potential trade-offs that will give every party more of what they want, creating a higher-value deal for both.

Let's look at an example of a negotiation I conducted on my own behalf. Several years ago, I was approached by a national law society (bar association) to conduct a two-day workshop on negotiation for lawyers. I was very pleased to take on the project, believing that the world would be a far less litigious place if more lawyers practiced relationship-based negotiation. However, we soon encountered a roadblock. When I quoted my fee to the society's head of professional development, she replied with embarrassment that normally they did not pay their speakers. That was patently unacceptable from my perspective, as we were discussing a two-day workshop that would involve flights and a hotel stay, not a short talk by a local member. When I replied that I couldn't take on a project of this scope on a pro bono basis, she said that perhaps they could make an exception if I would agree to do the seminar for one-quarter of my usual fee.

This could easily have turned into price haggling, but I didn't see how that would lead me either to a profitable arrangement for myself or to a sustainable relationship with the law society. Instead, I began probing for trade-offs. I asked the professional development director whether the objection to paying speakers was based on an organizational rule or overarching principle. No, she replied, it was because the professional development division's budget covered only advertising and administrative costs; all of their speakers up to that point had been either lawyers or service providers who were willing to speak for the exposure or prestige. I then asked if the society normally charged an attendance fee for their talks. She acknowledged that they charged a small fee to cover venue and refreshments.

These two questions had opened up a route. If there was no policy against paying speakers and it was possible to charge a fee, then it was clear by extension that if the fee was sufficiently high and enough people attended the workshop, it would be possible to pay a reasonable speaker's fee. The concern of the law society wasn't price; it was risk. Because the head of professional development had a very small budget and she didn't know how many people would pay a higher-than-usual fee to attend the workshop, she was afraid to commit to a figure for a speaker's fee that could put her department in the hole. In contrast, I was sufficiently confident of the level of interest (and of the generous expense accounts of law firms) to be willing to bear that financial risk in exchange for a higher potential payment. The door was open for a mutually satisfying trade-off.

After a little more probing on numbers, I made my counteroffer. The speaker's fee could be assessed on a per-person rather than a per-day basis, with a minimum number of eight registrations required to run the program. The law society would price the course at a rate that, at that minimum number of participants, would cover all direct expenses, including my travel and hotel. Thereafter, for every registrant beyond eight and up to sixteen, I would take home 75 percent of the revenue, which if we reached sixteen, would bring me my usual fee. For all additional enrollments up to the maximum number of twenty-four, I would collect 25 percent, with the remaining 75 percent going to the law society to cover future programs. In other words, above sixteen registrants I would earn *more* than my usual fee, while the society would come out even further ahead—which I had calculated would encourage them to market the program energetically.

We reached an agreement on these terms in one congenial phone call. By trading off the professional development head's concern for eliminating risk with my desire to earn a reasonable fee, both of us felt that we had gained what we most wanted. We also came away as partners in developing this project. That partnership paid off for me many times over. Not only did the initial training go well (with twenty-one participants), but over the years I have been invited back to give a number of additional trainings (at my usual daily rate). How differently the story would have turned out had I refused to budge in my fees or accepted a deeply discounted rate the first time around.

In relationship management, trading yields a far higher rate of satisfaction than cutting everything in half. Imagine that we share an apartment and want to divide the housework and expenses fairly. We could split everything down the middle: you do the chores one week, and I do them the next. But if you hated washing dishes and I made a mess of the ironing—or if you preferred to do less housework altogether and I wanted to get out of paying my half of the utility bill—wouldn't we both be better off (and happier with our living arrangement) if we traded obligations?

Trading can also mend a strained relationship. A commercial writer I know was asked by a friend of hers, a computer graphics designer, to partner on a website project for a large international company. Initially, they agreed to split the fees fifty-fifty, but after a few weeks the designer complained that the agreement wasn't fair. He should get a premium as he had been the one to bring in the client, he said. At first the writer was annoyed, both at the designer's reopening the agreement and, even more, at the implication that she had somehow cheated him. She knew that she was within her rights to refuse outright, as they had already signed a project contract, but she felt that to do so would seriously damage their relationship and maybe the project itself. Moreover, once she had gotten past feeling offended, she conceded that the designer did deserve something for bringing in the business. On the other hand, she was strongly opposed to renegotiating the fee split, because she didn't want to feed a bear or feel like a less-than-equal partner.

Instead of offering him a kickback, therefore, she acknowledged that the designer had brought more than she had to the project and offered to balance his contribution with one of her own. Knowing that the designer detested the business end of the project, she offered to take over all administration: collating expenses, sending out invoices, responding to client queries, producing printed prototypes, and so on. The trade-off gave the designer the recognition he had sought while releasing him from a job he found onerous; the writer retained her sense of equal partnership while staying on top of work that she feared might not get done otherwise.

As with giving in order to gain, trade-offs bring benefits even to onetime price negotiations. A few examples of possible trades that could raise mutual value include

- Quality guarantees

- Shorter or longer payment terms

- Quicker or free pickup or delivery

- Taking responsibility (for example, arranging for bids and liaising with the contractor if the neighbor will split the cost of a new fence)

- Assistance getting started (for example, giving a lesson in how to ride the motorcycle you are selling)

- Additional merchandise (for example, throwing in the poles, ski bag, or a still-valid lift pass as incentives for a price-conscious buyer of your used skis)

- After-sales service

True, it takes a lot less mental energy to cut prices, raise your offer, or even drop the whole thing, but the cost of taking the easy road is high. At best, you minimize your loss. Finding trade routes, in comparison, is the best way to maximize your gain.

Always Seek to Expand the Pie

The basic purpose of negotiation is to establish a more desirable state of affairs than the current one, be it having more cash and less inventory, getting a needed car at an affordable price, dividing office responsibilities more effectively, or resolving a tense and costly international water dispute. By logical extension, then, the more desirable you can make that new state of affairs, the better.

Of course, one way to get more of what you want is to grab the whole pie and leave the other party with nothing but crumbs. But as we have seen, that brings only fleeting rewards. Because it creates a more desirable state of affairs for one party only, it's simply not sustainable. Far more effective is to expand the size of the entire pie so that when it comes time to divide it, there is enough to satisfy everyone.

Here's a great example of expanding the pie, from a former participant in one of my seminars. In the negotiations for selling her upcoming crop of organic heirloom tomatoes, Dawn was unhappy with the price she was offered by her wholesaler, given the premium that gourmet tomatoes were commanding in the stores. When she raised her objection, the wholesaler, Jerry, explained that the price was deceptive. Because Dawn's tomatoes were picked ripe, they also spoiled considerably faster. He showed her figures to substantiate that he was losing around 25 percent of his earnings on her produce from having to buy back rotten tomatoes from the stores.

In the past, Dawn said, she most likely would have backed down, accepted the reality of the market and the limitations of the product, and taken the reduced price the wholesaler was offering. She admitted that she was not much of a fighter. It was easy to justify the lower price when she considered that the economy was weakening; what would she gain from fighting to increase her price by passing on the difference to the store and its customers? That would just eat into sales. However, after learning the GRASP method, she said she began searching for ways to expand the pie.

She started by talking to other organic growers in the area to see how they could collaborate to benefit both the growers and the consumers. To get Jerry's help in this effort, she looked for routes that would benefit the wholesaler as well. The breakthrough came when she learned that the wholesale processing system of collecting, cleaning, sorting, and packaging the produce took five to ten days before it was ready to be delivered to the stores. This was not a problem for bulk produce, which was picked green and so could withstand weeks in a warehouse, but for tomatoes that were already fully ripe at picking it was a recipe for disaster. Dawn suggested to Jerry that if they could work together to speed up the process, they would both lose less in spoilage—and therefore make more money.

Building on the ideas she and her neighboring farmers had come up with, Dawn proposed that the local organic tomato growers could clean and sort their own produce right at the farm under the guidelines of one of Jerry's quality inspectors, package it under a "really, truly, genuine vine-ripened" label, and have it ready to be collected and delivered straight to the stores by the next day. Dawn proudly recounted that everybody loved the idea. The wholesaler benefited from reducing his labor costs in processing this niche product, while being able to get the tomatoes onto the shelves before they started to perish. For the growers, although the new arrangement meant more work, it earned them the price premium they wanted and the personal satisfaction from getting their produce to market when it was at its most delicious. The stores had less moldy produce to deal with. And the customers benefited from being able to enjoy vine-ripened tomatoes at their peak. What an example of expanding the pie for everyone!

Another important way to expand the pie is to broaden the perspective. Remember that the central question in every negotiator's mind is "What's in it for me?" If the other parties feel that your proposals benefit them only marginally, they will be less willing to accept than if they feel they stand to benefit in a more significant way, even if not immediately or directly. It's the same thinking that gets the vendor to offer more flexible terms to a regular customer than to a one-time shopper, even when they're placing identical orders. To move the perception of the negotiation beyond immediate issues and onto aspirations will greatly increase your impact as well as your chances for success.

Here's an example of an impasse that was resolved solely through broadening the other party's perspective. Malina, a former international student of mine, had been accepted into a one-year diploma course at a well-known art institute in the United States. She had chosen the diploma in interior design, a part-time program, not because she wanted to take only three classes (nine hours) per quarter—she would have liked to take more—but because it was the only course at the institute that could be completed in a single year. Timing was the deciding factor. The advertising agency she worked for said it would grant her a maximum of twelve months of unpaid leave, and she had saved only enough money to pay for a year of school.

All was on track for Malina to attend the course when she got a letter from the art institute's head of admissions saying that because of changes in U.S. visa regulations, she was no longer eligible for the part-time program. The new regulations, a response to the attacks on the World Trade Center, limited visas only to those students enrolled in full-time programs (defined as at least twelve hours of classes per week). The admissions director suggested that she change her enrollment to the two-and-a-half-year full-time associate of applied arts program. Unfortunately for Malina, that was out of the question.

Desperate not to lose her chance to study at the institute, Malina wrote the director of admissions asking if it would be possible for her to earn a diploma by taking one year of the full-time associate program. The director said no, as the syllabi of the two programs were entirely different: a year in the associate program did not cover all the core subjects needed to earn a diploma. Malina then proposed that she take an additional art class or even a course in English composition on top of the nine-hour diploma curriculum, in order to raise her class-time commitment to the required twelve hours. The director replied that that also wasn't possible, as all the art classes fed into specifically designed, progressive programs of instruction. Students could not just take classes willy-nilly, she said, nor could they create their own courses that were not part of the regular curriculum. The only option available, she insisted, was for Malina to change her registration to the two-and-a-half-year associate program.

As a last-ditch effort, Malina called her old negotiation professor for advice. After hearing her story, I felt sure that the problem was that the administrators at the art institute just didn't see enough in it for them to go to all the effort it would take to enable one student to get a diploma. What we needed to do was expand their view of the pie.

As an interested party on Malina's behalf, I wrote a letter to the admission director to appeal the decision. Rather than wasting any ink on the merits of this one student, I widened the focus of negotiation to include *all* international students and, most significantly, the rich revenue stream they provided to the school. "Your policy as it stands now bars *any* foreign student from taking the diploma course," I wrote. "Is that your intention? Certainly such a policy would act as a barrier to international enrollments, both narrowing your pool of qualified applicants and limiting the diversity of your program." I proposed that they could prevent this costly loss of foreign students by adding a single elective to their diploma program each term, allowing students who needed visas to take four courses instead of three, and thus giving them enough credits to attend the institute.

I sent the letter less in optimism than in the spirit of "it never hurts to ask." Bureaucracies are notoriously difficult to move. I was unsure whether my unsolicited letter would even get a response. Well, it did and it didn't. Personally, I never heard back from the director of international admissions or anyone at the art institute. However, three weeks later Malina received an e-mail that read, in part:

> Good news! We are working on a schedule now
> that would allow you to take the interior
> design diploma program! We had to make some
> changes and came up with some solutions with
> immigration. You can now take four interior
> design classes a quarter. We had to get per-
> mission from education and make sure that
> they would allow this...but it looks like it
> will work! We are very excited!

Coincidence? Perhaps. We will never know if it was that big pie that tipped the scale. What we do know is the result—and that was good enough for Malina.

Is it possible to expand the pie in a one-time buy-sell negotiation? Of course. In sales it's known as bundling. For example, I will sell you my car for a certain price, but for slightly more I will throw in the custom-designed roof rack. For you, the price of the roof rack is a bargain; as for me, I am relieved of the hassle of advertising and selling the roof rack separately. Similarly, in a negotiation to take over my office lease, you might ask whether I would be interested in transferring the photocopier and broadband contracts to you as well. That way, you could get a deep discount on the service contracts while I am spared getting stuck with an early termination penalty.

Remember, the goal of relationship negotiation is to maximize mutual gain.

Planning and Presenting Routes

Although negotiations will always be dynamic, requiring flexibility and considerable on-the-spot thinking, the skilled negotiator nevertheless must prepare ahead insofar as possible. By entering the negotiation with a mental list of several potential routes or pieces of routes that would take the parties to their goals, you are far more likely to control the flow of the discussion, to avoid making panic-driven concessions, and eventually to emerge with a favorable settlement.

After brainstorming a list of routes, the next step is to rank them according to how well they would achieve your goals: from *most desirable* to the *least acceptable*. (Don't bother listing options you would find unacceptable.) I find it useful to jot down the advantages and disadvantages of each potential route, which helps me to clarify my own rankings and, more important, further prepares me to advocate a specific route under the pressure of the negotiation.

In a multiparty negotiation, where you have to bring a lot of competing parties with separate interests on board, it's wise to spend some time ahead of the formal negotiation, meeting privately with the various parties to solicit their ideas and test out their receptivity to routes you have come up with. This helps to fine-tune your proposals, while giving everyone a sense of ownership over them, so that they will be more readily accepted by all. People are far more likely to agree to and implement solutions they feel they had a voice in or will get credit for developing. In fact, one of the most valuable and least costly incentives a negotiator can give to his or her counterpart is credit for the outcome.

Just as if you were planning a group trip, once you have decided which route you like the best, that's the one you advocate at the start. Don't mention any of the other routes until your first choice has been completely ruled out. Why present only one route when you have gone to so much effort to think up many? First, because that's the outcome you most desire, you don't want to immediately open the door to less attractive alternatives. Second, if you present more than one idea at the outset, you stand a high chance of overwhelming the other negotiator, confusing the discussion, and bogging down the whole process. Negotiation is not a challenge to see who can come up with the most clever ideas. It's an attempt to settle on the best one.

Even if the other party rejects your initial proposal, you mustn't just drop the idea and move on to your next route. This is a rich opportunity to achieve a closer understanding of the person or institution you are dealing with. You need to ask open questions to uncover precisely what they find objectionable and to probe for modifications, if any, that would make the proposal more acceptable. Through this open questioning process you will learn much more about the other side's goals, which until now you have only been able to guess at. With that knowledge, you will then have a clearer idea of which of your secondary routes are most likely to appeal to the other side, so that you can work more confidently toward a mutually satisfying outcome.

That said, not all people respond well to open questions (those that cannot be answered with a single word, such as yes or no).

They may look on open questions from someone outside of their intimate circle as invasive and suspect a trick to get them to give away valuable information. These tight-lipped souls may reject a proposal as unacceptable, but when you ask them what specifically they object to, they refuse to tell you more. This can be pretty frustrating in a negotiation. One effective method for getting guarded negotiators to open up is to ask them choice questions instead. An open question ("What are your priorities?") may make them feel too exposed. If so, a choice question ("Are you more interested in maintaining the current wage level or minimizing layoffs?") will more likely get a useful answer. By asking a series of choice questions, building one on the other, you can often reach a sophisticated understanding of the other party's preferences, which will allow you to work toward an agreement.

Hotel Rate Case Study

Let's put all of this together by returning to the Empire Hotel room-rate negotiation introduced in the last chapter. As you may recall, the procurement head of Company A was generally happy with the hotel but expressed an interest in improving the speed and efficiency of the service. In particular, he mentioned having internet access set up and ready in the rooms on check-in.

This negotiation was looking like it would be relatively easy: to lessen any resistance to the price increase, the hotel would simply have to offer Company A the incentive of the higher level of service the procurement head had asked for, including having internet access preinstalled in the rooms. Both sides would come away with something they wanted. It seemed such a simple solution that it was doubly shocking when the hotel's general manager dismissed the idea out of hand. "We can't give free internet!" he said. "Our parent company doesn't allow it."

What was wrong with his reply? First, he hadn't even stopped to think about how it could be done before jumping to no. Second, he made no attempt to verify his understanding of the policy with the parent company. Third, and most fundamentally, no one had said "free." Company A's procurement head wasn't asking for a giveaway; he simply wanted an easier check-in experience for the company's employees. (Happily, once this final point was made clear to the general manager, he dropped his opposition.)

The general manager's initial response may have been unhelpful for the negotiation, but it is helpful as a lesson in what not to do in a negotiation. In fact, it teaches us three lessons:

- Never respond to an idea without thinking all sides through first.

- Always verify your understanding. ("Do you mean free internet?")

- Most important, *don't say no when you can say yes*.

What was the cost to the hotel of arranging to have internet access set up in the room whenever an employee from Company A was due to check in? Nothing. The hotel already had the internet cables and the technicians to install them. The solution simply called for a different procedure: installing the cable in advance of the guest's arrival instead of after. From Company A's perspective, however, what was the value of hassle-free service to the exhausted traveler who had been crammed into a crowded airplane for untold hours and just wanted to go to her room, be left alone, and check her e-mail in peace? Enough, in the end, to make Company A feel that the hotel was worth 32 percent more per night.

We had found an effective route for achieving both the hotel's and Company A's goals, but Company B called for a separate strategy. As you recall, their head of procurement hadn't shown the least interest in speed, efficiency, internet access, or even the end user. Her concern was about the way she and her team were treated. The three procurement staff who booked hotel rooms for the company wanted to feel that *they* were highly valued customers. To reach this unique goal called for a very different route.

How could the hotel management make Company B's procurement team feel more valued? The hotel's marketing department had a regular entertainment budget, which they primarily used to fund several gala events held throughout the year for key corporate clients. Why not peel off part of that budget to host an exclusive tea party for their single biggest customer to help repair the damaged relationship?

The sales director invited the three procurement staff from Company B to a private viewing of the recent renovations, followed by high tea. When they arrived, they were greeted warmly and by name, not just by the doorman but by their account manager, the sales director, *and* the general manager. The sales director and the account manager then led them on a personalized tour of the new facilities, soliciting their opinions throughout on what they liked, didn't like, and would like to see more of. This gave the hotel sales team indispensable information on how they could better please their major customer, while at the same time demonstrating how much management valued the booking agents' opinions. Afterward, the Empire's general manager treated the guests to a sumptuous tea fit for a queen.

Company B's procurement team came away from this event feeling valued as never before. They were gratified to learn that the hotel management appreciated the amount of business they provided and listened seriously to their ideas. Having repaired the damaged relationship, the Empire Hotel was now in a much better position to negotiate with Company B collaboratively rather than as enemies. What was the price to the hotel of giving their biggest customer a tea party? Only a little time on management's part. They already had the budget ... and the tea. What was the value to three midlevel corporate employees who spent their days booking five-star hotels that they probably could never afford to stay at themselves? I'll let you decide. In the next chapter we will see whether these routes brought the hotel any closer to achieving its price increase.

Conclusion

There are many ways to reach a destination. You can plow straight ahead, forcing your way, making others yield, perhaps ending up in a rut, and most certainly leaving bruises that will be slow to heal. Or you can find a creative route that will attain both your material and your relationship goals by helping all sides come away feeling that they have gained something. The latter route takes more mental effort, but the payoff is exponentially higher.

In the next chapter we will look at how you build trust and confidence using Arguments for your case, that is, justifying your proposals to the other party.

LESSONS FROM THIS CHAPTER

- Routes are sets of terms or trade-offs that will achieve all or some of your objectives while also satisfying the other party.
- Try to move from "either/or" to "both/and."
- When developing routes
  - Get more of what you want by helping others get what they want
  - Trade off instead of marking down
  - Always seek to expand the pie
- Even without material trade-offs there are a dozen ways you can give people what they want.
- Trading for more creates better all-around value and stronger relationships than settling for less.
- If you expand the size of the pie, there will be more to satisfy everyone when it comes time to divide it.

- Having a mental list of several potential routes prepared in advance helps control the flow of the discussion and keeps you from making panic-driven concessions.
- Rank your routes from the most desirable to the least acceptable, considering both their advantages and disadvantages.
- If your counterpart won't answer open questions, try asking choice questions.
- When responding to another party's suggested routes
  - Think it through before responding
  - Always verify your understanding
  - Don't say no when you can say yes

Chapter 9

ARGUMENTS — MAKING YOUR CASE

You have considered your goals and the best routes for achieving them. Now you need to marshal your *Arguments*—the explanations and evidence that support every proposal and every concession you make. In Chapter Five, I emphasized the importance of basing your negotiating position on reason and fairness instead of on feeding bears. Now let's look at how to do that.

Before explaining how to frame an acceptable argument, however, we need to have a clear idea of what an argument is and, just as important, what it is not. First, "argument" in the negotiation context does not mean a quarrel (a sure path to breakdown in a negotiation). Nor does it mean loudly insisting on your viewpoint or relentlessly building a case that "proves" you are right. (Aside from being pointless, trying to get others to admit that they are wrong and you are right creates fearsome resistance.) Rather, an argument in this context consists of (1) factual evidence that provides a legitimate basis for every position taken or (2) a mutually acceptable reason for everything asked for and every concession made. In short, arguments are what separate relationship-based negotiation from either bickering or dickering.

Second, although arguments are intended to be compelling, they are not the same as the fifth step of the GRASP method, Persuasion (the subject of Chapter Eleven). Arguments are employed to *validate* the legitimacy or fairness of the terms you propose or to *challenge* the legitimacy or fairness of the terms proposed by others, whereas persuasion seeks to *motivate* others to agree by showing them how the proposed terms would benefit them.

Here's a quick example that will demonstrate the difference between argument and persuasion. Imagine that you are a shopper at a craft fair, where I have a booth selling hand-knit wares. As you walk past my table, a sweater catches your eye. You pick it up but then express shock at the price tag of $200, telling me that the price seems pretty high for a handmade sweater. To support the validity of my asking price, I might tell you about the time-consuming work and expertise that went into knitting the complex pattern or perhaps describe the rare Himalayan wool yarn the sweater was made of. These are all reasonable arguments. They say, in essence, "This is a fair price. I am not ripping you off." Good arguments are intended to lower the other party's mistrust and make him or her more willing to accept the proposed terms as fair. However, while my arguments may convince you that I am a fair trader and the sweater is truly worth the price, they won't necessarily *persuade* you to make the purchase, which requires convincing you that you would be better off with the sweater than with $200 in your pocket. Arguments justify the speaker's position; they don't necessarily appeal to the listener's goals. That said, arguments are absolutely vital to relationship negotiation as they form the foundation of mutual trust and the sincere acceptance of the agreed terms.

Arguments Show Respect

Although we sometimes forget this when we're on the speaking side, taking positions without offering reasons for them is treating the listener as a child ("Because I said so"); an enemy ("I don't trust you enough to tell you"); a blockhead ("You couldn't possibly understand"); or a victim ("Just hand it over!"). It hardly needs saying that people rarely respond positively to being cast in any of those roles. (Even children hate the "because I said so" line.)

I recently went to the telephone company to change my mobile phone service. My own transaction proceeded without incident. However, while the sales agent was off setting up my phone, I found myself listening with increasing fascination to the conversation in the next booth. A man had come in to see about getting a new phone. He explained that he had signed up for mobile service the previous week and had purchased an upgraded phone as part of the plan, but over the weekend his phone had been stolen. So, he said, he'd come back to get a replacement. The agent replied curtly, "We don't do that." Taken aback by this impenetrable rejection, the man did what many of us do when the response we receive is out of line with our expectations: he repeated what he had said the first time. "No, no," he said. "I don't think you understand. You see, I just signed up for service last week . . ."

Unfortunately, the agent wasn't any more forthcoming the second time around. She simply repeated her four words in turn. With growing frustration, the man made one attempt after another to explain his request. He wasn't trying to cheat anyone to get a free phone, he said. He could show a police report to prove that his phone was really stolen. He was more than happy to pay whatever he paid previously for the phone. As the clerk just kept shaking her head to everything he said, his anger began to rise. "Is this how your company treats its so-called 'valued customers' once you've suckered them into signing a contract?" he snapped.

By now my transaction had concluded, but I remained glued to the conversation in the next booth. Why, I kept wondering, didn't she just tell him *why* she couldn't provide him with a replacement phone even if he paid the same price as he had for the initial phone? Her unwillingness to give him a reason for her refusal to sell him a new phone was obviously upsetting him as much as the refusal itself. Not only did he not understand why a request that made perfect sense to him was being rejected, but he plainly felt insulted at her denying him the courtesy of an explanation.

Undoubtedly, there were reasons for the refusal, which the clerk could easily have shared (or found out if she didn't know). She might have explained that the telephone company provided handsets to new mobile customers as a marketing tool and that the price that he had paid for the phone when he signed up for the service was below actual cost, so that even if he paid the same amount it wouldn't cover the real price. She might have explained that service providers were not legally authorized to sell retail phones except as part of new contracts, but that she could give him the names of some companies in the area that did. She might have assured him that once he got his new phone at one of those locations, she would help him set it up. Instead, by offering nothing but surly silence, she made him feel as if he were being victimized twice, first by the thief, then by the phone company.

The customer wasn't the only one who suffered because of the clerk's refusal to give legitimate arguments. He had kept her tied up for at least twenty minutes in a futile and increasingly loud argument. It couldn't have been pleasant for her, much less a productive use of her time. The company lost even more, as the customer eventually grew so frustrated that he canceled his service, despite being warned that he would have to pay a $250 early termination fee. "I don't care!" he shouted. "I would pay $500 to have nothing more to do with this company!" As the other customers in the store looked on with growing misgivings about their own dealings with this company, he slammed down his check on the counter and stormed out, taking his business to a competitor.

Some might call the man's behavior irrational. He was willing to pay $500 (and did pay $250) to break off his relationship with the company because one of its representatives didn't give him any arguments for the positions she had taken. In fact, his response was predictably human. As psychologist Abraham Maslow has shown in his renowned "hierarchy of needs," all people need to feel that they are respected.[1] The phone customer felt precisely the opposite. The resentment created by that sense of being disrespected trumped his concern about the extra cost he was incurring. It overrode any reluctance he may have felt about going through the hassle of signing up with a new phone company. It superseded any rationale (such as better coverage or lower price) he had had for choosing the original phone company in the first place. As illogical as his choice may sound from the cool remove of a cost-benefit analysis, I'll bet that you can remember a time when you felt dismissed and had a similar reaction, if perhaps you didn't express it at the same volume.

The positive lesson here is that the more arguments you're able to provide and the more open you appear, the more you confer respect on the other party, which in turn earns their goodwill and acceptance. As a result, the smoother the negotiation will proceed.

That said, what can you do if the person you are negotiating with is as tight-lipped as the phone clerk? Are you condemned to walking out in frustration, $250 the poorer, as the customer did? No. The outcome of their dispute was *absolutely avoidable*. Every negotiator possesses the power to change the dynamic of the negotiation. It doesn't take any special debating skills—merely the ability to ask questions. In the above case, the customer could have broken the logjam and saved himself a lot of broken blood vessels if he had politely asked the sales agent to explain herself. "Could you help me to understand why this is a problem?" is a vital sentence in any negotiator's repertoire (followed if necessary by, "Would you please call someone who could?"). When you're not getting any explanations, stop talking and start asking.

The Power of "Because"

Offering a simple explanation is a good start—and is sometimes all you need to break through resistance. In a famous series of studies carried out in the 1970s and 1980s, Harvard psychologist Ellen Langer showed that people asking to cut in front of others waiting in line at a copy center were granted permission two-thirds more frequently if they added "because . . ." to the request. If the request was small (the line-breaker was holding only one or two sheets of paper), the "because" alone was enough: the reason itself was virtually of no consequence. "Because I have to make some copies" worked as well as any other explanation. It was the respectful act of giving a reason that made the difference. Naturally, as the size of the request increased, so did the reluctance of the person being asked. However, even then, "because I'm in a rush" was effective nearly 95 percent of the time.[2]

I'll share a touching story that happened to my friend Nancy, which underscores Langer's findings. One evening Nancy was spending time with her mother, who suffers from senile dementia. Her mother asked for some ice cream, but there was none in the house. Wanting to grant this small wish, but fearing to leave her mom alone (as her dad was enjoying a rare night off), Nancy bundled her mother into the car and headed to the supermarket. When they got there, however, Nancy's mother didn't want to leave the car. There were too many strange people walking about. Thinking it would take only a couple of minutes, Nancy reluctantly agreed to let her mom wait in the car while she ran in to get the ice cream. Nancy bolted into the store, grabbed some ice-cream cups, sprinted toward the checkout counter . . . and stopped dead. Only two aisles were open, with a dozen customers split between them. Everyone looked annoyed at the long lines. Many were grumbling volubly. Nancy's heart sank.

She nearly gave up on the whole ice-cream mission. However, by the philosophy we had many times discussed that you should never say no for somebody else, she decided to lay her case before the sour-faced assembly and let them decide. "I'm very sorry to bother you," Nancy intoned. "I know you've all been waiting and want to get out of here as quickly as possible. But I'm buying this ice cream for my mother, who's in the car alone. She has Alzheimer's disease. I'm worried that if I leave her much longer she could become frightened or disoriented and wander away. Would anyone be willing to let me get in line in front of them?"

One by one, every single customer in line invited her to go in front. In a few moments Nancy was out of the store watching her mother's delight at getting her prize. That is the power of a sincere "because."

Arguments Build Trust

As we have seen, mistrust is a constant obstacle to productive negotiations. Although some insist that trust is not essential for dealmaking (giving the example that police can negotiate terms with hostage takers), unless you are holding a gun to someone's head (literally or figuratively), trust is a necessity for faithfully carrying out even the shortest-term deal. Even the criminal would be unlikely to release the hostages and turn himself in unless he trusts that the police will keep their promise not to shoot him when he does. Therefore, a primary mission of the negotiator is to increase the level of trust. And one of the most effective ways to do that is through offering credible arguments.

Let's look at it from a commonsense perspective. If one of your employees doesn't show up for work one Monday, you will naturally suspect that the employee is enjoying a three-day weekend at your expense unless he or she provides you with a legitimate reason for the absence. If you have a good relationship with the employee, the store of trust will probably be high enough for you to accept the spoken reason as sufficient. If, on the other hand, that same employee calls in sick repeatedly, your concern over being taken advantage of will be so elevated that a verbal explanation will no longer be enough. In that case you might require hard evidence to support the story, such as a doctor's note. In both instances you needed a credible argument, but the higher the level of mistrust, the more supporting evidence you would demand to give weight to that argument.

The same logic applies in negotiation, which naturally triggers people's fears of being exploited. Fear, mistrust, and opposition are inextricably linked. Therefore, it must be the goal of the negotiator to provide the arguments that will reduce others' fear of being taken advantage of, so that they feel sufficient trust in you to reach and carry out an agreement.

This was brought home in a negotiation I observed between Nan, whose family owns a small group of beach resorts in Thailand, and Heinrich, the agent for one of their biggest customers. Nan had returned from graduate school in Europe to head the resorts' sales and marketing team, which included negotiating rates with the large European travel companies from which they got most of their customers. Although she could speak fluent English and German, Nan admitted to being intimidated by the "pushiness" of the big and often brash European men she found herself facing across the negotiating table. Her nervousness didn't lead her to back down as much as to go stubbornly silent, leaving her with nothing to show for hours of meetings, phone calls, and e-mails but increasing misery. Depressed and bewildered by these repeated clashes, she asked if I would watch her next negotiation with Heinrich to see if I could figure out what she was doing wrong.

It took only minutes to pinpoint the problem. After a few warm opening words about how much each valued the other's long, supportive partnership, Nan presented her proposed contract—and Heinrich exploded. He demanded to know how she could raise prices just a year after the tsunami. "This is ridiculous! It makes no business sense!" he fumed. Nan responded timidly, "I don't want to fight; please don't yell at me," pushing the contract an inch or two closer to him.

Heinrich lowered his voice but did not change his position. "This is totally unjustified," he said. "My company lost a ton of money last year on canceled Phuket trips. Now we have to work together to bring the customers back. I'm ready to help you by promoting your property, but you have to help me by keeping prices as low as possible." Nan silently pushed the contract forward a few more inches.

"You'll kill your business if you do this," Heinrich warned. For an uncomfortable few minutes they just stared at one another. Finally, Heinrich broke the silence. "Is this take it or leave it?" he asked. Nan replied softly, without expression, "I don't want to put it that way, but . . ."

The "negotiation," if you could call it that, concluded with Heinrich refusing to sign the contract. His last words on walking out were that if she didn't make a better offer when he returned at the end of the week, he would drop the resort.

It was obvious from observing that short episode that Nan was sorely in need of some compelling arguments. However, the intensity of the mistrust and anger she stoked by her uncommunicativeness was only fully revealed that evening. In a stroke of luck, as I boarded the airport shuttle bus that evening, I saw Heinrich sitting a few rows back. He was still fuming and was more than happy to vent his frustrations on an eager listener.

"You can't trust these local family businesses," he said. "They take everything they can get and give nothing back. Nan smiles to your face, but she has no sense of loyalty to her business partners. I understand that they lost a lot in the tsunami, but my company suffered a beating, too. I don't know when my business will get back to its old level. Yet instead of sharing the burden and working as partners to lure back the customers, Nan wants to stick it to me. What's the point of raising prices now? Does she expect me and the other tour companies to make up for her losses? What about us?"

The next morning, I called Nan to share with her what Heinrich had said. "He believes that you're raising the resorts' rates to recoup your losses from the tsunami," I said. Nan was stunned. What was he talking about? The resort had borne the entire cost of repairing the flood damage. In fact, she said, they had used the opportunity to make some improvements, such as putting in the larger baths the European customers had asked for. The rate increase included none of that expense, she said. However, on the operations side, they now had to pay higher wages to attract staff, leery about working near the ocean. They also had to bear higher taxes to cover repairs to the island's infrastructure as well as increased utility fees. Excluding all the renovations, she said, the resorts' costs this year had gone up 12–15 percent, but they were asking for only a 7 percent increase. What was that if not burden-sharing?

The problem was that Heinrich knew none of that. Lacking any justification from Nan, he had done what we all do when we're fearful and mistrustful: he had invented his own negative explanation. If Nan wanted to win back his trust, she needed to share her reasons for the increase along with some hard evidence supporting them. Nan hesitated. Was it safe to share information with Heinrich? Wouldn't he use it to put himself in a stronger position over her? Her concerns revealed her own mistrust of someone so different from herself. If this kept up, they would surely never reach an agreement—and the resorts would lose one of their biggest customers.

In reality, Nan's fear made little sense. What advantage would Heinrich possibly gain from understanding the basis of the price increase? Nan wouldn't be opening up the hotel's books to him, merely illuminating the changes that had made it necessary to raise rates. Moreover, she would be revealing positive developments that Heinrich may not have known or thought about, such as how, rather than just bringing the resorts back to their previous standard before the tsunami, they had made improvements that he himself had requested in the past. Nevertheless, until she gave him another interpretation—and enough supporting information to make it convincing—Heinrich would continue to think that Nan's family was trying to take advantage of him. Eventually, Nan agreed.

She also prepared a calmly reasoned response to Heinrich's concern that a rate decrease was needed to bring customers back to the resort after the tsunami. Safety and price were separate issues, she would argue. If people were avoiding Thailand because they genuinely feared a repeat tsunami, a $10-a-night discount was hardly going to change their minds.

Finally, Nan needed to reassure Heinrich that she was indeed his trusted business partner. To do that she needed to face up to her own adversarial mind-set going into negotiations. When she started off with the negative (and passively accusing) "I don't want to fight," she sent the subtextual message to Heinrich and to herself that they were opponents engaged in a battle—not partners working to reach an agreement. Her subsequent silent treatment reinforced that perspective. Nan had to reverse that negative cycle by using arguments that showed a concern for Heinrich's goals. "Let me explain" invites communication, whereas "I don't want to fight" shuts it off.

Nan needed to explain that she had naturally considered the effect on Heinrich's business before deciding on the price increase, and that she had only gone forward after determining that it would not harm him. She would remind him that the key issue for the travel company was relative, not absolute, price. Heinrich's agency carried many properties around the world at different price ranges; if customers felt Nan's resorts were too expensive, they would simply choose another one of his destinations. The resorts bore all the risk. Heinrich's business would only be harmed if Nan charged his agency a higher rate than she charged its competitors, which she was willing to guarantee that she would not do. If he needed evidence of her sincerity, she was even willing to insert a best-price guarantee into the contract, specifying that as long as Heinrich's company remained the resorts' leading customer, he would always receive the lowest rate.

Feeling much more confident after this preparation, Nan awaited Heinrich's return. Two days later, I got her exultant call. "I met with Heinrich today, and he signed the contract at the rate we were proposing! It only took fifteen minutes! I can't believe it!" What had changed so dramatically between the first and this meeting? Openness—which in turn created trust. Nan's stock of legitimate arguments and her new willingness to share information and evidence had reduced Heinrich's misgivings that she was out to cheat him. He began feeling that they really were business partners.

Nan had the same impressive results in all of her subsequent negotiations that year. The following year's negotiations went even more smoothly, as she had already built up a foundation of trust with her regular customers. Today, Nan has become one of the best negotiators I've ever seen: firm but always with justification. In the process she has built strong and trusting relations with all of her business partners. In fact, she tells me Heinrich has become one of her closest friends in the business.

What Are Acceptable Arguments?

An acceptable argument is a reason (in support of a route) that pretty much everyone in the room would agree has some basis of merit. In order to support your request for a certain price, for example, you might talk about the cost of special materials, the quality of the product, distinguishing features, current market value, and so on. If you wanted to make the case that you deserve a raise, you might remind the boss of additional responsibilities you've taken on recently, successful projects you've completed, revenue you've brought into the company, first-rate evaluations you've received, comparative salaries across the industry, or increased market demand for your skills.

In these examples, all the listed arguments fall into cate-gories that *all parties* would agree are acceptable bases of valuation (although the other side may disagree with your calculations or counter your arguments with opposing ones). An *unacceptable* argu-ment is one that relates to fulfilling only one side's desires. "I need to reduce your payment terms because I'm having cash flow prob-lems," would be one example, as would, "I need a raise because I recently bought a new house and have to cover my mortgage." And there are my personal bugbears: "company policy," "our standard terms," and "the way we do things." (Tell me again what that has to do with me . . . .)

As in the experiment at the copy center, the bigger the request, the stronger the argument you need to provide. For comparatively minor or self-evident issues, a verbal explanation will normally be sufficient. ("I charge more for overseas training programs to compensate for the time lost in flying.") You should come into the negotiation prepared with an explanation for *every* position you take and every request you make. When the issue is significant or controversial, however, it is far more effective—and often necessary—to provide precise, *tangible* evidence. ("Here's a list of the awards we've won in the past three years," as opposed to, "We've won a number of awards.") The more written documentation you can prepare in advance and bring into the negotiation, the more compelling your case will be.

Although you may not have to mention them, 'you should come into the negotiation prepared with arguments in support of your less desirable routes as well as for potential compromises you may offer. In the give-and-take of negotiation, you may well have to yield ground on some of your initial positions, and you will retain far more credibility if you are able to share suitable reasons for making those concessions. As we saw in Chapter Five, a sure way to create bears is to imply through your silence that you are accepting less advantageous terms because you are desperate for a deal or because the offer you originally made was inflated. To avoid that outcome, you should base your concessions either on a suitable trade-off ("I can lower the price *if* you pay in full at delivery") or a defensible reason ("*Because* two-thirds of the dead tree lies on my property, I agree that it's fair for me to pay two-thirds rather than half of the cost of its removal.") Offering a suitable rationale for every shift will ensure that you retain the trust you have built up to this point.

Eliciting and Challenging Arguments

A sustainable agreement needs a strong foundation on both sides. Therefore, just as you ground every offer or concession that you make on solid arguments, you need to ensure that the other side does the same. This involves both *probing* and *challenging*: asking open (information-gathering) questions to probe the bases of the other side's positions and posing both open and closed (yes/no or single-word answer) questions to challenge arguments you feel are weak or miscalculated. (See page 198 for examples of open and closed questions.) Even in a dispute, however, probing and challenging should be a sincere process of positive questioning. Probing must never be confused with interrogation nor challenging with cross-examination, which only put people on the defensive. Remember, you are on a quest to understand and to reach agreement rather than to accuse or prove you're right.

The most consistent weakness I have observed among negotiators is that they ask far too few questions. When facing opposition, they will try to convince the other party of the rightness of their position; they will argue, attack, or defend, but they almost never ask why. As a result, they increase opposition rather than move toward problem-solving. The man at the phone store is an example. He started out by stating then reiterating his position, moved on to accusing, and finally threatened the sales agent with the loss of his business, but he never once asked her why she wouldn't sell him a new phone. Just as ineffectually, when many do ask questions, they move on to their next point without waiting for an answer. Heinrich did ask Nan how she could justify raising prices a year after the tsunami but then followed in the same breath with, "This is ridiculous! It makes no business sense!" As a result, the question came across as rhetorical and accusatory, part of a general outburst that certainly did not elicit a reply.

Two of the greatest skills of a negotiator are to be able to ask even tough questions politely, in an earnest desire to understand the other party's viewpoint—and then to wait as long as it takes to get an answer. Clarifying questions asked in a nonthreatening manner are virtually irresistible. It may take a while to get a reply—some people need time to think, and there's no benefit to be gained from rushing them—but in the end few are willing to answer a sincere request for explanation with, "I don't have a reason," or "I'm not going to tell you." In the more common instance that their answer isn't as forthcoming or revealing as you would like, you simply follow up with a more precise question, expressed with the same polite curiosity as the first.

To see how this process of probing and challenging can effectively chip away at flawed arguments, let's return to the story of Rich, the financial analyst in Chapter Three, who had broken his employment contract. To review, Rich had accepted a job with a bank, signing a contract in which he promised to start work in three months' time. However, a few weeks before he was to begin, Rich got a much higher-paying job offer from another firm, and so had tried to cancel the initial agreement. Having waited for him for over two months and feeling that Rich had used her offer to negotiate a better deal for himself, the bank vice president not only refused Rich's plea to get out of the contract but warned that if he didn't show up at work on the agreed date he would be sued for $27,000, plus court costs. I agreed to seek a negotiated settlement with the bank.

The negotiation, which took place with the bank's head of HR and the vice president of the department that had hired Rich, hinged on challenging arguments. To nip all pointless accusations in the bud and focus the negotiation on problem-solving, I freely admitted at the outset that Rich had broken the contract, that he had harmed them, and that he believed he owed the bank some restitution. The only issue we needed to work out was the amount of a reasonable assessment. "We don't understand the demand for $27,000," I said. "Can you explain how you came up with that figure?"

As I said a moment ago, when you politely ask a clarifying question, you will almost always get an answer. The head of HR replied that because Rich's base pay was to be $9,000 per month and he had kept them waiting for three months, they took the position that he owed them $27,000 ($9,000 per month times three months).

The probing question had made their reasoning clear. Now it was necessary to challenge the validity of that reasoning, again through asking informational questions. No matter how long this follow-up questioning process takes, it is vital to maintain the air of earnest and patient desire to understand throughout. "I'm sorry. I don't understand. Did you actually pay him $27,000?" (While you can always dispute an argument by making a direct statement—*That's absurd!*—or asking a sarcastic question—*What kind of sense does that make?*—attacking or humiliating the other party rarely leads to agreement.)

Once you ask the question, you must wait as long as it takes to get the answer before following up with the next question in the same genuinely curious, nonthreatening tone: "No? Then how can he pay you *back* $27,000?" Patience takes practice, but it always pays off in a negotiation. Negotiators who, in their impatience, leap in to supply an answer or give up and move on to a new subject waste their breath on lost opportunities for connecting.

The head of HR replied that the division had had to bring in a temporary employee from another branch to fill the job for the three months they had been waiting; so they were in fact out $27,000.

"This other person was needed to do the work for the department until Rich started?" I asked.

"Yes."

"Let me make sure I understand what you're saying. You want Rich to pay someone else's salary for doing regular bank work? Do you think, were this to go to court, that a judge would find that reasonable?" Well-posed questions can demolish specious arguments far more effectively and with less pushback than accusations.

Once the argument has been successfully challenged, you can then either offer a solution yourself or return to probing in order to elicit a more reasonable route from the other side. In this case, because the bank's vice president felt that Rich had made a fool of her, it was important to give her a sense of control over the outcome. Therefore, I put the question to the bank officers, "We're willing to pay compensation. But it has to be reasonable. What genuine expenses did you incur as a result of Rich's actions?"

By going through this process of probing and challenging, we eventually settled on a figure that everyone at the table could justify. Rich would make a contribution of $1,500 to the bank's community service fund. The $1,500 figure was derived from costs incurred by Rich's actions: $900 in transportation expenses paid to the temporary analyst over the three-month waiting period, $125 to cover Rich's medical exam for the company insurance policy, and $475 (a mutually accepted estimate) for administrative and legal expenses related to his hiring and the subsequent dispute. Of course, there were additional persuasive aspects to the negotiation that overcame the bankers' resistance and brought the dispute to settlement. But it was through probing and challenging arguments that we were able to reach a precise figure that all parties could agree was fair.

To become a more effective questioner, here are some polite but effective phrases every negotiator should have in his or her repertoire:

"Could you please explain?"

"Help me to understand . . ."

"I'm afraid I'm not grasping this. Do you mean . . . ?"

"Are you saying . . . ?"

"So what I hear from you is . . . Is that correct?"

Remember, your goal is not to win a debate but to achieve an agreement that all parties understand and feel is reasonable.

OPEN AND CLOSED QUESTIONS

Open Questions

Questions that encourage people to open up and say more:

What is the basis of that figure?

Why are you unable to do this?

Can you explain your company policy?

How do you think we can solve that one?

When to ask open questions:

To *probe* for more information

To understand the other party's attitudes, preferences, viewpoints, and goals

To show sincere interest in the other party

To find trade-offs and build synergy

Closed Questions

More-focused (often yes/no) questions that demand a clear answer:

Was that a direct cost?

Do you ever make exceptions?

Which clause are you referring to?

Does that make sense?

When to ask closed questions:

To *challenge* arguments

To test your understanding and clarify ambiguities

To show sincere interest in fairness and legitimacy

To come to a final settlement

Hotel Rate Case Study

Let's conclude by returning to our hotel negotiation. To recap, the Empire Hotel was negotiating with its top corporate customers to raise its room rates by 32 percent. There were very good reasons for the increase. The hotel had recently undergone a significant renovation, upgrading, and staff retraining initiative. The facilities and service were now among the best in the city. More significantly, three years previous the hotel had dropped its rates by about 20 percent in reaction to the SARS pandemic and had not raised them since, unlike the competing hotels in the city, which had increased their rates at an average of 10 percent a year. The Empire was currently so far below the market average that a 32 percent increase would still leave its rates at the very bottom of the five-star category.

The negotiation with the procurement head of Company A (who had wanted speed and efficiency and had asked to have internet access set up in the rooms on check-in) went remarkably smoothly. He was so pleased by the individualized service upgrades (based on his own requests) and the arguments the Empire's negotiating team provided to justify the increase that he offered no pushback on the price increase.

Company B, however, was a different story. Although the hotel management had succeeded in earning the goodwill of the local procurement team—even securing the coveted spot as preferred hotel in their annual poll—the Empire's negotiating team now had to face the company's regional negotiator, known to be a bear. The sales director anticipated the usual tough and unpleasant negotiation her counterpart always engaged in, marked by hardball tactics: insults, ultimatums, and a desire to win at all costs. However, this time, instead of either retreating before his onslaught or attacking back (both of which she had tried in the past with disastrous results), she would be armed with strong arguments.

To prepare for the meeting, the Empire's sales team compiled every piece of evidence they could lay their hands on to substantiate the new rate structure: charts to show that the increased rate would still be lower than those of competing hotels in the same category; historical figures demonstrating that the new rate was only 6 percent above the rate of four years previous; photos showing the extensive renovations; and information sheets on the increased staff-to-customer ratio, new restaurant, and various service upgrades. They compiled the evaluations that Company B's employees had given on the hotel's conference facilities and rooms (overall first-rate), photocopied dozens of spontaneous kudos letters, and made a list of the many awards the hotel and its restaurants had received since the last contract. When they were finished, the sales director told me she felt so confident of their position's legitimacy that she was no longer afraid to face even the toughest critic.

Company B's negotiator, as expected, came in armed with nothing but his usual ham-fisted tactics. His opening words were, "I hope you've come to me today with a good price, because I don't have time to play games." The sales director started to talk about the hotel's recent upgrades and services, but he cut her off, telling her just to get to the price. When she revealed the 32 percent increase, he leveled an ultimatum: "I won't accept anything over 10 percent! One point higher and we'll take your hotel off the list!"

Having anticipated and psychologically prepared for this response, the Empire negotiating team didn't panic or immediately start offering discounts, as they had in the past. Instead, they calmly heard him out, then the sales director explained why they were raising the rates. She handed him a copy of all the information her team had compiled, giving special attention to the facts that (1) the hotel had been completely remodeled and upgraded; (2) it was still less expensive than all the other hotels in its category; (3) it had been chosen by Company B's own procurement team as the best in its category; and (4) the actual rate increase from four years before was only 6 percent.

Simultaneously, she challenged the company negotiator's position. Was it reasonable, she asked, to apply a flat percentage increase as opposed to a price based on quality, value, or even market rate? She questioned whether it was fair to penalize the hotel for the sole reason that it had not raised its rates earlier, as the other hotels had. She asked him how he could justify dropping the hotel simply to replace it with a more expensive alternative.

I would love to say that those arguments and challenges immediately won the day, but with bears it's never so easy. The company negotiator had been rewarded too many times in the past for threatening. The Empire's new approach clearly shook him, but it wasn't yet enough to change a pattern of behavior that had worked for him for so long. "I don't care what your rates are compared to anyone else or to some number from years ago," he roared. "I only care about now! And I'm telling you now that I won't accept anything more than a 10 percent increase. Your choice: Do you want our business or not?"

Were the arguments useless then? Not at all. They just weren't sufficiently persuasive on their own. All five GRASP steps would be required in this negotiation. Eventually, the hotel's compelling and documented arguments would be key to enabling Company B's negotiator to justify his change of position when the hotel's team showed it was willing to walk away rather than take a bad deal. But that part of the story must wait until the next chapter.

Conclusion

It is impossible to exaggerate the importance of basing your negotiations on valid arguments, that is, compelling reasons backed by solid evidence. Arguments make the difference between a deal won through force, trickery, or endless concessions, on the one hand, and genuine agreement, on the other. People cannot genuinely agree unless they understand why they are agreeing. Arguments create that understanding. Moreover, through sharing information, arguments demonstrate trust and provide a solid, verifiable foundation for return trust. By connoting respect, they make others more willing to respect you in return.

That said, as we see in the hotel case study, there will always be those who don't want to listen to your arguments, share their own reasons, or give you fair terms. In the next chapter, on Substitutes, we will learn what to do in those cases.

LESSONS FROM THIS CHAPTER

- Arguments in negotiation consist of
  - Factual evidence that provides a legitimate basis for every position taken
  - Mutually acceptable reasons given in explanation
- Arguments are used to
  - *Validate* the legitimacy or fairness of the terms you propose
  - *Challenge* the legitimacy or fairness of the terms proposed by others
- An acceptable argument is one that everyone in the room would agree has merit.
- Prepare to give an explanation for *every* position you take and concession you make.
- The more arguments you are able to provide and the more open you appear, the smoother the negotiation will proceed.
- Offering explanations shows respect for the other side.
- When you're not getting any explanations, stop talking and start asking.
- The higher the level of mistrust or bigger the request, the more evidence you will need to support your argument.
- Ensure that the other side also makes solid arguments by
  - *Probing* for explanations and evidence
  - *Challenging* poor explanations and evidence
- Remember, your goal is not to win a debate but to reach an agreement.

Chapter 10

SUBSTITUTES — THE
BACKUP PLAN

I am often asked to tell about a negotiation I lost. My clearly unsatisfactory answer is that although there have been a number of disappointments (routes that didn't work out, relationships that couldn't be mended, counterparts who proved untrustworthy), I can't recall any time I or my clients have felt we lost a negotiation. That isn't because I'm particularly brilliant or lucky but because (1) I always base my agreements on verifiable arguments and (2) I never go into a negotiation without knowing my *Substitutes*. Substitutes are the backup plan: what you'll do if the negotiation doesn't yield positive results—and when you're better off moving to Plan B. I have come away from a negotiation with "no deal" and have accepted terms that fell short of my client's uppermost aims, but having a substitute has always saved me from a disastrous agreement.

As I have stressed throughout this book, the basis of negotiation is the belief that by working with the other party to the negotiation you stand a *better* chance of accomplishing your goals than by acting alone or working with someone else. However, that doesn't mean that reaching an agreement with a particular party is the *only* means through which you can satisfy your goals, or even that your initial belief that it is the best way will be borne out. The negotiation may not yield the results you had hoped for: you may want a higher price than the other side can afford; the other party may not be able to commit to your time frame. If you cannot reach an agreement that satisfies your basic needs or offers you more of what you want than the next best option, you are better off ending the negotiation and moving on to other parties or other means of achieving your aims; in other words, taking your substitute.

Suppose that you are negotiating terms with a prospective new hire in your division. The candidate you are talking to is Jill, who you believe would do a better job of achieving your various hiring goals than any of the other applicants you interviewed. Compared to the others, she has the highest qualifications and brings the most direct experience to the position. However, you have a strict salary ceiling of X. If despite all the creative routes you offer her, Jill will settle for nothing less than a salary of X+, then she is no longer the best choice. Affordability, in this case, is a need-to-have, while great experience is merely a want-to-have. If Jill exceeds your maximum price, you would be better off hiring Jack, whom you identified before the negotiation as the next best candidate. Jack may not be quite as qualified or experienced, but he is smart, eager to learn, and will accept a job within your salary range. Jack is therefore your substitute. And because you have that substitute in the back of your mind when you negotiate with Jill, you won't panic and get trapped in an unaffordable bidding war. Naturally, you will still do your best to negotiate an acceptable arrangement with Jill, who within your salary limit offers more advantages than Jack, but once it becomes clear that won't be possible, you are ready to move on to your substitute.

Negotiating with a substitute in mind is not cynical or disloyal. It's simply the mature understanding that not all relationships were meant to be and that you can't always get your first choice. The smart negotiator goes into every negotiation prepared to let go and move on when it becomes clear that it won't yield advantageous results. Without a substitute, the temptation is strong to lose sight of your goals and blindly offer anything to get the deal. The result is an unprofitable and often unsustainable bargain. Be forewarned: if you go into a negotiation thinking you will die if you don't get this deal, you are already dead.

Let's see how substitutes keep you from falling into a losing spiral by looking at the most common "negotiation" you conduct: a contract with yourself. We'll start with your having no substitute. Imagine that you are a devotee of "Gourmet Coffee." Every day on the way to work you stop by Gourmet for a grande latte, which costs $3.50. However, with the economy down you're beginning to question this expense. You decide that you're willing to continue paying $3.50 a cup, but if it goes up any higher you'll have to give up drinking Gourmet Coffee. A few weeks later you walk into your usual Gourmet outlet and see that the price of a grande latte has risen to $3.60. What do you do? You had promised yourself that you would pay no more than $3.50, but now that you face the pain of losing your daily coffee shot with nothing to take its place, that promise feels less and less binding. Maybe you're able to hold out for the morning, perhaps for a whole day. But in the end, you decide in caffeine-deprived despair, "Well, it's only a dime," and walk up to the counter to place your order. Although you had determined in advance that you couldn't afford the grande latte's higher price, with no other substitutes to turn to, you find yourself accepting it.

Now we'll replay the scene, but this time with a substitute. Instead of the negative, "I'll give up drinking coffee," which is trading something for nothing, this time you trade one option for another. "If Gourmet grande lattes go above $3.50," you say, "I am *better off* . . .

   . . . bringing my own coffee in a thermos."

   . . . reducing to a tall latte."

   . . . buying a less expensive brand."

   . . . switching to regular coffee and adding milk."

   . . . drinking tea."

These—and any other alternatives you may have thought of—are possible substitutes, as long as they involve *switching to something else* rather than simply *giving something up*. You then pick the substitute you like best and psychologically prepare yourself to redirect your preference if the cost of the first option exceeds your limit (price, specifications, time, and so on). Once that limit is reached, you will find that you move to the substitute quite naturally. Having a substitute allows you confidently to walk away from a fruitless negotiation or an unprofitable or lopsided deal. The substitute may not have been your first choice, but once cost is factored in, it has become the better one.

Having substitutes can also put a stuck negotiation on a more productive track. For example, a city transportation agency may really want the approval of the affected neighborhood committees before it finalizes its plan for a new subway line that will run through those areas. If the agency lacks any substitute for consensus, however, the negotiations could last an eternity. One disgruntled committee could effectively put a stop to the project by blocking approval, perhaps for reasons unrelated to the subway issue. An announced substitute would reduce this potential for obstructionism. The neighborhood committees would be more motivated to focus on the issues and reach an agreement in good time if the transportation agency explained at the start of the process that while it very much hoped to reach a consensus, if there was no agreement by a set date, the city would have to make the decision based on its own best analysis. (Disclosing substitutes, however, must be done carefully, so as not to come across as either a threat or a lack of sincerity in the negotiation. See section below, "How to Reveal a Substitute.")

Knowing Your Walk-Away Line

As you can see from the above examples, substitutes are inextricably tied to a set limit: the point at which you are better off ending the current negotiation and taking your backup option. This point is what I call your Walk-Away Line or WAL (pronounced "wall"). A WAL is similar to the overused expression "bottom line," except that in my experience so-called bottom lines are more frequently bluffs or, at best, very strong desires, as opposed to genuine stopping points. Countless negotiators have told me that X is their bottom line, only to plunge well past it before reaching agreement. There is simply nothing holding it up beyond hope and a few increasingly desperate adjectives. ("This is my *absolute* bottom line!")

A WAL, on the other hand, is solid, because it is based on a realistic assessment of your substitutes rather than on hot air. A WAL is built on the concrete understanding that beyond a determined limit, the negotiation you are pursuing would either fail to achieve your minimum requirements or would come at a higher cost or offer fewer benefits than your best substitute. Of course, a WAL is not absolutely rigid. It can grow or shrink as you gather more information or if circumstances change: in good economic times you can build it higher by finding ever more attractive substitutes; in bad times it can be lowered by weak demand or increasing competition (the other party's substitutes). But high or low, the WAL always stands as your barrier against folly, because you have determined in advance that once you pass that line, the current negotiation offers fewer rewards than pursuing your substitute.

There are various ways to establish a WAL. Most commonly, it is based on *absolute values:* the parts must be delivered by a certain date; you need a minimum price to cover material and labor costs; precise product specifications are required; the budget for the conference is X; the report is due Friday. If any of your needs cannot be fulfilled by your counterpart—and no alternative routes can be negotiated to resolve the problem—you have to move to your substitute.

Sometimes, however, there are no clear-cut values. In that case the WAL will be the minimum that you need to *feel good about the outcome.* In acquisition negotiations, in which valuation is highly subjective, I always ask my clients, "At what price, if you got anything less for your business, would you wake up the next day wishing you hadn't sold?"

"Sixty million," one company owner replied.

That sounded definite, but it wasn't enough. There is a big gap between what one feels when thinking calmly and rationally and what happens to those convictions during a high-pressure price negotiation. In order to have a solid WAL, he needed to have a substitute: "If you could not get that amount, what would you be better off doing?"

He thought for a while. "I would be better off putting off the sale for a couple of years until we had a more firmly established client base," he finally said.

"So, if you can't get at least $60 million for the company, you would rather walk away from the deal to give yourself time to build your business and raise its value?" I reaffirmed.

"Yes," he said without hesitation.

He now had a WAL—and a substitute—which would prevent him from agreeing to something he would regret later. If we could negotiate with the buyer to acquire the company for $60 million or above, the seller would feel he had achieved his goals. If we could not reach that level, he would be happier walking away. In either case, he would be satisfied that he got the best outcome under the circumstances.

The third and most robust category of WAL is the benchmark established by the *best competing offer*. This is a primary reason why you need to consider and develop substitutes before establishing your WAL. Without considering all possible alternatives, you are likely to settle for a low WAL that only just covers your needs. Finding substitute suppliers, buyers, employers, and so on raises the WAL beyond meeting basic requirements to maximizing value. (In some cases, the search for substitutes turns up an alternative that is better than your original choice.)

The company sale, above, is a good example of this. The owner initially had been approached by a possible buyer with an offer of $45 million for his company. Interested in selling, but unhappy with the offered price, he set his "minimum fairness" WAL at $60 million. This would protect him from selling for a price that would leave him with bitter regrets. But it would not maximize his returns. Without a competing buyer, his choices would have been limited to either convincing the initial suitor to bring his offer up to at least $60 million or waiting to put the company on the market in two years' time. Instead, by searching for substitutes before he began negotiating, he was able to expand the market to three potential buyers. As soon as one of them offered $62 million, his WAL went up by $2 million. The next offer brought the WAL to $65 million. Ultimately, he sold the company for $75 million—two-thirds higher than the initial offer.

Building a WAL

The *first step* in building a WAL is to consider your substitutes: the various ways of achieving your goals if you cannot come to a satisfactory agreement with your first choice.

Let's say you want to work more flexible hours. Your first choice (based on other goals, such as job stability and fondness for your colleagues) might be to try to negotiate flextime with your current boss. That would be great if it worked out, but what if it didn't? What if, despite all your creative routes and compelling arguments, your boss remained adamantly opposed to flextime? You need to have a substitute. Anticipating the possibility that the boss might say no, you compile in advance a list of every acceptable alternative available to you if you and your boss cannot reach an agreement. The items on that list are your potential backup plans. To choose the one that will become your substitute, you list the advantages and disadvantages or risks of each. Here is the list you come up with:

Advantages and Disadvantages

I could . . .	Advantages	Disadvantages, Risks
Switch to another division that offers flextime	• Would achieve my flextime goal • I'd keep my salary, colleagues, pension, and seniority • Might broaden my experience	• Not sure if another position is available • Would it be as interesting or challenging as my current job? • Would a change help or hurt my career?
Cut down to part-time work	• More control over my hours • Time to pursue other interests	• Not sure if boss would agree • Loss of income • Damage to career track
Find another job with flexible hours	• Would achieve my flextime goal • Might broaden my experience • Possible increased salary, position, and responsibility	• Is there an attractive and well-paying job out there for me? • Would it be as interesting or challenging as my current position? • Would a change help or hurt my career? • I would lose my colleagues and perhaps have to commute farther
Accept the status quo and use up my leave if I need time	• I'd keep my position, salary, colleagues, pension, and seniority	• Wouldn't actually achieve my goal of flexible hours • I wouldn't get a vacation

You can see that all of these potential substitutes, with the exception of "accept the status quo," have a number of unknowns. The *second step* in building a WAL, therefore, is to get the answers to as many of those unknowns as possible. For example, you might quietly ask around to see if other divisions that offer flextime are hiring and, if so, in what types of positions. You might seek advice from a more experienced colleague on how to map your ideal career track. Concerning the external job, you could start by checking the want ads or consulting an employee search firm. At minimum this will give you a reality check: If jobs are scarce, leaving your current company may not be a good substitute. However, searching for other employment opportunities may also open your eyes to some excellent positions.

Suppose that through this search you find that an interesting job is available in another division of your company? Given that you would prefer to remain with your current employer if possible, that other job will then become your substitute.

Having established a substitute, the *third step* is to build up your WAL by making your substitute more concrete. You might schedule a confidential meeting with HR to find out more about the job, how it compares to your current position, the qualifications required for the position, and whether you would be seriously considered for it. You might talk casually with employees of the other division to get a feel for whether it would be a good fit for you. Each piece of information that makes the substitute a more viable possibility increases the strength of your WAL.

Through this process, you will have strengthened your negotiating position with your boss from the anemic, "If this division isn't able to offer more flexible hours, I will have to reconsider my options," to

"I am considering taking a position in another division," to

"I heard from HR that there is a position open in X division," or even to

"I will have to accept the offer I received from X division."

Having a convincing substitute and WAL will not guarantee that you get what you want, but it makes your case much stronger. Had you come into the negotiation with no tangible substitute, the boss would likely have felt there would be no serious downside to refusing your request. Now you have brought the downside into the open and raised it as a plausible risk. If your boss truly prefers the status quo, having to find and train a new employee would be a very strong incentive to reach an agreement on flextime, now the lesser of two evils.

The more specific your substitute, the less likely the other side will mistake your WAL for a bluff. More important, the more spe-cific your substitute, the stronger you will feel throughout the nego-tiation. Knowing that you have a bona fide backup plan if things don't work out, you won't feel desperate to get this deal at all costs.

When my friend Sue was setting up her professional services firm, she used a substitute and a WAL to negotiate a good price on her office. She started by doing an informal survey of office rents, employee salaries, and business start-up costs, then budgeted out what she was safely able to pay for office space. Given all of her other expenses, Sue decided that the most she could spend on rent was $2,000 a month, so that would be her Walk-Away Line. Then she set out to reinforce her WAL by finding a substitute.

With the help of her real estate agent, she found a number of office spaces that fell safely under the $2,000 limit, and finally settled on one unit that was listed at $1,700. It was smaller than she was hoping for and the building was rather run-down, but it was located in the heart of the neighborhood where she wanted to set up her office. So she decided that if she couldn't find anything more desirable at $2,000 or less, she would be better off taking this place—and using her savings for other expenses—rather than busting her budget on rent.

Then she raised her standards, telling her agent to show her places listed between $2,000 and $2,500. She told me she knew, as soon as she walked into the third place on the list, that it was exactly what she had been looking for. A heritage building with big, airy rooms and old-world charm, it was listed at $2,300. Sue's agent told her that he could try to get the rent decreased, but that $2,250 was probably as low as the owner would go. Sue later admitted that had she not had a substitute, she would have agreed to pay the extra $250–$300 a month and made a deal on the spot. But because she had a substitute firmly in mind, she was able to remain cool. The substitute unit may not be in as attractive a building, she reminded herself, but by taking it she would save over $6,000 a year in rent that she could put to more directly beneficial business costs, such as advertising or furnishings.

She kept one other important fact firmly in mind: her agent, despite his promises to get her the lowest price, had no real incentive to do so. As his commission was the first month's rent, he personally would be better off if Sue accepted the lease at the higher price. Therefore, the substitute would also be needed in order to motivate him to negotiate the price to the level she wanted. She told her agent that she would take the nicer unit if he could get the owner to reduce the price to $2,000; otherwise, she would take the first unit at $1,700. Now the agent took her seriously. First, her substitute showed that she wasn't simply pleading to get a better price; she was presenting a determined choice. More important, the choice she presented changed the agent's options. No longer did he face the alternative of earning a commission of $2,250 versus $2,000, which would hardly encourage him to negotiate a lower price. His choice now was making $2,000 or $1,700. He was now materially motivated to make a genuine effort to help her get the price down to $2,000.

An hour later, Sue got a call from her agent telling her that the office was hers at $2,000. Of course, there were a number of factors that helped her succeed: the rental market was softening; it was the end of the month; the landlord had no ready substitute. All of these reasons went into the landlord's decision to accept Sue's offer. However, it was having a solid WAL that kept Sue from getting sucked into paying more than she could afford and that kept her agent, and ultimately the landlord, from trying to dicker for a smaller reduction.

How to Reveal a Substitute

The power to walk away is the basic component of free will: a vital element of any respectful relationship. At root, free will keeps us treating each other fairly. Having a substitute and WAL are essential safeguards for ensuring that the relationship you are negotiating is based on reciprocity and mutual gain, rather than on one-sidedness and force. Yet, while you absolutely need to keep those safeguards in mind, you most often won't need to reveal them to the other party. When it does become necessary to do so, it must be done prudently. Handled poorly, revealing substitutes can come off as condescending ("You are just one of the possible business partners we're considering") or even bullying ("We have other suppliers who would be happy to take over this commission if you don't give us the terms we want"). Neither of these approaches will contribute to the development of positive working relationships. Worse, revealing a WAL too early will drive the other parties to reduce their offer to that minimally acceptable point, preventing you from achieving greater value.

The basic rule is that *a substitute may be raised at any time within the negotiation.* As just mentioned, however, it should be done carefully so as not to belittle the other side. Don't forget that you're talking to someone with whom you are trying to reach agreement and, in the process, develop a working relationship. Imagine how you would react if the person across the table were to say, "We're comparing a number of vendors and want to see what you can offer us." Would you feel particularly forthcoming? How differently might you feel if the person had put it like this: "In looking at different vendors, we have been especially impressed by the quality of your products. While we have to bear in mind our cost restrictions, we're really hoping to find a way to work together." In both cases you have indicated to the other party that you have other options. However, in the second example you have also shown honest admiration for the other party. Some people fear that showing admiration gives away a negotiating edge. In my experience, it just makes the announcement of substitutes less damaging to the relationship and encourages the other party to search for ways to work things out.

While a substitute can be alluded to at any time, *a WAL should be laid down only as a final warning*, after all other routes have been exhausted and you are on the very brink of walking away. (The exceptions are when the Walk-Away Line is a set time limit or required specifications.) As disclosing a WAL is a direct warning that unless there is a change in the other side's position, the negotiation will end and the parties will go their separate ways, a WAL should be stated more firmly than a substitute. Even then, however, it should be explained calmly, factually, and regretfully, not as a threat or angry accusation. Walking away is a disappointment—an admission that the relationship you had hoped to create could not work out, given the separate goals of the parties on this occasion. But it does not mean that you might not be able to work together at some future point. You rarely gain anything from burning bridges.

In fact, a useful side benefit of having a substitute is that it allows you to walk away from a negotiation without rancor. Instead of saying accusingly, "There's no way I am going to agree to that ridiculous price!" you can say, calmly and regretfully, "I'm sorry, but your price is significantly higher than the other quote I received. While I do appreciate the quality you put into your products, given our cost restrictions on this project, I'll think I'll have to go with them." In many cases, that will lead the other party to reconsider its terms. Even if not, you still end things amicably.

The company sale I described at the beginning of this chapter provides a good example of an effective use of a substitute and

WAL. One potential buyer, a private equity firm, became irate when we rejected their offer of $60 million for the company. In a very loud conference call, the firm's acquisition team took turns berating me: "You've got your head in the clouds if you think you can get more than that, lady! We've run our numbers and your company's not worth a penny over $60 million! Forget it. We're wasting our time talking to someone who doesn't have the slightest idea how to value a company!" It went on like this for a while. They were obviously trying to intimidate or embarrass me into accepting their offer.

Because I had a substitute, however, I was immune to emotional pressure. Nor did I have to out-shout them to make my point. When their rant finally died down, I was able to say easily, "Look, if you think the company is only worth $60 million, that's what you should offer. I'm not going to tell you to do something that doesn't make any sense to you. I will tell you that we've received an offer of $62 million from another buyer. But you should make your decision based on your own calculations." There was a pleasing silence, after which they asked for a postponement to reconsider. The next day they raised their offer to $65 million.

What If You Have No Substitute?

A question I always can count on when training negotiators is, "What if I have no substitute?" There are three possible answers:

1. You are dealing with a monopoly—fortunately, a rare occurrence.
2. You are under such time pressure that you have reduced your options to one—a more frequent but avoidable situation.
3. You haven't looked hard enough—by far the greatest likelihood.

Let's start with the third and easiest scenario. Most often a negotiator doesn't have a substitute because he or she hasn't taken the time to find one. Impatient bargainers who like to plunge straight into the thick of things may find the advance effort of coming up with a backup plan to be too cumbersome. However, by not having a substitute, they are going in with no leverage, leaving themselves with no positive way out if the negotiation isn't bearing fruit and, if they do reach an agreement, with no benchmark to establish whether it was the best possible resolution.

Sometimes people fail to have a substitute because they psychologically limit their range of choices to the most familiar or obvious, closing their minds to other possibilities. One participant in a seminar told me with complete conviction that in her case there was simply no substitute. She explained that she was studying with the best piano teacher in the city, and although she could no longer afford to pay the teacher's increased rates, she had no alternative. "There is no substitute for the best," she said. "Well," I recall replying with bemusement, "there is always the second best."

Remember, a substitute will not initially be as desirable as your first choice. That's why you start by negotiating with choice number one. You move to your substitute only when choice number one crosses your Walk-Away Line.

Although a substitute doesn't offer the same level of satisfaction as the original choice in certain key areas, it may offer uniquely attractive qualities of its own. Had the woman who rejected all other piano teachers as less than the best actually looked around a bit for a substitute, she may have found another teacher who excelled in specific techniques that she would like to develop, or who could help her expand her repertoire. Similarly, your first choice of car-leasing companies may beat out the competition in terms of brand name and the range of models to choose from, but the substitute might provide direct-to-door delivery. In any case, the substitute offers you a fundamental point of comparison so that you can negotiate the best outcome overall.

The most common reason for genuinely having no available substitute is time pressure. You may have waited so late to negotiate for an item of limited supply that you require almost immediately that there are no alternatives remaining or, if there are, you have no time left to locate them. You're in pretty much the same position that you would be in if you showed up at the sold-out game shortly before it started and found only one scalper holding one pair of tickets. It's a self-created predicament. The obvious solution is to plan ahead and not wait until the last minute to negotiate for something you know you will need by a specific date.

If you're already in the trap, however, your best hope comes through having a relationship. If the negotiation is a onetime transaction, like the scalper example, you're pretty much up a creek. If you have dealt with the other party aggressively or selfishly in the past, you'll be in even worse shape, as they will now be in a position to balance the score. On the other hand, if you have a positive relationship, you will at least have a cushion of goodwill that can help you over the bump in the road. Moreover, even in a first-time negotiation, if you can realistically offer the other party a continuing business relationship, you will be able to get a more favorable outcome than were the negotiation to be seen as a single transaction, even though you have no immediate substitutes.

In the very rare instance that no substitute exists, as when there is a monopoly, the only solution is a radical one: creating your own substitute. That's what we saw Maersk do in Chapter Three, when it developed the Port of Tanjung Pelepas to challenge the domination of the Port of Singapore. Closer to home, when small, local growers couldn't get supermarkets (used to buying in bulk from agribusinesses) to pay what they felt was a reasonable price for their produce, they started their own farmer's markets, began selling directly to restaurants, and even developed subscription programs called Community Supported Agriculture, in which consumers pay in advance for weekly deliveries. The point is that even in the most difficult scenario there is usually a substitute out there somewhere, if you just exercise your imagination and a little initiative.

Remember That Both Sides Have Substitutes

A necessary word of caution, however: you are not the only party with a substitute. If you are house-hunting in a tight real estate market, the seller will have more potential buyers and thus more negotiating power than if there is a housing glut. If you are applying for a highly desirable job straight out of college, you will be competing against comparable job-hunters, giving the employer a much higher WAL than if you were a seasoned expert in a specialized field. Most fundamentally, if what you are offering is less appealing than what the other party's substitute offers, the other party will take that substitute. Even the most relationship-based approach to negotiation won't lure the other side into choosing dross over gold.

I will never forget the salesman of a newly privatized power company, who asked me, "How do we negotiate the price we want if we're more expensive than our competitors?"

"Price isn't the only consideration," I replied. "Do you have a more consistent supply record than others?"

"Umm, I don't think so," he reflected. "We had two blackouts last year."

"Okay. Do you provide better service?"

"Not really. Our phones are manned from 9:00 to 5:00. After that, customers can leave a recorded message."

This was getting difficult. "Do you have a better environmental record?"

"Actually, we recently got fined for excessive emissions."

Out of frustration I finally asked, "Is there anything at all that makes you stand out?"

After a long pause, he popped up enthusiastically, "We give $10,000 a year to the local soccer team!"

That wasn't going to cut it, I had to tell him. This wasn't a negotiation problem. It was a bad case of unrealistic price expectations tied to a second-rate product. Negotiation isn't about using magic words that make the other party behave irrationally. If you want to negotiate more profitable contracts, you have to give the other side more of what they value than they can get from their substitute.

It's imperative that you consider in advance what the other side's substitutes are likely to be so that you can negotiate from a realistic understanding of your competitive position and your competitor's advantages over you. In the best case, where you find no comparable substitutes for your product or service, that knowledge will give you greater confidence going into the negotiation. In the worst case, you will get an important reality check so that you can reassess your expectations. In every case, being aware of likely substitutes will help you to match or even overcome their advantages.

Hotel Rate Case Study

Back at the Empire Hotel rate negotiation, the sales director and her negotiating team were facing a bear. Despite all of their strong, fact-based arguments and evidence supporting the 32 percent rate increase, Company B's negotiator remained obdurate: "I don't care what your rates are compared to anyone else's or to some number from years ago. I only care about now! And I'm telling you now that I won't accept anything more than a 10 percent increase. Your choice: Do you want our business or not?"

The hotel negotiators were rattled. The sales director slipped out for a quick phone conference with me. "What should we do?" she asked nervously. "He's threatening to pull the whole account. Do you think he's bluffing?"

Yes, I said, he was probably bluffing. It was certainly unlikely that he would drop his company's highest-rated hotel to replace it with one that was more expensive and less popular. That said, people sometimes react vindictively when they are thwarted—or will refuse to give in because they fear losing face if they back down. I couldn't guarantee that he wouldn't drop the hotel simply to prove his power. However, I said, the important question wasn't what he would do, which was his own decision, but rather what was best for the hotel. The answer to the latter consideration lay in two simple questions. "First, does this company's business matter so much to you that you are willing to be the perpetual victim of a bear? Second, is the 10 percent increase that he says is his final offer better than your substitute?"

The answer to both questions was no. In preparing for the negotiation, the sales team had done a study of corporate customers who in the past had offered to raise their allotments if they could be put in the premier rate category. While none of them could generate the room-nights that Company B did, if two or three of them were to increase their room-nights by 25 percent each—in exchange for getting the premier corporate rate—the combined total would cover the shortfall. It was a bit of a risk, the sales director admitted, but not as risky as continuing to feed this bear.

With renewed confidence, the Empire's sales director returned to the negotiating table and said that they were holding to their rate. In the nonthreatening language she had planned in advance, she said, "You are one of our most valued partners and we very much want to continue that partnership. But we have to get our rates back to market level if we want to maintain the quality your employees expect when they stay with us. As our other key accounts have agreed to the new rate and we have had requests for more allotment, we cannot change the rate structure, but there may be other ways we could satisfy your concerns. Would it help if we offered you a lower daily rate that did not include breakfast?"

Very gently she had laid out her WAL and her substitute. She had called his bluff and shown she was willing to walk away under the terms he proposed. Yet she also proved herself accommodating to his concerns about keeping the price increase to an acceptable increment over the previous year by suggesting that the hotel could provide a lower rate by eliminating the inclusive breakfast. Although he rebuffed it, her offer demonstrated the hotel's goodwill and created less of a showdown than a take-it-or-leave-it position would have sparked.

Being a bear, he didn't meekly give in, of course. But he also didn't pull the account as he had threatened to do. Instead, he growled that he was not going to waste any more time dickering with them and that the local procurement head would take over the negotiation. In other words, he passed the buck.

That was good news for the hotel, as they had developed a much more positive relationship with the local procurement head. Now the only challenge was to persuade her—and avoid creating another bear. We will see how that was done and conclude the case in the next chapter.

Conclusion

A substitute doesn't have to be a precise *who:* "If I can't get a deal with Pat, I will sell to Sam." It is rather *whatever* you feel you would be better off doing than continuing the current negotiation. A substitute might be as vague as, "If I can't get a commitment from Pat after three meetings, I am better off spending my time looking for new investors." However, instead of you saying, "I will give up," it sends you in a positive direction.

In the same way, a WAL doesn't have to be a precise *how much.* It can be any *condition* that is necessary to an acceptable outcome from your perspective. You may determine that you will invest in a company only if it adopts certain green technologies; if they refuse, you walk away. You decide that you would rather go to court than accept the blame for something you did not do. In short, the WAL is the point beyond which you no longer believe that you would stand the best chance of accomplishing your goals by working with the other party.

Strong, positive relationships must be based on mutual benefit and free choice. Substitutes provide you with an informed choice (and sometimes a reality check) so that you can derive the most value from your negotiation. You may not always win everything you want, but by having a strong substitute and Walk-Away Line, you will never come away a loser. In the next chapter, on Persuasion, we will see how to communicate your message in a positive way that will most appeal to the other party.

LESSONS FROM THIS CHAPTER

- Substitutes are your backup plan: what you'll do if the negotiation doesn't yield positive results.
- If you go into a negotiation thinking you will die if you don't get this deal, you are already dead.
- Explaining substitutes can put stuck negotiations on a more productive track.
- The Walk-Away Line (WAL) is the point at which you are better off taking your substitute.
- WALs are based on at least one of three categories:
  - An absolute value (price that covers costs, due date, and so on)
  - A strong sense of what you need to feel good about the outcome
  - The benchmark established by the best competing offer
- Reveal your substitute and WAL with care so as not to offend unnecessarily:
  - A substitute may be disclosed at any point in the negotiation
  - A WAL should only be divulged at the last moment before walking away
- If you think you have no substitute
  - You are dealing with a monopoly — a rare occurrence
  - You delayed so long that you've run out of options — a self-inflicted injury

- You haven't looked hard enough — by far the greatest likelihood
- Relationships or promises of future business help when there is no immediate substitute.
- In the case of confronting a genuine monopoly, you may need to create a substitute.
- Remember that the other side has substitutes too.

Chapter 11

PERSUASION — WINNING THEM OVER

If you were to think of relationship-based negotiation as a living organism, the first two steps of the GRASP method, Goals and Routes, would be the brain: the focus of your creative energy. The next two steps, Arguments and Substitutes, are the muscles: they strengthen and support you, preventing you from falling. The final step, *Persuasion*, is the heart of negotiation: the emotional core that connects you to the other party. Persuasion, in short, reaches out from your goals to theirs.

Persuasion, the art of winning someone over, is the easiest step in the GRASP method to define. Unfortunately, it's the hardest to master. First, it requires that you focus the conversation toward the interests of the other party, which goes against our natural tendency to perceive the world from our own viewpoint. Second, it obliges you to adopt a more positive way of speaking than comes naturally in a disagreement, when you are feeling self-protective, especially if the other party is glowering at you. Third, despite the generally held view that convincing someone means "talking him into it," good persuading balances speaking, questioning, and listening. Most fundamentally, persuasion entails creating an atmosphere that leads the other party to want to cooperate with you.

It's a big challenge to go from planning in isolation to interacting with other people. When there are two or more parties involved, it's no longer enough to justify why *you* deserve something. You need to show other parties what's in it for *them*. It's not even enough to demonstrate how they might benefit materially; you need to earn their trust that those benefits will actually materialize. And you have to create enough goodwill to make them agreeable to sharing the benefits with you. Ultimately, no matter how compelling you feel your position to be, it will gain you nothing unless you can persuade the other party.

A while back I conducted a negotiation workshop at one of the leading European business schools. The centerpiece of the event was a trio of extemporaneous role plays. While the first two concerned business and career issues, the third was a domestic negotiation between a wife who felt she was taking on too much of the burden of housework and a husband who wanted to maintain the status quo. Both parts were played by volunteers from the audience.

The negotiation started off badly and went downhill from there. The "husband" was sitting casually in a chair onstage when the "wife" walked in and challenged, "Do you think the division of housework between us is fair?"

His face recorded shocked surprise, quickly followed by defensiveness at the implied charge that he was unfair. Given the choice of either admitting that he was behaving selfishly or denying the idea altogether, the husband said what virtually anyone put into that corner would say: "Yeah. Pretty fair."

The wife rolled her eyes visibly enough to be seen from the back rows of the auditorium. "How can you call it fair?" she charged. "I have a job that's as demanding as yours. Yet when I come home, I am the one who cleans the house. I make dinner. I do the shopping. I help our daughter with her homework ... " And on it went, a litany of "I, I, I," until at the end she said, "And I want to know what YOU intend to do about it."

The husband looked back at her with a mixture of defiance and feigned boredom. "Why are you asking me? I'm not the one with the problem," he replied, at which point the wife became so genuinely angry that I had to call an end to the role play. (Clearly this was hitting a nerve in the real life of the woman playing the wife, which is probably why she had eagerly volunteered for the role play.)

Once things calmed down enough to discuss what we had seen, a member of the audience asked the woman why she hadn't made any effort to show the husband how it would benefit him to free her from some of the domestic burden. Still seething, the role player glared back at the questioner, hands on hips. "I'm already doing all the housework," she snapped. "Do I have to think for him, too?"

What's in It for *Them*

The answer is no, she didn't have to think *for* him; but if her goal had been to persuade him to take ownership of the problem and work with her in finding a solution, she had to think *about* him, to show that she had his interests in mind as well as her own. And if she wanted his help in crafting a joint agreement that he would carry out willingly, she had to think *with* him. If the only result she was after was to get all of her resentment off her chest and to let the husband know that she thought he was a selfish jerk, her approach was fine. However, had she continued along the same me-oriented, blaming vein, it would never have led to agreement, much less to mutual gain or an enhanced relationship. When was the last time you were persuaded by someone attacking you?

Let's look at a more other-centered approach. First, the wife could have begun by asking the role-play husband if now was a good time to talk. This is not a question of power, but of sensibility. We must never assume that just because we're ready to make our case, others are ready to receive it. They may be in the middle of something they don't want to interrupt. If we force them to pay reluctant attention to our concern, they will be distracted or irritated, certainly not positively focused on resolving our issue. Or they may be the sort of people who need time to think about an issue before discussing it and will clam up if verbally ambushed. In either case, asking first sets a positive tone and, not insignificantly, starts the negotiation off with a yes.

The wife might then have opened with something like, "I know I haven't been very fun to live with lately. I always seem to be too busy or tired to enjoy a glass of wine with you in the evenings and laugh about our day, like we used to. I feel like I have no time for us." She is helping him to see how what heretofore had been an issue that bothered only her also affects him. Once they agree that they have a mutual interest in solving the problem of the overworked wife, they can move to a nonblaming discussion of what actions they each might take to balance the housework.

The sample opening I suggested above is not intended to be manipulative or insincere. Rather, the point is for her to start out by focusing on where she and her husband's interests align rather than where they conflict. She would also be describing the issue impartially as opposed to casting blame. And she would be empathizing with his perspective. Are impartiality and empathy insincere?

The husband/wife example underscores the difference between arguments and persuasion. Arguments justify your position: "I do X amount of housework per week while you only do Y amount." Persuasion focuses on why the other party should take action: "I am too tired to do anything at night but sleep." To put it in the commercial context described at the beginning of Chapter Nine, arguments establish why the selling price of $200 for a hand-knit sweater is fair; persuasion centers on how you would benefit from owning it.

Most negotiators seem to be better at arguments than persuasion. They are happy to give a list of all the reasons why they feel they deserve something, but will put it in such a self-centered way that the other party can't understand what it has to do with him or her. "I'll need early payment on this because I have a lot of expenses coming up." Or "We need to move up the due dates on this project because I'm going to be taking a ski trip the week before the presentation." Neither one of these examples connects at all with the other party.

I believe that this failure to connect to others was behind Paris's loss to London in its bid for the 2012 Olympics. Going into the final round, Paris was the clear front-runner, holding a perfect score.

Both France and the United Kingdom sent their highest officials to push for the deal. In the end, the London team proved more persuasive. Let's look at *how the focus of the two pitches differed.*

The culmination of Paris mayor Bertrand Delanoe's presentation was, "Paris needs the Games. Paris wants the Games. Paris loves the Games." President Jacques Chirac added, "The heart of Paris and the heart of France are beating in unison in the hope of becoming Olympic ground in 2012." Whom are these speeches about? Paris, and the French.

Representing London, Lord Sebastian Coe, the British Olympic gold medalist, told how he was inspired to become a runner because of seeing the Olympics on TV as a child. "Thirty-five years later, I stand before you still inspired by the Olympic movement," he said. "London's vision is to reach people, young people, all around the world and connect them with the power of the Games." Coe's speech was about the Olympic movement and its ability to inspire people around the world.

Another common mistake is to try to persuade another party based on reasons you assume matter to them purely because they matter to you: like the mobile phone salesman who tried to get me to upgrade to a more expensive handset because it could download games, videos, music, and little cartoon creatures. How much more time-efficient would his sale have been if he had started by asking me what I care about?

The failure to connect was brought home vividly in a presentation I observed in which a large and well-established but financially struggling Korean manufacturing company sought to persuade an American investment group to acquire a significant portion of its business. The Koreans spoke proudly of the company's market share, rapid expansion, production capacity, and massive network of satellite companies—all of which are signs of success in the Korean conglomerate-based business system. The Americans, however, were concerned with profitability and debt. What is the value of market share if you get it by dropping your prices so low that you lose money with every sale? they asked. What is the value of rapid expansion if you base it on crippling debt? The Koreans were totally unprepared for these questions, having assumed that the buyer's interests were the same as their own. Instead, the Korean company's persuasion points were seen by the American investors as liabilities. The talks never got beyond the first stage.

A more successful example comes from a participant in one of my training programs, José, who persuaded his neighbor, an elderly woman, to chop down a dying tree on her property. Before taking the course, José had raised the issue with the neighbor but had gotten nowhere because he had spoken only about his own concerns. As he recounted the story to the class, "I told her that I was worried that the tree was rotten and could fall on my garage in the next big wind," he recalled. "She refused to have it cut down. So I told her I would pay half the cost of cutting it down. She still wasn't interested. Heck, she even rejected my offer to pay for the whole thing! I give up. There are some people you just can't negotiate with!"

I recommended that he give it another try. His neighbor was probably neither irrational nor pigheaded. José had simply failed to persuade her because he hadn't shown her what was in it for her. He had opened by focusing on his personal concerns over a potential (unproven) risk to his garage. When the neighbor showed no interest in that, he had made the false presumption that her reluctance was about cost. When his offers to foot the bill didn't move her, he wrote her off as irrational. But her refusal of his offers didn't mean she was irrational, only that he wasn't speaking to her goals. Instead of guessing what her concerns might be, I advised, he needed to *ask her* why she didn't want to remove the tree.

A couple of weeks later I got an excited call from José telling me that he had resolved the issue. He'd gone over to talk to the neighbor just to talk—not to talk her into something—and had learned that she'd lived in that house since she was a child. She recalled how she had grown up swinging from that tree, how her children had climbed it, and how her grandchildren were now talking about building a tree house. She saw no reason to cut down a perfectly healthy tree just because it was getting on in years!

"You're right," José said. "Perhaps I jumped to conclusions in assuming that the tree is unsafe. But if it *is* sick and in danger of falling, you sure wouldn't want your grandchildren playing on it." Only then did he have her positive interest in the issue. "I'll tell you what," he suggested. "Why don't I arrange for a tree specialist to come out and determine the health of the tree? If it's fine, I'll admit I was wrong and do penance for taking up your time by helping build that tree house. If they say it's dangerous, though, would you agree to have it removed?" She accepted gladly.

Here are some examples of how you can rephrase your words to speak to the interests of the other party. (Every statement in the left column is something I have actually heard.)

Me-Centered Versus Other-Centered Speech

Me-Centered	Other-Centered
I'd like to get through this meeting as quickly as possible.	I don't want to take up too much of your time, so I'll be as brief as possible.
Because our recent renovation reduced the number of rooms from 400 to 350, we have to charge more for each unit.	In our recent renovation we expanded the size of our rooms by 15 percent. The increased square footage does mean a slightly higher price.
You'll need to get me the material at least two weeks in advance.	Customizing everything to your specifications will take two weeks. Can we agree on a due date of the 15th for the material?
There's no way I'll accept clause 13. You have to delete it.	My concern with clause 13 is X. Help me to understand why you've included it, then we can work together to craft some language that satisfies both of our concerns.
A chief attribute of this house is that it's in one of the best school districts.	Do you have children?

Finally, you must be negotiating with someone who actually has something to gain from coming to terms with you. There is no point trying to talk a sales clerk into refunding your purchase after the return deadline if that employee only risks getting in trouble for doing so. You can threaten staff all you want with the loss of your business; their interest is in keeping their jobs. Instead, you need to speak to a manager, as he or she will have a more personal stake in retaining you as a customer and promoting good public relations. Similarly, if the other party has no authority to agree to changes from a preestablished position (for example, a midlevel bureaucrat or almost anyone below the most senior management in hierarchical countries), any attempt to lure concessions out of them is wasted. Your goal instead should be to gain their goodwill and understanding, in the hope that they will pass on a message that will persuade the people who are empowered to make decisions.

Be Positive

There is no doubt that showing appreciation and respect for one another helps people work together or that creating a positive atmosphere leads to positive results. Here are some other ways to set a positive tone.

Say, "Yes, if . . ."

"Yes," even with a qualifying "if" attached, creates a more cooperative mood than "No" or "No, but . . ." Imagine you were planning to buy four tickets to a show and asked the clerk at the box office whether you could get a group discount. Which response from the ticket seller would make you feel more motivated to buy a fifth ticket?

"No discounts without a minimum purchase of five tickets."

or

"Yes, we have a group discount if you buy five or more tickets. Do you think you could find one other person who would like to join you?"

Both say the same thing, but one says it so much more positively.

Point Out Gains Rather Than Losses

Have you ever noticed how much people enjoy telling you what you can't have? Unfortunately, their momentary pleasure is gained by souring your mood. "If we don't get your agreement by this Friday, we can no longer guarantee these terms" is just a negative and, frankly, irritating way of saying, "We can guarantee these terms for you until Friday."

I once had a client walk out of a sales negotiation when the buyer said, "If you can't increase our allotment this year, we'll have to cut you from our brochure." Later I replayed the incident and asked the client if he thought the buyer's position was unreasonable. He replied that in principle, he understood that retailers needed to secure sufficient stock before launching promotions. "I just didn't like the way he threatened me," he said. "Why couldn't he just have said something like, 'We're working hard to keep you in our brochure?'" It was a fair question.

In negotiating disputes, clients will typically issue instructions along the lines of, "Tell those bums that there's no way they're getting a quarter of the demands on this list!" Assuming that the goal of the negotiation is to get a resolution, not a walkout, I will rephrase the message to something like, "Obviously we want to reach an agreement that's fair to both sides, so let's go through this list and see what's possible." A dispute will still involve plenty of disagreement, but a constructive approach is more likely to nudge the parties toward solutions.

In a lengthy negotiation, you will create forward momentum if you periodically remind the other side of the agreements you have reached and the progress that you have made together so far. Here are a few examples of how to show progress in a positive way:

- "We've agreed on the scope of the report, the structure, and the time line. All that's left is to divide the responsibilities."

- "We've crossed the most important hurdle. We're all in agreement that we want to reach a negotiated settlement. Now we've just got to hammer out the details."

- "Great! We've now settled five out of the twelve issues we had on the agenda. Almost halfway there!"

Another important tip for building a sense of momentum in a lengthy or difficult negotiation is to start out by reaching a few small agreements early on rather than going straight to the most contentious issues, which are sure to bog everything down. If your negotiation does get bogged down, you might try the following method for keeping things positive, told to me by a senior diplomat: "In a difficult, drawn-out negotiation, where there may be no tangible outcome for weeks, I'll display any sign of movement publicly, both to show progress and to prevent backtracking. For example, if one country's delegate says, 'We're not 100 percent insisting on this, but we would strongly prefer . . .' I will immediately highlight their willingness to consider other options and thank them for their flexibility. It gives them face rather than making them feel they've given in."

Rephrase Affirmatively

As every Monday-morning quarterback knows, it's easy—and fun—to criticize. However, within a negotiation, criticism just obstructs the search for a solution. Not only do you need to avoid criticizing, but sometimes you have to nudge the other party in a more productive direction. Rephrasing their language from negative to affirmative can help.

Imagine the other party says, "I won't agree to this." The reactive reply would be to stay on the negative by asking, "What don't you like about it?" However, that question is sure to set off a litany of criticisms and may even harden their opposition as they take full advantage of the invitation to tear apart your proposal. Instead, you can turn their thoughts in a more productive direction by asking, "What *would* you agree to?" In many cases, they will actually come up with something that is not too far from what you had proposed.

Another effective language change was mentioned earlier: moving from "either/or" to "both/and." We have a natural tendency to narrow arguments down to an all-or-nothing choice: either we do it your way or mine. Take, for example, this negotiation between division heads over which new computer system to purchase. An either/or question would be, "Shall we adopt the full-service system that the IT division is advocating or go for the less expensive system that Purchasing has proposed?" By putting the issue in either/or terms, the stage has been set for battle. Even if agreement can be reached, the end result will be one winner (either IT or Purchasing) and two losers (the second loser being the company, which will end up with a system that doesn't address all of its interests).

Now let's turn this into a both/and proposition. "IT has emphasized the importance of after-sales service. While Purchasing shares that interest, they are primarily concerned with budgetary constraints. So let's set our goal at finding a solution that maximizes both service and affordability." Switching from either/or to both/and encourages the parties not merely to be more positive but also to deal with the whole range of issues, rather than focusing only on their pet concerns.

Finally, instead of asking whether other parties have a problem with an idea that has been raised or a solution that has been suggested (which invites people to think about problems), ask whether they feel the proposal would help achieve their goals. If they reply along the lines of "Not really," don't take it as a complete rejection. Instead, ask them what they would add or subtract to the proposal to make it more effective. The effect in most cases will be to move naysayers from blanket condemnation, which shuts down discussion, to expressing agreement with at least some aspect of the proposal, which you can then build on.

Reject Intimidating Language

Sometimes you will meet a negotiator who hasn't yet learned the power of positive language. Sadly, there are people who try to get their way through shouting, cursing, or intentionally insulting you. If the other party becomes verbally abusive, you will need to stop their intimidating tactics in order to return the negotiation to a productive path.

Although standing up to abuse can be especially difficult for appeasers, withdrawers, and splitters (see descriptions in Chapter Four), the failure to do so will make you a target for further victimization. Bears thrive on rattling people. For forcers, the danger is that you will get sucked into a reactive cycle, losing sight of your negotiation goals. Therefore, if you do encounter a bully, instead of lashing back, getting visibly upset, or suffering in quiet misery, try one of the methods for nipping the behavior in the bud. All are effective. Choose the one that works best with your personality:

- *Laugh it off*. Rather than escalate threats by getting angry, try breaking the tension by treating threats as nothing more than a good try. "Come on, Sam," I heard one lawyer chuckle good-naturedly to a colleague who had just smacked him with a take-it-or-leave-it demand. "How many clients would I have if I accepted deals like that?" Moments later they were back on friendly terms.

- *Wait for the tirade to pass.* If you don't react to an emotional outburst, eventually the yeller will realize that he or she is the only person in the room out of control and will usually wind down sheepishly. Don't cower; just wait calmly, maintaining eye contact if possible. Once the other party has quieted, you can return to the discussion from the point it left off before the eruption.

- *Take time out.* When emotions start to boil over, ask the other party if this is a good time for a break. Be careful, however, that this doesn't come across as condescending. "Should *we* take a break?" will always be more effective than "Do *you* need a break?"

- *Ask the other party to stop.* If someone uses offensive language (racist or sexist slurs, shouting, excessive swearing), you need to recognize it and stop it. It's imperative that you don't get emotional yourself when doing this, however, or things may go from bad to worse. Tell the offender in a calm voice that such language is both unnecessary and unproductive, remind all parties of the purpose of the talks, then ask whether everyone will agree to keep the discussion courteous. People will feel bound more to keep an agreement they have made of their own accord than to obey your commands. Moreover, you will have just turned an attack into an agreement!

Stop Talking and Start Listening

In Chapter Nine, I brought up the importance of asking questions as a means of challenging arguments. Asking and listening are also critical persuasion skills. All people like to be asked their opinions, and they love being listened to. When they feel you are truly listening to them, they become more receptive to your opinions in turn. Moreover, in the process of talking, they give you a rare firsthand glimpse into how they see the world.

No matter how much planning you do, when it comes to identifying the other side's goals, you necessarily will rely on assumptions. They may be educated guesses, but they are still guesses. Only by getting people to talk do you have a source of information right from the horse's mouth. If by listening to the other party you learn that you were largely right about their concerns, then you can proceed with greater confidence. If you learn that you made some false guesses, you now have the information you need to correct your approach and possibly come up with some new routes. In either case, the more you know about your counterpart's goals and attitudes, the more persuasive you can be.

Many people confuse persuasion with a sales pitch. In fact, lengthy monologues on why the target party should do what you want are most effective at creating resistance. "Winning someone over" is rarely accomplished by beating them over the head. You win someone over by respecting them enough to listen to them, by genuinely trying to understand them, by showing how what you are offering fulfills their expressed desires, and by alleviating their concerns. If you find yourself talking on and on while the listener hasn't said a word, chances are they've turned off. It's time for you to stop the onslaught and ask them about *their* priorities, concerns, and opinions.

Ten Keys to Successful Listening

Active listening means more than just letting other people talk. It means doing everything you can to *hear* what they are saying and, just as important, *encouraging* them to communicate more. Here are ten key skills of a successful listener.

- **Open your mind.** Make a concerted effort to close off the judgmental thoughts and emotions that get in the way of hearing what others have to say. Don't get distracted by their style, accent, appearance, or even tone of voice. Focus on the message they are conveying through words.

- **Pay attention.** Set aside whatever other issues are preoccupying you at the time and give your full attention to the speaker. The other party will sense — and take offense — if your mind is wandering.

- **Don't try to predict what others are going to say.** You'll most likely be wrong. Just wait for them to speak — and then listen attentively.

- **Don't plan your reply while the other party is speaking.** You can't hear properly when you are busy formulating ripostes in your head. By reacting before the speaker has finished, you miss hearing important points or nuances. Moreover, people dislike overly quick replies, much preferring the feeling that you have both heard *and thought about* what they have said before you respond.

- **Stay calm.** This is especially important if the other party gets emotional. If a hardball negotiator is using aggression as a tactic to rattle you, a calm response creates nothing to react against. If the speaker is truly upset, listening calmly not only will reduce tension but may give you new insights into the problem.

- **Don't interrupt** — especially when crossing language barriers, even when the speaker seems temporarily lost for words. Control your desire to finish others' sentences. This is especially important when the topic is complex or uncomfortable. Interrupting is distracting, annoying, and frustrating.

- **Show you're listening.** Not interrupting doesn't mean sitting statue-like while the other party speaks into a void. Dead silence can be even more off-putting than interrupting. Even though only one person is speaking at the time, active listeners respond with visual (such as nodding your head) and vocal ("uh-huh") cues.

If the topic is serious, taking notes shows a high level of interest and a desire to follow up.

- **Ask questions.** Asking questions is vital to ensure that you fully understand the speaker's meaning. Done correctly, it also shows your interest in the other party's thoughts, and it acts as a conversation stimulus. However, questioning is effective only when it is a genuine attempt to advance the conversation or seek clarification, as opposed to an indirect attack ("Is that offer serious?") or an interrogation with a barrage of questions, either of which will create a defensive reaction.

- **Watch your body language.** Looking around the room while another person is talking to you sends the humiliating message that the speaker is boring or insignificant. You should also avoid making dismissive or irritated facial gestures, such as rolling your eyes or shaking your head, which set people off far more than negative words will.

- **Reply to what was said.** Don't just launch into what's on your mind. Reply to the other party's point before moving on to yours.

It's impossible to overemphasize the importance of getting the other party to open up. Admittedly, it can be difficult listening to some people talk, especially if they speak at a much slower pace than you or tend to veer from the point. Still, you must resist the temptation to hurry them along. People who speak in a roundabout way most likely think in a roundabout way, and attempting to control the flow of their thoughts will only confuse them or shut them off. Just be patient; they will get there. (Take notes if it will help you keep things straight.) If they seem to drone on or flood you with details, don't cut them off or let your mind wander. Listen hard, because they're giving you a gold mine of information. Even if they're complaining, they are telling you what is important to them. As they talk, they may give you something you can grab on to to use as an opening to an agreement. But you will only catch it if you are listening.

Adapt to Their Communication Style

Successful communication requires flexibility. We all have preferences as to how we like to interact with others, to receive and process information, and to make decisions. Those preferences can vary dramatically from person to person. However, variances don't need to be a bar to effective communication. My husband and I have radically different communication and decision-making styles. I am direct and outspoken, while Joe is indirect and restrained. I tend to make quick decisions, while he likes to mull things over. I hate putting things off; he hates to be rushed. Yet we have remained happily married for over thirty years and through untold negotiations. How? By adapting to each other's style.

I have learned, for example, that I will only create resistance by pushing Joe to make decisions at my pace. So I build in more time. He has learned that I don't always pick up his subtle signals. So when something is important, he will speak to me more directly than he is naturally inclined to do. Neither of us is being phony. We are merely recognizing that there is more than one way to say something and that while my way of expressing things may be the most natural for me, it is not the most comfortable for Joe, and vice versa. Our goal is to express ourselves in the way the other can best hear it.

Adaptation begins with self-awareness. There are many good books, tests, and internet sites on personality types, such as the Myers-Briggs Type Indicator and DISC Assessment. These and other individual measurement tools can give you important insight into your behavioral, communication, and decision-making styles. By showing you how you are distinct, they also indirectly raise your awareness of how others are different from you. Every negotiator would benefit from taking a personality self-analysis at some point.

However, self-awareness alone will not make you persuasive. To win someone over, you need to be *other-aware*, so that you can adapt to their style. Although unfortunately you can't make your counterpart take a personality test before you negotiate, uncovering another person's preferences is surprisingly easy. People are constantly giving signs to indicate how they want to be treated. Once you spot these signs, all you need to do is to adjust your style to match their preference.

In negotiation, the five most important communication categories to watch for are

- *Fact-oriented versus people-oriented:* Do they get straight to business, stay on the issues, and speak in unadorned language ("The outputs need to be clearer")—or do they start out with friendly small talk and pepper their conversation with personal asides, humor, or polite, positive phrases ("Please," "Thank you," "This is a good proposal, but do you think we could be a bit clearer on the outputs?")? When they describe issues, do they stick to the relevant facts—or do they put them in a larger context (tell a story)?

- *Direct versus indirect:* Do they openly, assertively, and unambiguously express their thoughts and opinions ("There's no way we can have that ready by that date")—or are they more quiet, cautious, and circuitous ("Okay. We can certainly aim for that date. It should be possible. There may be some difficulties, but we will do our best.")?

- *Big-picture–oriented versus detail-oriented:* Do they prefer bullet points and brief data, with a focus on action and consequences—or do they like as much background and procedural information as possible, with a focus on understanding causation?

- *Fast-paced versus slow-paced:* Do they talk rapidly, interrupt, and make and push for quick decisions—or do they take their time, pause before speaking, show a good deal of patience, but clam up when rushed?

- *Achievement-driven versus risk-averse:* Do they get excited by opportunities and potential success—or do they respond cautiously and show concern over what could go wrong?

Don't worry if you can't identify your counterparts' preferences in every one of these categories. As soon as you have identified even one or two preferences, you will greatly increase your persuasiveness if you model the same style in communicating with them. The following chart offers tips on how to work with different types of communicators.

Key Communication Categories

If they are . . .	Fact-oriented	People-oriented
You should . . .	•Stick to business	•Be friendly, smiling
	•Keep side notes, personal comments, humor to a minimum	•Intersperse business with side notes, personal comments, humor
	•Have facts at your fingertips	•Provide context
If they are . . .	**Direct**	**Indirect**
You should . . .	•Raise the main issue immediately, minimizing background	•Approach the issue tactfully, starting with background
	•Be clear and assertive	•Be implicit and sensitive
If they are . . .	**Big picture–oriented**	**Detail-oriented**
You should . . .	•Use brief data, charts	•Provide lots of information
	•Speak in bullet points	•Be precise and thorough

(*Continued*)

Key Communication Categories (Continued)

If they are . . .	Fast-paced	Slow-paced
You should . . .	• Get quickly to the point	• Lead in deliberately and calmly
	• Respond swiftly to questions	• Wait patiently for responses
	• Ask for a quick decision	• Give time to think before deciding
If they are . . .	Achievement-driven	Risk-averse
You should . . .	• Focus on results, action	• Focus on manageable steps
	• Stress potential gains	• Stress avoidance of problems
	• Be confident	• Be calm

Hotel Rate Case Study

The Empire Hotel's rate negotiation with Company B was now in its final stage. The bear had retreated, handing over the role of negotiator to the local procurement agent. All of that was good news for the hotel management, which had worked hard to develop a more friendly relationship with the procurement head and her staff, an effort that had proved so successful that Company B's procurement team had ranked the hotel as their favorite in the five-star category.

Nevertheless, the Empire's sales director couldn't assume that the procurement head would simply acquiesce to the new rates. Preparing for this final round with the new negotiator, she asked herself, "What's in this negotiation for her?" The sales director understood that Company B's procurement head was under tremendous pressure to prove herself as a negotiator by getting some sort of discount. However, since the company had already failed to get a major price cut, the new negotiator's ambitions would almost certainly be more humble than her predecessor's. The hotel's biggest advantage would be that while the new negotiator had to consider price, her personal interests as procurement head were more about quality and relationship.

In preparing for the meeting, the sales director planned her opening words carefully. She would start by congratulating the procurement head on her new assignment and stress how much she and the Empire management looked forward to working together with her. She would emphasize that although there were a few matters to be ironed out, she foresaw a quick and successful outcome. Once the friendly tone had been set, the negotiation gotten under way, and the sales director had explained the reasons for the rate increase, she asked Company B's negotiator what her concerns were. The procurement head replied frankly that she understood and even accepted the hotel's reasons for raising the rates, but she had to get some sort of discount or she would be viewed as having failed in her first assignment. The sales director empathized, saying that she was under the same sort of pressure herself. "So what can we offer you that would give you the discount you need, while still allowing me to get the rate my general manager has set for the next contract?" she mused.

Putting their heads together, they came up with a win-win solution. The sales director proposed the idea (developed earlier with her general manager) of offering Company B a special discounted rate in the low season. Because the hotel catered primarily to business customers, it had two high seasons (mid-January to May and mid-September to November) and a five-month low season, when corporate business dropped off by as much as half. If the hotel offered Company B a dual rate—the regular 32 percent increase in the high season but a smaller increase, say 20 percent, in the low seasons—the procurement head could claim that she had won a reduction of the average yearly rate increase to 27 percent (a 15 percent discount from the original 32 percent across-the-board increase). The sales director justified the lower off-season rate as an incentive to attract business during periods of low occupancy. The procurement head was persuaded but asked for a few days to discuss the revised offer with her management and to go over with them the arguments the hotel had compiled to explain the rate increase. Two days later she called to say that they would sign the contract.

So which party won? Both did. The procurement head got her psychological victory, while the hotel kept its biggest customer *and* got the full 32 percent increase in the period that principally affected its bottom line. Moreover, both parties emerged with an even stronger and more supportive business relationship, which would bring them mutual financial benefits during the life of the contract, starting with increased hotel bookings for rooms and conferences by Company B.

Yet, perhaps the happiest party was the formerly downtrodden sales director, who had once seen no winning choice between giving in to a bully or having her hotel dropped by its major customer once again. "We did it!" she cheered, her voice a mixture of pride and relief. "After this, no more feeding bears!"

Conclusion

Remember, negotiation is an attempt to resolve conflict, to reach a mutual agreement now, and to work together tomorrow. It isn't a war. You will always benefit by showing respect to the other side. Even when you disagree, you can be empathetic. Even when you're drawing a line, you can be polite. And it never hurts to express regret when you have to walk away.

You will stand a far higher chance of reaching a favorable resolution if you always give others the benefit of the "3 A's" described in Chapter Three:

- *Admiration*—showing respect for who they are

- *Affiliation*—approaching them as partners, colleagues, or friends

- *Acknowledgment*—appreciating the value of their thoughts, feelings, or actions

In the timeless words of Abraham Lincoln,

> When the conduct of men is designed to be influenced, per-suasion, kind, unassuming persuasion, should ever be adopted. It is an old and a true maxim, that a "drop of honey catches more flies than a gallon of gall." So with men. If you would win a man to your cause, first convince him that you are his sincere friend....
>
> On the contrary, assume to dictate to his judgment, or to command his action, or to mark him as one to be shunned and despised, and he will retreat within himself, close all the avenues to his head and his heart; and though your cause be naked truth itself, . . . you shall no more be able to pierce him, than to penetrate the hard shell of a tortoise with a rye straw.[1]

Read Lincoln's words closely. He did not advocate posing as a friend. He said, "convince him that you are his *sincere* friend." While positive, respectful, and empathetic communication is a central part of persuasion, it must be matched by positive, trustworthy, and relationship-oriented behavior. Being pleasant is critical, but a relationship depends on more than nice words. Words have to be sincere. Promises have to be fulfilled. And the outcome has to be just.

Lessons from This Chapter

- In the art of winning someone over, persuasion is the hardest of the five steps to master.
- To persuade successfully you must
  - Focus on the interests of the other party (what's in it for him or her)
  - Earn the other's trust
  - Adopt a more positive way of speaking

- Balance speaking, questioning, and listening
- Create an atmosphere of goodwill that leads the other party to want to cooperate
- Asking if now is a good time to talk sets a positive tone and starts the negotiation off with a yes.
- A persuasive opening to a negotiation
  - Focuses on where the parties' interests align rather than where they conflict
  - Describes the issue impartially rather than casting blame
  - Empathizes with the other side's perspective
- To set a positive tone
  - Say "Yes, if . . ."
  - Point out gains rather than losses
  - Rephrase affirmatively
- Reject intimidating language.
- Asking questions and listening to the answers are the best ways to learn the other side's goals and attitudes.
- Effective persuaders adapt to others' communication and decision-making styles. The five most important communication categories are
  - Fact-oriented versus people-oriented
  - Direct versus indirect
  - Big-picture–oriented versus detail-oriented
  - Fast-paced versus slow-paced
  - Achievement-driven versus risk-averse

Part 4

CONCLUSION

Chapter 12

YOU CAN NEGOTIATE!

I have often been told by nervous clients that the very thought of negotiating intimidates them because they have no experience at it. Nonsense. They've simply bought into the common misperception that negotiation is a formal face-off involving buying and selling or treaty-making. In fact, those are only a tiny fraction of the negotiations that are going on all around us all the time. Every one of us negotiates, whether consciously or not, because every human relationship involves negotiation. Though you may not always be aware of it, if you work in a large institution you negotiate nearly every day. Even if you work from home you have to reach agreements with other people from time to time. The challenge, therefore, is not acquiring a wholly new skill set, like learning to skydive or write computer code. It's doing what you already do, only more consciously, thoughtfully, and therefore, effectively.

Through the many varied examples in this book, I've tried to show that negotiating beyond the deal brings long-term benefits, from the boardroom to the bedroom. By negotiating with an eye on building strong and mutually profitable relationships—rather than on fighting to win short-term skirmishes—you will win the far more lasting victories of improving customer relations, achieving team goals, getting the most out of business partnerships, resolving punishing disputes, better managing your career and workload, and having a happier home life, to name just a few.

Naturally, these great benefits don't come free. Relationship-centered negotiation does demand a greater investment in time, consideration, planning, empathy, patience, and self-control than does the old transactional method of plunging in and hoping to talk your way into a deal. Some of these endeavors may go against your natural inclinations, requiring conscious effort and practice to master. I'll confess that for me, the challenge is maintaining emotional self-control, responding calmly when I feel attacked. Keeping my reactions in check is something I focus on in every negotiation, formal and informal. It can be hard work at times, but I put in that work because I've seen the benefits it has brought me. For you, the biggest challenge might be speaking up, or slowing down, or putting yourself in another party's shoes. Yet, if you make that investment in the art of relationship negotiation, you will be repaid many times over, both materially and psychologically. Not only will you see immediate results, but a negotiation that builds a positive relationship will continue to pay off long past the signing—or even the completion—of the deal.

This book was written with two goals in mind. First, I have sought to share with you the five life-changing lessons I have learned from observing and taking part in countless negotiations across the globe—and from monitoring their outcomes after the ink has dried:

1. For ensuring reliable and lasting outcomes, building strong working relationships must be a central goal of negotiation, not a mere step in the process.

2. By building relationships that reach beyond the deal, you will reap far higher rewards in both your business and your life than will those who engage in short-term, win-lose transactions.

3. Fairness, openness, honesty, and appropriate trust are not naïve aspirations; they are the nuts and bolts of long-term success.

4. Time spent up front in preparation will reward you tenfold in value returned.

5. Effective negotiation needn't be aggressive, scary, or painful.

Fundamentally related to the fifth lesson, the second goal of this book has been to provide you with a set of proven tools to enable you to negotiate with confidence and success. I hope I've convinced you that becoming an expert negotiator doesn't involve mastering verbal tricks or cunning strategies or developing an intimidating personality. On the contrary, it's merely a process of *understanding* (starting with yourself), *anticipating*, and *connecting* with others in an effort to reach a mutually profitable agreement.

Thousands of people from every corner of the world and all walks of life who have attended my training seminars have already achieved success far beyond their expectations or past experience by following the five-step GRASP negotiation method. As a group, these people had no exceptional oratorical skills, educational background, IQ score, sense of self-esteem, or personal charisma. The only thing they had in common was that before they negotiated, they all asked themselves the same five questions:

Goals—What do I/they want to achieve or avoid?

- Identify, prioritize, and weigh your goals.

- Imagine and learn the other side's goals.

- Consider long-term as well as immediate interests.

Routes—How can I best achieve my goals by supporting theirs?

- Consider all possible avenues to satisfy both sides while maximizing your goals.

- Consider the advantages and disadvantages of each path, then choose your *preferred* route.

- Plan fallback routes in case you find the road blocked.

Arguments—What reasons support my/their proposals?

- Develop valid and compelling arguments to back each proposal you make.

- Provide evidence to support those arguments.

- Insist that they provide equally valid and supported arguments.

- Focus on fairness and reason.

Substitutes—How else could I/they accomplish my/their goals?

- What other ways *outside of this negotiation* are you able to achieve your goals?

- Establish your "Walk-Away Line" (WAL).

- Consider the other side's WAL and substitutes.

Persuasion—What is in it for them?

- Speak to other parties' goals and perspectives.

- Listen and ask questions to better understand their goals and perspectives.

- Focus on problem-solving, not fighting or game-playing.

- Be flexible, open, and honest while holding firm to legitimacy.

By following these five simple steps, you too will find that negotiation can be a truly rewarding experience. Of course, negotiation will still involve disagreement. That's why you're negotiating after all. But through focusing on the relationship, those differences will go from being head-to-head clashes to mere problems to be discussed, weighed, and in most cases, solved. Differences, handled with an open mind, create synergy. The payoff is not only a higher-value immediate outcome but an agreement that will be honored over time, and that very often will lead to future agreements.

Negotiation is a fundamental business and life skill that goes far beyond dealmaking. As you become a stronger negotiator, you will not only maximize the value of your agreements; you will also build confidence, develop more satisfying and lasting relationships, become a better communicator, grow more efficient at getting things done, face less fighting and stress, save time that you would have spent searching for new business partners, experience fewer disappointments now and shocks later, and generally become more successful in life and work. Your only challenge is to go out there and try.

To get you started, the step-by-step GRASP Negotiation Planner in Appendix A will help you prepare for your next negotiation. Afterward, use the Post-Negotiation Evaluation (Appendix B) to analyze your negotiating effectiveness and assess the areas you feel you need to work on.

In just five steps, you will be on your way to becoming an expert negotiator, with the results to prove it. The first step, which you've already begun by reading this book, is to know your goals.

Appendix A

GRASP NEGOTIATION

PLANNER

What is this negotiation about?

For example: *"To negotiate an extension to an existing two-year purchasing agreement with one of our largest suppliers, with a minimum price increase and extended payment terms."*

Who will take part in the negotiation, and what do you know about them?

	Negotiators	Description (position, characteristics, and so on)
My Side		*How will they see me/us?*
Their Side		*What do I/we know about them?*

Step One: Goals

GOALS		
What are MY needs, desires, and aspirations in this negotiation? Which are most important?		
	Priority	
	1.	
	2.	
	3.	
	4.	
	5.	
	6.	
What do I imagine THEIR goals to be? How do they compare to mine?		
	Same, Opposed, or Distinct?	

Step Two: Routes

I could…	Advantages	Disadvantages
1. My *best possible outcome*		
2.		
3.		
4.		
5.		
6. My *least acceptable outcome*		

ROUTES

Step Three: Arguments

ARGUMENTS

Reasons to justify the merit of *every* position I take:

I am justified in asking for _____ based on the following:

1.

2.

3.

4.

Supporting information I could share or documentation I could provide to strengthen my argument:

1.

2.

3.

4.

I can justify changing my terms to _____ for the following reasons:

1.

2.

3.

4.

Questions I plan to ask to probe and challenge their anticipated arguments:

If they argue _____, I will ask:

1. Probing:

2. Challenging:

Step Four: Substitutes

If this negotiation doesn't work out...		
I could...	Advantages	Disadvantages
1.		
2.		
3.		
4.		

My Substitute: _____

My Walk-Away Line: _____

THEIR likely substitute:	Advantages over me:	Disadvantages compared to me:

SUBSTITUTES

Step Five: Persuasion

PERSUASION	**How will I phrase my key message to appeal to them?**

Observed communication preferences (circle one in each column):

Fact-oriented	Direct	Big picture	Fast-paced	Achievement-driven
or	*or*	*or*	*or*	*or*
People-oriented	Indirect	Detailed	Slow-paced	Risk-averse

Appendix B

POST-NEGOTIATION
EVALUATION

Overall, do you consider this negotiation a success?   □ Yes □ No

Why or why not?

_____

_____

Did you achieve your top-priority goals?   □ Yes □ No

If no, what could you have done differently or better to get a more
   favorable result?

1. _____

2. _____

3. _____

Did you strengthen the relationship with the other   □ Yes □ No
   party?

If no, how could you have approached the party differently or more
effectively?

1. _____

2. _____

3. _____

What did you do during the planning and execution of the negotiation
that . . .

was particularly useful?	you feel you need to improve?
1. _____	1. _____
2. _____	2. _____
3. _____	3. _____

What are some lessons that you have learned from this negotiation?

1. _____

2. _____

3. _____

Notes

Introduction

1. Jim Cathcart, *The Eight Competencies of Relationship Selling* (Washington, DC: Leading Authority Press, 2002).

Chapter One

1. Jeffrey K. Liker and Thomas Y. Choi, "Building Deep Supplier Relationships," *Harvard Business Review*, December 2004.
2. See, for example, Robert Cialdini, *Influence: The Psychology of Persuasion* (New York: HarperCollins, 1998).
3. Lee Alan Dugatkin, "Discovering That Rational Economic Man Has a Heart," *Cerebrum*, the Dana Foundation e-journal, July 2005, http://www.dana.org/news/cerebrum/detail.aspx?id=748
4. Alan B. Goldberg and Bill Ritter, "Costco CEO Finds Pro-Worker Means Profitability," ABC News 20/20, August 2, 2006, http://abcnews.go.com/2020/business/story?id=1362779

Chapter Two

1. Sarah Brosnan and Frans deWaal, "Monkeys Reject Unequal Pay," *Nature*, September 18, 2003.
2. Much work has recently been produced by the behavioral economists countering the myth of man as "homo economicus," a perfectly rational economic calculator. I recommend as a starting place, Daniel Ariely, *Predictably Irrational: The Hidden Forces that Shape Our Decisions* (New York: HarperCollins, 2008).

3. Joel Brockner, "Why It's So Hard to Be Fair," *Harvard Business Review*, March 2006.

4. For a fascinating account of this episode, see Priya Ghandikota, "When 'Power Failures' Undermine International Business Negotiations: A Negotiation Analysis of the Dabhol Power Project," master's thesis, Fletcher School of Law and Diplomacy, 2002, http://nils.lib.tufts.edu/Fletcher/PriyaGhandikota1.pdf

5. James Luckey, "Lessons from Dabhol," *Energy Markets*, October 2001, p. 20.

6. *Times of India*, January 25, 2002, http://timesofindia.indiatimes.com/Agreeing-to-Enrons-tariff-was-a-mistake-Govt/articleshow/358654838.cms.

Chapter Three

1. KPMG, "Unlocking Shareholder Value: The Keys to Success," *Mergers and Acquisitions: Global Research Report*, 1999, http://pages.stern.nyu.edu/~adamodar/pdfiles/eqnotes/KPMGM&A.pdf

2. See, for example, Roderick M. Kramer, "Trust and Distrust in Organizations: Emerging Perspectives, Enduring Questions," *Annual Review of Psychology*, 50, 1999, pp. 569–598.

3. KPMG, "Alliances and Joint Ventures: Fit, Focus and Follow-Through," *Transaction Services Advisory*, June 2005.

4. Nirmalya Kumar, "The Power of Trust in Manufacture-Retailer Relationships," *Harvard Business Review*, November 1996.

5. E. W. Larson and J. A. Drexler Jr., "Barriers to Project Partnering: Report from the Firing Line," *Project Management Journal*, 1997, pp. 46–52.

6. Author's interview with Dr. Kim Yong-Ho, June 23, 2008.

7. "Singapore's Port Faces New Competition from Malaysia," *Asian Economic News*, August 28, 2000, and "Singapore Port Faces Up to Competition," *Financial Times*, July 2, 2002.

8. Dale Carnegie, *How to Win Friends and Influence People* (New York: Pocket Books, 1998).

9. Geert Hofstede, *Cultures and Organizations* (New York: McGraw-Hill, 1997).

10. William James, *Principles of Psychology* (Cambridge, MA: Harvard University Press, 1981), p. 313. (Originally published in 1890.)

Chapter Four

1. "Negotiating Without a Net: A Conversation with the NYPD's Dominick J. Misino," *Harvard Business Review*, October 2002. Officer Bruce Wind of the Seattle Police Department's Hostage Negotiations Team, however, makes it clear that the "little something" Misino refers to is definitely modest: "When a subject demands '$1 million,' the negotiators actually hear 'a 6-pack of soda.'" Bruce A. Wind, "A Guide to Crisis Negotiations," *FBI Law Enforcement Bulletin*, October 1995.

Chapter Five

1. Quoted in Stephen L. Vaughan, *Encyclopedia of American Journalism* (New York: Routledge, 2007), p. 70.

Chapter Nine

1. Abraham Maslow, *Motivation and Personality*, 2nd ed. (New York: Harper & Row, 1970).

2. Ellen Langer, *Mindfulness* (New York: Perseus Books, 1989).

Chapter Eleven

1. Abraham Lincoln, address to Springfield Washington Temperance Society, February 22, 1841.

Acknowledgments

I developed most of the concepts in this book during my years as senior partner of Global Resolutions, a Singapore-based negotiating and consulting firm. I wish to thank my partners at Global Resolutions, Jonathan Yuen and Hasanand Napasab, as well as my exceptionally talented associate Nok Tamphanuwat, for providing insights, suggestions, and criticism for my germinating ideas—and for relentlessly motivating me to put those ideas onto paper.

I also wish to thank my many clients, executive trainees, and students at the Master of International Management program at Portland State University and at Sasin Graduate School of Business Administration of Chulalongkorn University in Thailand for generously sharing their viewpoints and experiences with me, providing a treasure trove of examples to learn from.

While writing this book, I have greatly benefited from the advice and support of my ever-diplomatic husband, Joseph Yun; my persuasive colleague, Kathy O'Brien; my dearest friend and critic, Diane Rynerson; the queen of networking, Tami Overby; my astute agent, Ted Weinstein; and my editor at Wiley, Karen Murphy, who truly understands the value of negotiating relationships. They have made this book so much better than I would have done on my own. All faults are mine alone.

About the Author

Melanie Billings-Yun, PhD, was founder and senior partner of Global Resolutions, a Singapore-based consulting firm providing negotiation strategies, representation, and training to international businesses and individual clients. Formerly a research director and lecturer on history at Harvard's Kennedy School of Government, Dr. Billings-Yun has spent most of the past two decades assisting Western and Asian companies, NGOs, and public agencies in improving their internal and external relationships through negotiation.

Billings-Yun has a PhD from Harvard University, specializing in diplomatic history, an MSc from the London School of Economics, and a BS with high honors from Portland State University. She is the author of *Decision Against War* (Columbia University Press, 1988), as well as numerous articles on negotiation, mediation, and dispute resolution. She regularly speaks to professional associations and business conferences around the world about negotiation and relationship management.

A native of Portland, Oregon, Billings-Yun has lived and worked in London, Paris, Bangkok, Hong Kong, Seoul, Indonesia, and Singapore. She currently works from Washington, D.C., and teaches at the Master of International Management program at Portland State University.

Index

A

Acceptance: gaining, 63, 71; honoring relationships and, 63–64
Achievement-driven communications, 243, 244
Acknowledgment: persuasion and, 246–247; resolutions using, 66–69
Active listening, 238–240, 248
Adaptability: in communications, 241–244, 248; importance of, 11, 23–24
Admiration: persuasion and, 246–247; resolutions using, 66–69
Affiliation: defined, 13–14; persuasion and, 246–247; resolutions using, 66–69
Aggression, 13
Agreements: developing trust in international, 59; handling inequitable, 41–46; implementing fairly, 37; importance of understanding in, 54–55; needs in, 144, 145; negotiated with force vs. respect, 40–41; reviewing terms of, 83. *See also* International agreements
Anticipating, 118, 119, 123–126
Appeasing: decision making and, 138–139; tactics for, 91–92, 102
Arguments: about, 202; acceptable, 192–193, 202; adding "because" to, 185–187; building trust with, 187–192; communicating valid, 110–111; defined, 181; eliciting and challenging, 194–198, 202; in GRASP model, xix, 181–182, 254; including respect in, 182–185; persuasion vs., 181–182, 228; used in Hotel Rate case study, 198–201

Aspirations: negotiation and, 145, 146–147; understanding other side's, 149–150
Authority to negotiate, 128, 129

B

Bear traps: about, 99–100; avoiding, 99–100, 109–112; encountering grizzly bears, 112–114; honey bear negotiations, 114; negotiating beyond mistrust, 103–108; rejecting intimidating language, 236–237, 248; training bigger bears, 108–109; using substitutes in, 220–222; walking away from, 113
"Because" requests, 185–187
Best competing offers, 208
Big picture-oriented communications, 242, 243
Bluffing, 15–16
Body language, 12–13, 240
Bottom line. *See* WAL
Breaks during negotiations, 237
Broun, Heywood, 102
Bundling, 164, 173
Bush, George, 43–44
Businesses: adding value in vendor relations, 60; importance of playing fair, 31–35; long-term relationships in, 57–59; profitability and trust relationships, 57

C

Care for counterparts, 17–18
Carnegie, Dale, 63
Case study. *See* Hotel Rate case study
Cathcart, Jim, xv
Challenging arguments, 194–198, 202

Chamberlain, Neville, 92
Chirac, Jacques, 229
Clone myth, 148, 149
Closed questions, 198
Coe, Lord Sebastian, 229
Collaboration: about, 19–21; as aim of negotiation, 98; creating, 78–79
Commitment, 24–25
Communications: adapting to counterparts' style of, 241–244, 248; avoiding bear traps with, 109–110; body language and emotions, 240; categories of, 242–244, 248; effect of negative body language in, 67; honest, 11, 15–17; listening to other's, 237–241, 248; me-centered vs. other-centered, 227–232, 247–248; negotiation as, 75; positive, 15–17, 232–237, 248; rejecting intimidating language, 236–237, 248; rephrasing affirmatively, 234–236; transforming resistance in, 64–65
Competition, 120
Concessions: avoiding repeated, 112–113; making valid, 111–112
Conduct: fair implementation of agreements, 37; keeping agreements faithfully, 45–47
Confidence, 120, 129
Conflict: dealing with, 79; finding solutions vs., 85–87; negotiating styles and, 87–90; resolving disputes with 3 A's, 66–69
Connecting: illustrated, 119; importance of, 118, 119, 126–127; ways of, 127–129
Cooperation, 62–63
CostCo, 20–21
Counterparts: adapting to communication style of, 241–244, 248; basing negotiation on emotions of, 112; encountering overbearing, 112–114; establishing care for, 17–18; finding goals enabling trade-offs, 153–155, 156; goals of,

147–155; helping them get what they want, 159–163; learning and providing values of, 151–155; listening to, 237–241, 248; priorities of, 149–150; pursuing mutual gain with, 168–173, 178; responding to their routes, 176, 179; substitutes for WAL, 215–216, 224; substitutes of, 219–220, 224; understanding, 119–123
Courtesy, 162–163

D

Dabhol Power Plant project, 41–44
Deal-centered negotiations: avoiding bear traps, 99–100, 109–112; focus of, 99; limitations of, 3–4; moving to relationship negotiations from, xvi; negotiating relationships vs. deals, 6–10; relationships extending beyond, 69–70; transactional basis of, 7–8
Decision making: emotional basis of, 65; game about, 137–140
Delanoe, Bertrand, 229
Dependability, 11, 25–26
Desires: in negotiations, 145–146; understanding other side's, 149–150
Detail-oriented communications, 242, 243
Direct communications, 242, 243
DISC Assessment, 241

E

Emotions: anticipating, 124–125; basing negotiation on counterpart's, 112; body language and, 240; dealing with in negotiations, 237; decision making based on, 65; positive emotional contagion, 69. See also Reactions
Empathy: building agreement with, 18–19; transcending conflict with, 79
Enemy myth, 148–149

Enron International, 20, 41–44, 82
Equity: about, 36–37; imbalances in deal's, 41–46
Ethics, 31–35

F

Fact-oriented communications, 242, 243–244
Fairness: defined, 35–36; imbalances in equity, 36–37, 41–46; including in negotiation, 14–15; monkeys need for, 29–30; in negotiations, 36–37; negotiations and, 11; as pillar of negotiation, 78, 95–97; playing fair, 31–35; process, 36, 37–41. *See also* Process fairness
Fast-paced communications, 243, 244
Favors, 114
Fear: dispelling with arguments, 187–192; removing from negotiations, xvi–xvii
Forcing: goals, 138–139; negotiations, 91
Ford Motor Company, 13
Four pillars of negotiation: building productive relationships, 78–81; defined, 78, 97; fairness in, 78, 95–97; illustrated, 78; outcomes in, 81–85; solutions in, 85–87
Friendliness, 12–14

G

Gain. *See* mutual gain
Gaining acceptance, 63, 71
General Dynamics, 57, 58–59
Getting to Yes, x
Goals: about, 156; aspirations, 145, 146–147; author's, 252–253; clarity from, 136–140; desires for, 145–146; developing, 133–136; examining, 143–144; finding and providing counterpart's, 150–155; finding underlying, 140–143; focusing on, xiii–xiv; in GRASP model, xix, 133, 134, 253; learning other

side's, 147–155; missing forest for trees, 139, 141–142; myths of other side's, 147–149; needs, 144, 145; resolving conflicting, 75, 76–77; selecting routes from, 173–175; short-term, 4–6; stereotyping other's, 147–149; types of, 144–147
GRASP model: arguments in, xix, 181–182; benefits of using, 51–53; building trust with arguments, 187–192; coming up with routes, 157–163; communication categories, 242–244, 248; defined, xix, 133, 253–255; developing acceptable arguments, 192–193, 202; developing goals, 133–136; eliciting and challenging arguments, 194–198, 202; examining goals, 143–144; expanding size of pie, 168–173, 178; finding equitable trade offs, 163–168; finding underlying goals, 140–143; GRASP Negotiation Planner, 255, 257–262; Hotel Rate case study, 150–155; illustrated, 134; knowing and building WALs, 206–214; learning other side's goals, 147–155; negotiating without substitutes, 216–218, 223–224; persuasion in, xix, 225–227; planning and presenting routes, 173–175, 179; Post-Negotiation Evaluation form, 255, 263–264; revealing substitutes, 214–216, 223; substitutes in, xix, 203–206
GRASP Negotiation Planner, 255, 257–262
Grizzly bears, 112–114

H

Hardball negotiators. *See* one-sided demands
Harvard Business Review, 13, 77
Hitler, Adolph, 92
Hofstede, Geert, 64

Honesty: avoiding bear traps with, 109–110; balancing tone of, 16–17; relationships and, 11
Honey bear negotiations, 114
Hostage negotiators, 77
Hotel Rate case study: arguments used in, 198–201; offering substitute and WAL in, 220–222; persuasion as used in, 244–246; routes offered in, 175–178; understanding counterparts' priorities, 150–155
How to Win Friends and Influence People (Carnegie), 63
Humiliation, 39

I

IBM, 64
Indirect communications, 242, 243
International agreements: developing trust in, 59; pace of developing, 24–25

J

James, William, 67
Jung, Carl, 65

K

KPMG, 53, 56

L

Langer, Ellen, 185–186
Laughter, 236
Likeability, 12–14
Liking in relationship negotiation, 12–14
Lincoln, Abraham, 247
Lockheed Martin, 58–59
Loyalty: building, 70

M

Maersk Sealand, 60, 61–62, 96
Maharashtra State Electricity Board, 42, 43
Manipulative behavior, 114
Maslow, Abraham, 164–165
McDonnell Douglas, 57, 58, 59

Me-centered vs. other-centered communications, 227–232
Mind-reading negotiations, 112–113
Miser myth, 148
Misino, Dominick, 77
Missing forest for trees, 139, 141–142
Mistrust: negotiating beyond, 103–108; preventing, 115; situations cultivating, 103
Monkeys, 29–30
Monopolies, 216, 223, 224
Mutual gain: courteous negotiations for, 162–163; expanding size of pie for, 168–173, 178; negotiations with, 77
Myers-Briggs Type Indicator, 241

N

Nature, 29–30
Needs: in agreements, 144, 145; respect as, 184–185; understanding other side's, 149–150
Negotiation: acceptable arguments in, 192–193, 202; adaptability in, 23–24; anticipating in, 123–126; appeasing tactics, 91–92; benefits of relationship, 49, 70–71; beyond mistrust, 103–108; collaboration in, 19–21, 78–79; coming up with negotiation routes, 157–159; communications in, 15–17; confidence in, 120, 129; connecting in, 118, 119, 126–129; defined, 75–77, 97; dependability and, 11, 25–26; disclosing WAL, 215, 223; empathy in, 18–19; establishing care and concern in, 17–18; fairness and, 14–15, 29–31, 36–37; focusing on short-term goals in, 4–6; forcing, 91; honey bear, 114; knowing substitutes in, 203–206; learning about, 251–253; limitations of deal-centered, 3–4; missing forest for trees, 139, 141–142; mixture of goals in, 148–149; moving

from deal-centered to relationship, xvi; mutual gain in, 77; myths of other side's goals, 147–149; nature of relationship in, ix–x; negotiating against self, 112–113, 115; persuasion vs., 77; preparing for, 117–119; problems-solving in, 92–93, 98; process of, 6–8; relationship rules for, 10–12; respect in, 12–14; responding in, 176, 179; revealing substitutes and WAL, 214–216, 223; role of reciprocity in, 11, 21–23; splitting, 90–91; stages in, 118–119, 129; styles of, 87–90; transactional basis in deal-centered, 7–8; using WALS in, 206–214; walking away from, 113; withdrawing in, 92; without substitutes, 216–218, 223–224. See also Deal-centered negotiations; Four pillars of negotiation; GRASP model; Negotiators

Negotiation routes. See routes

Negotiations: successful, 53, 66–69, 71, 246–247

Negotiators: active listening for, 238–241, 248; anticipating negotiations, 123–126; appeasing tactics for, 91–92; asking questions, 185; avoiding bear traps, 99–100, 109–112; communicating objective and fair view, 96–97; connecting in negotiations, 126–129; decision-making game for, 136–140; errors establishing power, 41; forcing negotiation, 91; handling grizzly bears, 112–114; hostage, 77; problem-solving for, 87, 92–93, 98; relationship rules for, 110–112; responding in negotiations, 176, 179; splitting approach for, 90–91; styles of negotiating, 87–90; success rate using understanding, 53; 3A's for, 66–69; using fairness, 45–47; withdrawing

in negotiation, 92. See also Counterparts

New York Police Department, 77

O

One-sided demands: about, 99–100, 115; avoiding, 99–100, 109–112, 115; encountering overbearing negotiators, 112–114; encouraging, 108–109; manipulative negotiations, 114; negotiating beyond mistrust, 103–108; walking away from, 113

One-time negotiations: expanding pie for, 173; trade-offs for, 164

Open-mindedness, 11, 23–24, 239

Open questions, 198

Other-centered speech: adapting to counterparts' style of speech, 241–244, 248; developing other-centered approach, 227–232, 247–248; using positive communications, 233–234

Other side. See counterparts

Outcomes: negotiating intended, 81–85

P

People-oriented communications, 242, 243–244

Persuasion: arguments vs., 181–182, 228; developing other-centered approach, 227–232, 247–248; in GRASP model, xix, 225–227, 254; listening to other's opinions, 237–241; mastering, 225, 247–248; negotiation vs., 77; positive communications in, 232–237; rejecting intimidating language, 236–237, 248; rephrasing affirmatively, 234–236; 3 A's and, 246–247; used in Hotel Rate case study, 244–246

Planning: anticipating, 118, 119, 123–126; GRASP Negotiation Planner, 255, 257–262; routes, 173–175, 179

Points of negotiation: avoiding polarizing effects of, 85–87; outcomes vs., 81–85

Port of Sinagpore (PSA), 60–62, 96

Port of Tanjung Pelepas (PTP), 60, 61–62

Positive communications: honest, open , and, 15–17; positive emotional contagion, 69; using, 233–234, 248

Post-Negotiation Evaluation form, 255, 263–264

Praise, 14

Preparation, 117–119

Price, 148

Priorities: reviewing negotiation, 140–147; understanding other side's, 149–150

Probing, 194, 195–197, 198, 202

Problem-solving: moving from fighting to, 93–95; negotiating with, 92–93; as skill for negotiators, 87

Process fairness: about, 36; example of, 37–41; keys to, 40

Project Management Journal, 57

Q

Questions: during active listening, 240; need to ask, 185; open and closed, 198; probing, 194, 195–197, 198, 202

R

Reactions: to aggression, 13; understanding, xvi–xvii

Reasonableness, 95–97, 98

Reciprocity, 11, 21–23

Relationship negotiation: about, ix–x, xv–xvi; adding care and concern in, 17–18; agreements built with empathy, 18–19; benefits of, 49, 70–71; building productive relationships, 78–81; clarity gained from goals, 136–140; collaboration in, 19–21, 78–79; defined, 75–77; developing goals, 133–136; examining negotiation goals, 143–144; fairness and, 14–15; finding equitable trade offs, 163–168; four pillars of, 78–87; getting beyond mistrust, 103–108; handling grizzly bears, 112–114; increasing understanding via, 50–55; learning about, 251–253; learning other side's goals, 147–155; moving from deal-centered to, xvi; pursuing outcomes, 81–85; respect, friendliness, and liking in, 12–14; using substitutes in, 222–224. *See also* Counterparts; Four pillars of negotiation; GRASP model; Negotiators

Relationships: adding value to, 176–178; allowing dominance in, 100–103; building productive, 78–81; crafting proposals with understanding, 121–123; developing trust in, 24–25, 55–59, 70; extending beyond deal-centered negotiations, 69–70; gaining acceptance in, 63–69; gains with courteous negotiations, 162–163; getting beyond mistrust, 103–108; honoring beyond negotiations, 69–70; importance of in negotiations, 252–253; long-term business, 57–59; maximizing value in, 59–63; negotiating as reflection of, 113–114; negotiating deals vs., 6–10; reciprocity in, 21–23; rules for, 10–12; training bigger bears, 108–109; understanding dynamics in negotiation, 119–123; understanding in, 51–53

Repairing relationships, 176–178

Resistance, 61–69

Respect: adding to arguments, 182–185; asking for courteous communications, 237; effective questioning with, 197, 198; forced negotiations vs. agreements with,

40–41; need for, 184–185; negotiating with, 11, 12–14
Risk-averse communications, 243,
244
Routes: about, 178; coming up with,
157–159; defined, 157; finding
equitable trade offs, 163–168; in
GRASP model, xix, 253–254;
helping others get what they want,
159–163; planning and presenting, 173–175, 179; pursuing mutual
gain, 168–173, 178; responding to
counterparts' routes, 176, 179

S

Sinegal, Jim, 20–21
Slow-paced communications, 243,
244
Solutions: approaches to, 87–90; pursuing, 85–87
Splitting: difference in goals, 138;
negotiating using, 90–91
Stages of negotiations: about,
118–119; anticipating, 118, 119,
123–126, 129; connecting, 118,
119, 126–129; illustrated, 119;
understanding in, 119–123, 129
Substitutes: about, 203, 222, 223;
building WALs, 209–214; in
GRASP model, xix, 203–206,
254; how to reveal, 214–216, 223;
knowing walk-away line, 206–209;
offering in Hotel Rate case study,
220–222; reviewing advantages and
disadvantages of, 209–210; understanding counterparts,' 219–220,
224; what to do if unavailable,
216–218, 223–224. See also WAL

T

3 A's, 66–69, 71, 246–247
Tit-for-tat strategy, 21–23
Trade-offs: about, 178–179; equitable,
163–168; finding goals enabling,
153–155, 156

Transactional negotiations. See
deal-centered negotiations
Trust: building with arguments,
187–192; developing in relationships, 24–25, 55–59, 70; importance of, 55–59; moving beyond
mistrust, 103–108; negotiating with
respect, 182–185; understanding
and, 121; ways of losing, 58
Tupper, Earl, 63
Tupperware, 63

U

Understanding: building agreement
with empathy, 18–19; importance
in agreements, 54–55; increasing,
50–55; as negotiation stage, 118,
119–123, 129; trust and, 121
United Nations, 83–85

V

Vajpayee, Prime Minister, 43–44
Values: adding to relationships,
176–178; establishing WAL on,
207–208; learning and providing
counterpart's, 151–155; maximizing, 59–63
Veolia Water, 24

W

Wal-Mart, 20
Walk-away line (WAL): about, 223;
building, 209–214, 222; disclosing,
215, 223; knowing your, 206–209;
offered in case study, 220–222;
reviewing advantages of substitutes,
209–210; substitutes for counterpart's, 215–216, 224; walking away
from bear traps, 113
Whole Foods Market, 60
Wise, Bonnie, 63
Withdrawing in negotiation, 92
World Bank, 42

X

Yong-Ho, Dr. Kim, 57–59